# JOURNALISM TECHNIQUES

# JOURNALISM TECHNIQUES

**Monita Singh**

CENTRUM PRESS
NEW DELHI-110002 (INDIA)

**CENTRUM PRESS**
**H.O.:** 4360/4, Ansari Road, Daryaganj,
New Delhi-110002 (India)
Tel: 23278000, 23261597, 23255577, 23286875
**B.O.:** No. 1015, Ist Main Road, BSK IIIrd Stage,
IIIrd Phase, IIIrd Block, Bangalore-560085 (INDIA)
Tel: 080-41723429
*Email:* centrumpress@gmail.com
*Visit us at:* www.centrumpress.com

*Journalism Techniques*



First Edition, 2010

ISBN 978-93-80836-15-7

PRINTED IN INDIA

*Printed at* Mehra Offset Press, Delhi

# Contents

# Preface

Technical communication strives to convey information in ways to best help the reader, whether a jet-engine mechanic with manual in hand, a physicist reading a peer-reviewed article, or the new owner of the latest computer or coffeepot. Ideally, it presents information that people will read, understand, and find interesting. "Just writing a document isn't enough to ensure that people will read it.

Technical communication could also draw from another field, journalism, which uses story structure and writing styles that readers everywhere are familiar with. And journalism is adept at adapting to an array of audiences. Like technical communication, journalism has countless practitioners and a crucial role. It enhances our lives, with newspapers, magazines, radio, television, and the Web, informing us on everything from a local school-board vote to Central Asia politics.

Journalism encompasses many techniques. A basic one used to structure articles is called the "inverted pyramid," which has a long history. It simply means that a story begins with the most important facts, with the rest in descending order of importance.

Technical communication is less personal. But could a technical document contain some glimpses of, for instance, an inventor of a new lab machine, the thoughts that went into designing an interface, or those who would benefit from a new medical device?

Certainly these would just be asides to the core of any technical document, but they could be brief enough to not only spark interest -- and further reading -- but give readers some background on what they are reading. Imagine a question-and-answer interview with a Nobel laureate appearing in a highly regarded journal. It may seem out of place, but it would offer a fascinating look into how a genius approaches problems.

## Chapter 1

# Public Journalism Techniques

Labels of elitism and egalitarianism are useless because there are elements of each in both objective and public journalism.

Each advocates a different level of constraint on the press. The past 50 years have witnessed much scholarship and debate regarding the practice of objective journalism. This discussion has been intensified with the advent of public journalism, whose advocates boldly assert that objective journalism is fundamentally flawed.

Not surprisingly, much heated debate has emerged in which proponents of either journalistic practice accuse the other of being negligent, misleading or culpable in the erosion of democracy. Of key concern to this chapter is the propensity for participants in this debate to talk past one another - to be too quick to judge and dismiss the other practice as intrinsically broken, and thus, something to be immediately recanted and forsaken.

The debate concerning objective and public journalism is flawed because it focuses almost exclusively on the final products of each approach, usually demonstrating how each fail to achieve desired goals. This is because there is no fair and standardized way to compare and contrast the processes of each approach.

The study of journalistic practices as techniques overcomes this problem. Analyzing objective and public journalism as techniques affords the opportunity to focus on the means, not simply the end results, of each approach. This is a necessary step in enriching the debate over objective and public journalism. Without this focus, debate will continue to produce more derision than deliberation.

## FOCUS ON PROCESS

In discussing the impossibility of true objectivity, Denis McQuail asserts that objective journalism is more of "an approach... than an Achievement." Jorgen Westerstahl states that "maintaining objectivity in the dissemination of news can... most easily be defined as adherence to certain norms and standards. It is not a question of basing conclusions on some definition of the inherent nature of objectivity." Each of these scholars has emphasized the need to focus on objective reporting as a process rather than becoming distracted by the philosophical debate over the possibility of true objectivity.

Because public journalism is still very young, there is no single set of procedures which the approach advocates. However, using a series of case studies, some scholars have outlined how different organizations approach the practice of public journalism.

Other researchers have gone so far as to outline some common practices (i.e., public forums, public opinion polling, etc.) typical of public journalism projects and some urge the creation of a systematic approach for public journalism. Thus, while each public journalism project is unique, there remain some common practices which are consistently espoused. As a result, public journalism also yields itself to the study of technique.

## STUDY OF TECHNIQUE

The study of technique is the study of process. Jacques Ellul states that the study of technique incorporates an examination of means, values and resources. First and foremost, the study of technique allows scholars to focus on the actual practices of any activity.

Second, technique examines how value structures dictate the practices of an activity. Finally, although Harold Lasswell alludes to the fact that the study of technique should involve the topic of resources, this study focuses exclusively on means and values.

## FOCUS ON MEANS

Ellul asserts that "our civilization is first and foremost a civilization of means... the means, it would seem, are more important than the end." The means or practices of any activity are nothing more than steps taken to achieve a desired goal. Importantly, focusing on the means of an activity requires an examination of the efficiency of the means. Ellul claims that "technique is the totality of methods rationally arrived at and having absolute efficiency" and that techniques are designed to "search for the greatest efficiency." Clearly, the matter of efficiency is very important to the time-constrained world of journalism. Thus, in Ellul's terms, both objective and public journalists seek out the one best means to achieve their goals.

## FOCUS ON VALUES

Lasswell stresses that a defined value structure is a necessary but not sufficient condition for the initiation of a given technique. Because value orientations necessitate the employment of a given technique, a complete analysis of a technique must entail a thorough explication of the goals and values that provoked the creation of any particular set of practices. Indeed, if an individual or organization does not have some set of values or desired goals in mind, then specific practices will not be generated.

Further, these goals and values must be conscious realizations of individuals or organizations. The conscious nature of these values brings a human element to the activity. Indeed, the study of technique "attempts to take human nature into account in order to keep man from being crushed by technique." It is not the technique that drives people, but the values constructed by people which initiates the process. People are not beholden to any one technique - any technique can be altered to suit changes in the value structure of an individual or organization. This gives technique a flexibility that allows for a more humanist approach to the study of human activities.

## Objective Journalism

If you mean by objectivity, absence of convictions, willingness to let nature take its course, uncritical acceptance of things as they are... the hell with it. If you mean by objectivity a healthy respect for the ascertainable truth, a readiness to modify conclusions when new evidence comes in, a refusal to distort deliberately and for ulterior or concealed motives, a belief that the means shape the end, not that the end justifies the means, all well and good.

Opponents of objective journalism argue that pure objectivity is unobtainable and that the notion of objectivity is, at best, a shield devised by corporate America to insure a sanitized version of the truth, and at worst, an ideological weapon used to maintain the status quo. However, studying objective journalism as technique avoids this philosophical debate and concentrates on the means and values of the approach; instead, it is the practices employed to achieve this unobtainable goal which become most important. It is important to take note of the fact that objectivity is an ever-evolving term.

Richard Streckfuss makes this point clear in his tracing of the historical underpinnings of the term as it relates to the profession of journalism. Although objectivity is often treated as a synonym for neutrality by today's proponents of public journalism, its initial use was more closely associated with the growth of scientific naturalism in the 1920s than any notion of the need to remain neutral or detached. Objective journalism as a technique is based both on the original meaning as outlined by Walter Lippmann and the more recent practice of this form of newsgathering; studying each of these aspects is essential to understanding the values and means of this form of journalism.

Values of objective journalism Objective journalism is often seen as the successor to the sensationalistic journalism which was common in the 19th century. Wishing to avoid heavily skewed, sensational and propagandistic news, many journalists, most notably Lippmann, realized the need for a standard of journalism which would simultaneously ascribe credibility to the field and provide an intrinsically different news product.

This new standard took the form of objective journalism, a technique modeled after the.social sciences. Its ultimate goal was to expunge the biases and ideologies that journalists bring to reporting. Objectivity, it was heralded, was a way to delineate facts from feelings, truths from opinions. Penultimately, it was hoped that the extraction of reporter biases would yield a more pure form of news reporting based singularly on facts - not absolute facts, but verified, consensual facts.

Further, it was believed that objective journalism would benefit the public by providing unembellished and unbiased presentations of facts from which people could formulate their own conclusions.

In short, the basic tenets of objective journalism are: To extract reporter biases from journalism; to present factual information in order to best inform the public; to protect the public from duplicitous or biased journalism; to eschew emotional or slanted reporting; and to raise the credibility of the profession of news reporting. Means of objective journalism It was Lippmann who best argued for the application of a systematic scientific study to journalism. He believed that "there is but one kind of unity possible in a world as diverse as ours.

It is unity of method, rather than of aim; the unity of the disciplined experiment." Mirroring the social sciences, journalists like Lippmann devised rigorous procedures which, if followed, would consistently yield facts on which all reporters could agree. Herbert Gans writes, "like scientific method, journalistic method is validated by consensus. Equally important, the methods themselves are considered objective."

Similarly, Everette Dennis states that objective reporting is possible if "procedures are followed providing for systematic decisions." Thus, the values of objective journalism were translated into a technique meant to produce unprejudiced, evidence-based reporting. If the method is properly followed, objective reporting should allow 10 different reporters to reach similar conclusions from a set of consensually agreed-upon facts. Hence, "objectivity, in this sense, means that a person's statements about the world can be trusted if they are submitted to established rules deemed legitimate by a professional community."

The influence of scientific method is clearly seen in all introductory journalism textbooks. Students are taught to dogmatically follow procedures of fact verification. Melvin Mencher writes, "An objective report contains material that everyone would agree is based on fact.

Stories are objective when material in them is borne out by evidence." As the basis of objective journalism, facts must be rigorously checked for validity, attribution, and accuracy. This is accomplished by checking every fact against multiple sources of information, including records, experts and other relevant information sources. Further, only after all the facts have been gathered should reporters comment upon them.

Gans states that reporters should "strive for opinions based on 'subjective reactions' which follow from gathered facts. Journalistic values are seen as reactions to the news rather than a priori judgments which determine what becomes newsworthy." Neophyte reporters are also admonished to gather as many facts as possible before conducting an interview to prevent news sources from using the media to disseminate mis- or disinformation; an informed reporter should be able to spot information discrepancies immediately and investigate them.

Further, students are told to strive for complete accuracy, which includes: Verifying the spelling of all names; understanding the information to be reported; avoiding unwarranted assumptions; placing the story in the most relevant context; and consistently seeking statements from all relevant parties in a story. The adherence to these practices is meant to mirror that of the scientist; reporters meticulously gather, question, verify and re-question information until they are convinced of its authenticity.

Only after this process is complete are reporters permitted to draw conclusions. In sum, objective journalism strives to use the scientific method of systematic fact-gathering and fact-verification to remove reporter biases from news coverage. Westerstahl succinctly expresses the need for objectivity when he comments, "objective news reporting is not accomplished without conscious will," and "when that will is missing, then the requirement of truth will occasionally be affected, but relevance decisions, balance between the parties in the conflict, and the presentations of the parties will always be affected."

## PUBLIC JOURNALISM

By their [reporters'] actions, they should try to create the conditions in which the public can learn its business and find solutions to its problems. Public politics, public discussion, public involvement by public-minded citizens - these are the announced goals.

Values of public journalism Public journalism is an inchoate technique that has been steadily evolving over the last several years. Jay Rosen writes, "Public journalism is not a settled doctrine or a strict code of conduct but an unfolding philosophy about the place of the journalist in public life." Put less eloquently, public journalism "is ambiguous and messy work."

Charlotte Grimes comments that public journalism "aims to fix American public life and to fix American journalism, both of which it deems to be sadly, badly broken." Grimes is referring to the fact that the advent of public journalism was initiated by research highlighting that key American institutions are simultaneously eroding: newspapers' loss of readers, the decline in voting, the national loss of a sense of place, declining civic membership, the rising disgust with politics and the decay of public discourse were all speculated to be related in some way.

Several journalists and scholars assert that part of the

problem stems from an objective press which has alienated itself from citizens by its code of detachment. The argument runs like this: People feel attachment to each other when they share certain core values; objective reporting champions itself as detached, thus implicitly claiming that it shares core values with no one; thus, citizens feel alienated from the news media, and this aids in the erosion of civic and political involvement.

For decades, journalists have worked under the assumption that credibility stemmed from an unwillingness to care about outcomes, and the result is a cynical, disempowered polity. Public journalists assert that credibility does not spring from detachment but from shared values and interests with their communities.

Necessarily, journalists must move beyond the simple telling of news and take a proactive stance on addressing problems and generating deliberative solutions to them. Arthur Charity writes, "Public journalism is nothing more than the conviction that journalism's business is about making citizenship work." Similarly, Monica Bowman asserts that public journalism "seeks to engage citizens in public discourse, foster civic responsibility, and encourage citizens to take ownership of community problems." Thus, the fundamental characteristic of public journalism is its emphasis on aiding the public in addressing and solving mutual problems.

Many public journalists have been inspired by Daniel Yankelovich's writings on generating public judgment. Public judgment is the outcome of informed citizens deliberating about social-political problems with the goal of creating viable, consensually-supported solutions. It stands in stark contrast to the term mass opinion and all of its cynical, negative connotations.

Yankelovich argues that there are three stages to reaching public judgment: Consciousness raising, working through and resolution. Public journalists realise that the news media are very good at accomplishing consciousness raising, as demonstrated by the numerous works on agenda-setting. However, to accomplish the second and third stages, public journalism "provides the information people need to engage in informed discussion of the items on that agenda" and it "moves beyond agenda setting by providing information relevant to the clarification of core values and organizing a discussion with that goal in mind."

The stage of working through assumes that journalism can assist people in making educated decisions on tough issues. Finally, once these decisions have been made, public journalists believe that it is the responsibility of journalism to champion these ideas to the public.

Bowman eloquently summarizes the stance of public journalism: "The goal of civic journalism is to provide citizens with the news and information they need to function fully as participants in our democratic society." According to public journalists, the accomplishment of these goals means going further than objectively supplying information to the public.

## MEANS OF PUBLIC JOURNALISM

Currently, the practice of public journalism is just as nebulous and diverse as its philosophy. Nonetheless, there are several core practices which differentiate public journalism from objective reporting.

As Jay Rosen and Davis Merritt make clear, public journalism requires a fundamental change concerning the way that audiences are viewed. Rather than thinking of them as simply consumers or readers, public journalists attempt to think about the audience as a collection of citizens. Consequently, public journalists attempt to discover the core values shared by the community; these values will become the cornerstone of news coverage. As Richard Harwood points out, "the most fruitful insights from tapping into civic life emerge when journalists actively engage people in uncovering the essence of what they are thinking." This, of course, requires journalists to move beyond reporting and observing; they must adopt a pro-active and involved role in the community.

Most importantly, public journalism insists on a focus on solutions as opposed to problems. For instance, public journalists eschew the horse-race coverage discussed by Thomas Patterson, and they refuse to talk about politics in terms of tactics and machinations. Instead, they focus on the needs and concerns of the citizens, attempting to encourage discussions centered around the core values of the citizenry.

Merritt aptly points out that this requires "developing a new journalistic talent: the ability to understand and write clearly about the competing beliefs and priorities that underlie each public problem. Rosen and Merritt highlight four of the most intrinsic practices of public journalism: Sorting out the core values of citizens; encouraging constructive, deliberative citizen debates; providing in-depth reporting of particularly tough issues; and, reporting news stories which demonstrate the successes and potential of an active public.

Clearly, the above list is necessarily broad and vague; there are numerous ways to go about public journalism. In some communities, public journalism has taken the form of press-sponsored neighborhood round-table debates, while in other communities it has involved town hall meetings or mock legislatures.

But no matter how it manifests itself, the basic practice of public journalism always requires instigating citizens to confront and solve problems. Rosen states, "Public journalists thus try to challenge, cajole, and otherwise disturb the complacency of any community that has work to do, choices to make, opportunities to seize control of its future in a democratic manner."

It is important to emphasize that public journalists do not equate their breaking away from detachment with the breaking away from neutrality. Indeed, Rosen readily states that the pledge of neutrality is vital to public journalism because "it separates 'doing journalism' from 'doing politics'." Similarly, Ed Fouhy states that the essential values of traditional, objective journalism - accuracy, seriousness, context, and independence - are retained by public journalists.

Thus, the objective is to initially foment deliberation, after which the public journalist will allow the citizens to reach their own conclusions. However, due to the need for efficiency in journalism, it is difficult for journalists to emphasize simultaneously both thorough fact-verification and provocation of the public. Rather, journalists must decide which goal they wish to emphasize most, and this choice will fundamentally determine which style of journalism they embrace.

## COMPARING AND CONTRASTING

It should be obvious that there is an intrinsic difference between objective and public journalism. The former places a premium on providing the most accurate and factual information possible.

It involves reporters quickly gathering and confirming facts and presenting them to the public in a detached manner. The latter places a premium on playing a pro-active role in communities.

It asks reporters to discover which issues concern the public and to then provide a forum in which these issues can be discussed, debated and resolved. These competing primary goals have led to the creation of the two distinct techniques marked by their own unique set of practices. Yet, recent debate reveals a fundamental lack of appreciation for what each technique offers to journalism.

## ELITISM VERSUS EGALITARIANISM

One nuance of the debate between objective and public journalism entails the dichotomy of elitism and egalitarianism. While objective journalists have often been called elitists, public journalists herald themselves as egalitarians seeking to give the people a voice.

Placing labels on either of these forms of journalism is limiting and debilitates the debate over their relative merits. The study of technique allows the realization that both objective and public journalism contain elements of elitism and egalitarianism.

Public journalism strives "to re-engage readers, listeners and viewers with the public life of their communities" in order to encourage them into confronting issues. Further, public journalists are willing to actively promote public decision-making "even if journalists must create the public space where those decisions are discussed."

The fact that public journalists are attempting to force the creation of civic capital while simultaneously setting the conditions within which this capital can be exercised suggests elitist tendencies. William Woo, commenting on public journalism, states, "I think about the possibility of developing an elitism in which the non-voter, the non-participator, becomes not merely a second-class citizen but also a second-class reader."

Just as in the myth of Plato's cave where only those who apprehend the form of the good are fit to rule, public journalists are defining what a public good consists of and they are constructing the stage upon which the good is to be revealed. While this sort of issue prompting may be necessary, perhaps even beneficial, it still suggests elitism.

Clearly, the elitism/egalitarianism dichotomy is far too simplistic and misplaced to aid in the debate over objective and public journalism. The issue is not which approach is more egalitarian or elitist; the issue involves examining how each technique perceives its role in society.

## THE ROLE OF CONSTRAINTS

The study of technique affords the opportunity to take note of an important difference between these forms of journalism; their varying notions of constraints. The practices developed in objective journalism were created out a perceived need for constraints to be placed on the press. Lippmann, criticizing the state of the press prior to the advent of objective journalism, states,

It [tabloid journalism] selects from events of the day those aspects which most immediately engage attention, and in place of the effort to see life steadily and whole it sees life dramatically, episodically, and from what is called, in the jargon of the craft, the angle of human interest.

For Lippmann, the only way for journalists to see life steadily and whole was to incorporate a set of constraints, mostly based on social scientific study. Thus, journalists do not utilize the technique of objectivity simply because it allows them to accurately gather facts; rather, they use objectivity because without it, they argue, no pure facts would exist. Conversely, proponents of public journalism are looking to break free of the constraints created by objective reporting.

Fouhy observes that "they [public journalists] are finding that some of the 'ancient' and 'sacred' practices of journalism are simply habits best done away with." It is very difficult for a reporter to disturb the complacency of a public or cajole the polity into making a decision while remaining detached, nor can a reporter urge action while remaining impartial. Charity points out that the ideals of detachment and impartiality have no sacred meaning or utility for journalists who wish to aggressively engage the public.

The study of these two journalistic practices as techniques has shed light on the fact that each form of journalism has a very different set of notions about the necessity of constraints. Objective journalism was conceived out of the desire to reel in a sensationalistic press whose sole focus was to create outrageous and attention-grabbing stories.

It advocates the use of constraints to set the press apart from the public and social institutions in order to ensure fairness and detachment. In contrast, public journalism was born out of a perceived need to reinvigorate the polity. It advocates the breaking of prior constraints in order to directly engage and mobilize the public.

The first technique institutes constraints on reporters and news organizations in order to best serve society, and the other is looking to emancipate itself from those bonds in order to do the same. Any debate over the merits of these techniques must confront their divergent understandings of the role of constraints on the press.

## DEFINING QUALITY JOURNALISM

Another issue of key importance involves the quality of news coverage. The examination of objective and public journalism as techniques reveals that each approach has a fundamentally different definition of a quality news product. Of primary importance to objective journalists is the presentation of reliable information. Conversely, public journalists place prime importance on presenting information that voters can find useful in making decisions important to their community.

This is not to say that objective journalists do not wish to provide useful information to the public or that public journalists do not strive to present reliable information, but that these two techniques vary in where they place these concerns along a continuum of importance. Again, time constraints force journalists to decide what is most important to them - extremely reliable information which may sacrifice some usefulness, or extremely useful information which may sacrifice some reliability.

These different ideals of quality are at the heart of much of the criticisms leveled against both forms of journalism. Objective journalism has been accused of making information useless by presenting it in a detached and aloof manner. The charge is that while objective reporting may indeed strive to provide accurate and unbiased news, this does not adequately assist the public in interpreting and using this information. Without such guidance, the argument runs, the public becomes disenchanted, disillusioned and cynical. Inherent to the criticisms is a belief in the primacy of making sure the information being provided spurs civic engagement.

Critics of public journalism question whether it is wise to allow the press to lose the detachment inherent to objective journalistic practices. Frankel claims that "the emphasis on 'solutions' and 'connections' will inevitably distort the news agenda, devalue problems for which no easy remedy is apparent, and end up compromising the newspaper and its independence." Further, he asserts that journalists should work harder at better reporting while leaving reform to the reformers.

Dennis offers a similar sentiment when he claims that "journalists should cover the parade, not march in it" because community organizing must remain separate from journalism.

Clearly, these criticisms stem from a deep-seeded belief in a need to keep the press detached.

The discussion of quality hints at tenuous assumptions made by each journalistic approach. Objective journalists assume that the public will make good use of the information provided to it.

Merritt takes issue with this assumption, stating that "if journalists view their job as merely providing information - simply telling the news in a detached way - they will not be particularly helpful to public life." There is no guarantee that the public intrinsically knows what to do with all of the information it receives, which is why public journalists believe that information must be provided in a manner that is well-suited for the creation of a deliberative democracy. According to public journalists, detached news reporting does not provide the necessary assistance the public requires to understand its business.

Conversely, Michael Schudson points out that public dialogue does not ensure a healthy democratic process. He states, . when we criticize the reality of the mass media, we do so by opposing it to an ideal of conversation which we are not inclined to examine.... We have developed a notion that all communication should be like a certain model of conversation, whether or not that model really exists or not. This is where public journalism has a problem: The ability of the public to generate a quality debate should not be treated as gospel.

Schudson points out that "there is an unspoken sense among students of the mass media [and the same can be said of public journalists] that the world of face-to-face communication is the world of rich and complicated interaction," but this idealized version of debate may not exist in the real world. In summary, both approaches to journalism rest on challengable assumptions.

This study of technique has afforded the opportunity to focus upon the means and values that are the driving forces behind both objective and public journalism. Rather than compare the final products of each approach with its self-professed goals - a comparison which is unproductive - this examines both through consideration of their values and means. As stated previously, a debate focused only on final products leads to a fruitless argument in which each side showers the opposition with labels, insinuations, and professional debasements. The study of technique, by focusing on the means and values of each form of journalism, has revealed some important points which need to be recognized in the debate over the relative (de)merits of each journalistic approach. Specifically, quibblings over elitism and egalitarianism must be replaced with discussions of constraints and quality.

## Chapter 2

# Visual Communication in Public Journalism

A comparison of the design and photography of public journalism projects with non-public journalism shows there is a difference, but not a radical one. Between 1990 and 1996, more than 400 media outlets in the U.S. had undertaken public journalism projects. Much has been written about the philosophy behind public journalism, its goals, and techniques.

Individual public journalism projects have been analysed and compared against these goals and philosophies, and also compared to traditional journalism to see what, if any, difference exists. However, no study has yet focused on the visual communication of public journalism in newspapers. Public journalism practitioners and theoreticians argue that the content of stories generated through public journalism methods is significantly different from the content generated by traditional reporting methods. News designers are taught that the form of their designs must reflect the content of the stories rather than artistic preference or trends.

This prompts the question: If the content of stories generated through public journalism methods is different, and design is driven by content, doesn't it follow that design for public journalism will be different than design for non-public journalism? This is a key question that visual communicators and public journalists must address if the final product is to truly integrate verbal and visual meaning.

The purpose of this research, the first of a two-phase

study, is to explore how public journalism projects have been visually communicated in newspapers practicing this approach, and how they differ from the visual communication of non-public journalism.

Through content analysis, textual analysis and telephone interviews, this exploratory study examined the design and photography of projects at six newspapers; four practicing public journalism and two practicing non-public journalism to explore how public journalism projects were visually communicated in newspapers that practiced the genre, and whether the visual communication of public journalism differed from the visual communication of nonpublic journalism.

Public journalism is a product of the 1990s — its first well-documented experiment was in late 1989 in Columbus, Georgia. Even a decade later, there are as many operational definitions of public journalism as there are media outlets that practice it. For a conceptual definition that speaks to the developing theory of public journalism Jay Rosen has said: "Journalism can and should play a part in strengthening citizenship, improving public debate and reviving public life." Public or civic journalism is widely understood as an approach designed to address issues that readers say are important, rather than only those issues identified by experts. It seeks to promote a public conversation about those issues that will result in a collective working through of the problem to resolution. Among its goals are strengthening citizenship, improving the quality of public debate, and reviving public life. It proposes a more active role for the press than has traditionally been adopted.

Public journalism derives many of its philosophical foundations from the social responsibility theory of the press and agenda-setting theory. While some scholars of public journalism trace its roots as far back as Thomas Jefferson, John Locke and John Stuart Mill, it seems unarguable that the development of the ideas that infuse public journalism were an outgrowth of the debates between John Dewey and Walter Lippmann over the proper role for the press in a democracy.

Dewey and other scholars helped lay the foundation for a gradual shift toward the emerging social responsibility theory of the press, which was akin to Dewey's proposal of the role of the press in helping build a more pluralist and tolerant society. The evolution of the social responsibility theory culminated in the Commission on Freedom of the Press' report in 1947.

The Hutchins Commission's work can be seen as a forerunner of public journalism in that it called for the press to offer "a method of presenting and clarifying the goals and values of the society" and for reporting to project "the opinions and attitudes of the groups in society to one another." Although social responsibility theory has been challenged as a product of its time, the developing concept of public journalism has drawn heavily from the Hutchins Commission and expanded on the role of the press by incorporating ideas from Dewey, philosophers Jurgen Habermas and Hannah Arendt, and political scientist Michael Sandel. Arendt, Habermas and Sandel all acknowledge the important role media play in society – without communication there is no public sphere. Contemporaries whose thoughts have added fuel to the public journalism fire include Daniel Yankelovich in Coming to Public Judgment, Russell Neuman, Marian Just and Ann Crigler with Common Knowledge, Clifford Christians, John Ferre and Mark Fackler's Good News, James Carey, Jay Rosen, and Davis Merritt.

Public journalism also incorporates aspects of agenda-setting theory, which says that one of the effects of mass communication is to direct the audience's attention to certain problems or issues. By conducting focus groups and taking polls of what the audience considers important before reporting on issues, public journalists make a self-conscious effort to avoid agenda-setting by the media or others, including government and special interests.

While there is no consensus on what public journalism is, or even on what to call it, the premise that all agree on is that it is the duty of the press is to improve the quality of public life by fostering public participation and debate. Some of the methods and techniques public journalists are best known to have used toward these goals include focus groups and citizen advisory boards to discover issues of importance to people; avoiding conflict framing of stories; using ordinary citizens as sources as well as officials and experts; seeking to clarify the core values behind opinions and underlying causes of problems; focusing on solutions and success stories; and taking an active role in promoting discussion among citizens with public forums and town hall meetings.

While public journalists are still focused on inventing their craft, they are understandably concerned with fine-tuning the proper reporting and writing techniques. As is historically typical in journalism, the visual aspects of journalistic storytelling — photography and design — are postponed for attention after the verbal aspects have been worked out.

While they may momentarily forget this essential element, journalists have come to realise that visual communication can be just as important, if not more so, as verbal communication. Inherent in all definitions of design is the idea that it is not simply decoration or dressing up a page, but that form carries a content of its own. The literature laments the use of designs that overemphasize form to the detriment of communication. Originally, design developed in response to the mechanical needs of page make-up. With the advent of photocomposition, mechanical concerns were eliminated as well as the design conventions they necessitated. Today, the story content and needs of the reader drive design.

It is the consensus in design theory that form is inextricably linked to message meaning. The form, or design, of news changes the perception of its content. If newspaper page design is truly to be used to communicate meaning derived from the story's content, and if public journalism has changed that content, then design must change to reflect that. Design must now communicate the public agenda.

If public journalism is an attempt to better address the goals laid out by the Hutchins Commission, how can design and photography encourage this? Perhaps public journalism photographs should reflect citizens more often than candidates. Photojournalists might also refuse to participate in photo opportunities organized by public relations people in the interest of letting the public set the agenda, rather than PR professionals. Public journalism design could also make use of design elements which help communicate its goals, such as summary boxes describing the values in conflict over a certain issue, or graphics telling readers how to get involved, express their opinions, or get more information on an issue. These and other topics must be addressed by public journalism's visual communicators if the final product is to truly integrate verbal and visual meaning.

There is some indication in the public journalism literature that design is beginning to be considered. Most are references made in passing with little follow-up as to how the goals of public journalism might be achieved with visuals. Others offer some specifics. For example, in a speech to the Regional Reporters Association, Jan Schaffer of the Pew Centre for Civic Journalism suggested building in "graphic devices that invite and encourage readers and viewers to contact the news organization and react to an issue, a controversy, a public problem." Jay Rosen made the connection between public journalism's goals and design when he commented that, "If the pages of the newspaper are thought of as a public space designed by journalists, then what the (Wichita) Eagle did is arrange this space so that the proper concerns of politics (`issues in depth') shone through." He then described how the Eagle accomplished this with visual elements.

For each of the major issues, the Eagle published a list called Places to Start, with the names, addresses and phone numbers of organizations and agencies working on the problem. Repeated invitations were issued to readers to contact the paper with their comments and suggestions. At the Charlotte Observer, the Where They Stand feature was more than a voter's guide. If candidates refused to answer the questions the public posed, then a blank appeared under the candidate's name. This was a powerful use of space, charged with visual meaning.

A survey found that one of the most useful features was the Where They Stand box. The Pew Center's Schaffer also reported that a focus group at one newspaper responded differently to information conveyed graphically than when the same information was reported in a bylined story: "They loved the voter's guide in a grid and asked why we didn't give it to them earlier and repeat it often.... It seemed to them fairer and more factual. There was no byline and no news peg, just distilled information. Even though it was from bylined stories, the way it was presented seemed to make a difference in how much people believed it."

At the Virginian-Pilot in Norfolk, a new feature was inaugurated on the front page to stimulate more productive dialogue about controversies in the news. The paper also created a new design element that graphically conveyed its new treatment of controversy. After summarizing the themes of the issue, readers were directed to question themselves. For example: "If you tend to disagree... in what part of (his) argument can you find merit? Even if you tend to agree... what part of (his) argument do you have problems with? Where is the common ground?" It is much harder to find discussions of photojournalism that promotes the ideals of public journalism. One example that was widely discussed appeared in the Wisconsin State Journal when citizens gathered in the seats of their representatives at the state capitol to question candidates. The result was "a startling visual," according to Rosen, a visual symbol that things had changed.

The value of visual communication to public journalism's goals is even beginning to be addressed tangentially in some scholarly research. Paul Riede concluded that, in the Wichita Eagle's The People Project, the most journalistic depth came in the form of the graphics: "the graphic goes beneath the surface, personality-based coverage of politics typical of traditional journalism." This same study called the "innovative use of the `core values' graphics'... the project's most promising attempt at depth in coverage." In order discover how public journalism projects have been visually communicated and whether they differ from that of non-public journalism, one research question and six hypotheses regarding visual communication were developed based on public journalism characteristics derived from the literature. *They are:*

*H1:* Public journalism will visually convey more mobilizing Information to help citizens participate in their communities than non-public journalism.

*H2:* Public journalism will visually convey more interactivity, i.e.: ways to contact the media.

*H3:* Public journalism photographs will use fewer managed photo opportunities than non-public journalism.

*H4:* Public journalism will use more photographs of citizens and "real people" versus candidates or experts than nonpublic journalism.

*H5:* Public journalism will use more visual devices to convey views of citizens and "real people" than non-public journalism.

*H6:* Public journalism will use more visual devices to convey common ground and solutions than non-public journalism.

*RQ1:* Does the visual communication of public journalism differ with circulation size?

The unit of analysis was all the stories on the public journalism topic in one day's issue of the newspaper. Forty-one newspaper issues were sampled. The 41 issues were drawn from six newspapers in two circulation sizes using one week from each paper. For this study, large newspapers were defined as greater than 200,000 daily circulation. Small newspapers were defined as less than 100,000 daily circulation. Medium newspapers, 100,000 to 200,000 daily circulation, were not included in order to maximize comparisons. It was postulated there would be little difference, for reasons such as resources, between medium and large papers, but the difference would be greater between small and large papers.

One week's issues from two large-circulation non-public journalism newspapers were compared against one week's issues from four public journalism newspapers (both large and small circulation sizes); one week's issues from two small-circulation public journalism newspapers were compared against one week's issues from two large-circulation public journalism newspapers; and one week's issues from two large-circulation public journalism newspapers were compared against one week's issues from two large-circulation nonpublic journalism newspapers.

This allowed comparison of the presentation of public journalism against non-public journalism two ways, and also allowed comparison of the presentation within the genre of public journalism.

Sampling time was limited to one week because one newspaper's series ran for only six days. In addition, the large number of variables examined made a larger sample unwieldy. All elements associated with the stories in each issue, including stories, headlines, photos, illustrations, sidebars, boxes, logos, refers, graphics, charts, maps, tables, schedules, lists, pullquotes, readouts, and jumps, were coded for size and presence of public journalism criteria.

Since the purpose of this exploratory project was to learn as much as possible about a subject which has not previously been studied, examining all relevant appearance variables was deemed to be more important than a large sample. If even small differences were detected, the results of this exploratory study could help point the way toward future research.

The public journalism stories were sampled using the latest public journalism projects at each newspaper; the non-public journalism stories were sampled using the newspapers' latest series that was on a similar topic as the public journalism series in its comparison paper, or, if that was not feasible, a project that ran as a series of similar magnitude was chosen. This study analysed the content of the appearance variables of all stories dealing with the subject except opinion pieces and letters to the editor.

The focus of this study was on differences in photography and design. Editorial pages are highly formatted and generally do not vary in presentation, so they were not deemed suitable for this study. Purposive sampling with newspapers stratified by circulation size and chosen for their experience with the public journalism approach was used because it is better suited the purpose of comparing the visual presentation of public journalism to see how it varies within the genre, and of comparing the visual presentation of public journalism to non-public journalism.

The four public journalism newspapers were initially chosen for a different study by the Pew Centre for Civic Journalism. The basis for this decision included the level of experience each paper had with public journalism philosophies and techniques, and Pew's director's and assistant director's assessment that these particular papers were doing some of the more interesting work within the public journalism genre.

Because of their early entry into the movement, the philosophies and practices of public journalism at these papers are assumed to be more highly developed than those of papers just beginning to practice public journalism.

Therefore, the visual communication of public journalism stories should have achieved a deeper level of consideration in these newsrooms. Also, by experimenting with the photographiy and presentation of public journalism for a longer period, their practices should be more finely tuned and may represent the direction that other newspapers will take in public journalism.

The two large circulation newspapers not practicing public journalism were chosen by this researcher for their similarities with the public journalism newspapers in circulation size, morning publication, and market demographics, and also to represent specific regions of the country. Their editors have publicly stated their opposition to the public journalism approach.

The differences in design styles across the different newspapers were taken into account in the textual analysis.

The characteristics of each newspaper sampled are:

*Public journalism - large circulation:*

- San Francisco Chronicle: 489,238 daily circulation. Public journalism project on commuter transportation. Published October-December 1996.

The public journalism stories were sampled using the latest public journalism projects at each newspaper; the non-public journalism stories were sampled using the newspapers' latest series that was on a similar topic as the public journalism series in its comparison paper, or, if that was not feasible, a project that ran as a series of similar magnitude was chosen. This study analysed the content of the appearance variables of all stories dealing with the subject except opinion pieces and letters to the editor.

The focus of this study was on differences in photography and design. Editorial pages are highly formatted and generally do not vary in presentation, so they were not deemed suitable for this study.

Purposive sampling with newspapers stratified by circulation size and chosen for their experience with the public journalism approach was used because it is better suited the purpose of comparing the visual presentation of public journalism to see how it varies within the genre, and of comparing the visual presentation of public journalism to non-public journalism.

The four public journalism newspapers were initially chosen for a different study by the Pew Centre for Civic Journalism. The basis for this decision included the level of experience each paper had with public journalism philosophies and techniques, and Pew's director's and assistant director's assessment that these particular papers were doing some of the more interesting work within the public journalism genre.

Because of their early entry into the movement, the philosophies and practices of public journalism at these papers are assumed to be more highly developed than those of papers just beginning to practice public journalism.

Therefore, the visual communication of public journalism stories should have achieved a deeper level of consideration in these newsrooms. Also, by experimenting with the photographiy and presentation of public journalism for a longer period, their practices should be more finely tuned and may represent the direction that other newspapers will take in public journalism. The two large circulation newspapers not practicing public journalism were chosen by this researcher for their similarities with the public journalism newspapers in circulation size, morning publication, and market demograph.

## COMMON GROUND AND SOLUTIONS

Results showed that the public journalism issues sampled in this study used significantly more visual devices to convey common ground or solutions than non-public journalism issues. None of the non-public journalism issues sampled used visual language to convey common ground or solutions, while 21 per cent of the public journalism issues sampled did so.

Reporting common ground and solutions is fairly unique to public journalism, with non-public journalism traditionally focusing on past events. Common ground and solutions speaks to Yankelovich's idea that media should facilitate a working through stage that ultimately leads to solutions, rather than stopping at the consciousness-raising stage. That none of the non-public journalism issues sampled visually conveyed common ground or solutions reinforces the belief that non-public journalism limits itself to issue-raising.

Even though there is a significant difference between public and Nonpublic journalism in this sample, fewer than one-quarter of the public journalism newspaper stories sampled (21 per cent) used visual devices to convey common ground and solutions. It is hoped that higher ratios would be achieved as public journalism develops. However, this is a sign there is beginning to be an awareness of the need to visually communicate this information. This hypothesis also showed a marginally significant difference between small and large papers within public journalism in this sample.

Larger papers in this study used visual devices for common ground and solutions in 36 per cent of their issues, while only 7 per cent of issues sampled in small papers did so. Perhaps this speaks to the difference in resources between small and large papers. It may be that common ground and solutions are harder to conceptualize, thus, small papers with smaller design staffs, more inexperienced designers, and less time to design each page, will not have the resources to devote to such complex issues. The other side of this argument is that a box conveying possible solutions with typography is neither hard to conceptualize nor time-consuming to execute.

Alternately, it could mean that reporters and editors at small papers are not including common ground and solutions in stories, thus the designers are not either. This seems to be the case with one small public journalism paper sampled. In the textual analysis, the Wisconsin State Journal's We the People project on the fall 1996 election showed no common ground or solutions in either the text or visuals.

The possibility that the topic may not lend itself to exploring common ground and solutions is unlikely since the other public journalism paper that covered the election, the Charlotte Observer, did visually present common ground and solutions. On most days, the Observer had a box on the issue of the day (i.e.: crime, school vouchers, etc.) that outlined different sides, gave background, and told where there was agreement or not. The solutions box on school tuition vouchers explained three reasons for supporting vouchers and three for opposing them. Common ground was explained this way: "Critics and supporters agree that school vouchers, if offered on a national scale, have the power to dramatically change the face of public education. Where both sides disagree is whether those changes will improve or ruin public schools."

Public journalism election coverage in the Wisconsin State Journal more closely resembled non-public journalism in the Omaha World-Herald. Both focused on differences in the candidates' positions rather than where there was agreement on issues. The main difference was that the public journalism election treatment included forums for citizens to question candidates, whereas the non-public journalism coverage did not.

This difference between the small public journalism issues and the large non-public journalism issues could still be partly due to staff resources. But the possibility that journalists at the small paper did not have as great an understanding of public journalism is another likely explanation. In the informant interviews, two designers at the small public journalism paper indicated they had received no training in the philosophy, goals and techniques of public journalism, while the design director at the large public journalism paper said design staffers had been included in educational sessions with one of the founders of public journalism, Prof. Jay Rosen.

## READER-REPORTER INTERACTION

The hypothesis that public journalism designs would visually convey interactivity between readers and the media more than non-public journalism (H2) was also significant. Seventy-five per cent of the public journalism issues in this sample used visual elements to encourage readers to contact the media, while 46 per cent of non-public journalism issues sampled did so. In addition, the number of different ways public journalism provided for readers to contact them (address, phone, e-mail, web site, fax) was highly significant. Small circulation mean = 2.1, large circulation mean =.5. There were no significant differences between small and large circulation issues on this variable, as would be expected if all size papers were practicing public journalism the same way.

## PHOTO OPS AND PHOTOS OF 'REAL PEOPLE'

The two public journalism characteristics that were not significant when public and non-public journalism issues were compared but whose means were in the direction hypothesized both dealt with photographs; whether public journalism relied on managed photo opportunities less often than non-public journalism (H3), and whether public journalism photos featured citizens and real people more often than candidates or experts (H4). The non-significant findings may be due to the low number of cases sampled (N = 41), but it is important that for both hypotheses the mean ratios of non-managed photos and photos of real people to total photos showed that the public journalism issues sampled used fewer photographs from managed photo opportunities and also used more photos of citizens and real people than candidates or experts.

Comparisons within public journalism showed no significant differences between small and large papers' photos in this sample regarding photo opportunities or the use of citizens and real people in photos versus candidates or experts. Textual analysis revealed both small public journalism papers, Binghamton and Wisconsin, used all photos of real people from non-managed photo sources. In the large public journalism category, San Francisco used all non-managed photos featuring citizens in its series on transportation.

Since Binghamton's series was on the local economy and primarily covered the citizen's forums, and San Francisco's series was on commuter woes, it is perhaps not surprising that they were able to find photo subjects that did not involve officials and experts. It is more unusual for election coverage to avoid photos of candidates, yet that is just what the Wisconsin paper did. It achieved this goal mainly by running only one photo (citizens at a forum) over all seven issues; six issues had no photos at all. In the large non-public journalism genre, Omaha used all photos of candidates, as would be expected for traditional journalism.

The variation is mainly explained by the non-public journalism Philadelphia paper's use of all non-managed photos of real people, and the public journalism Charlotte paper's heavy use of managed photo ops of candidates — findings that are counter to what would be expected in ideal public journalism. The story subjects provide partial explanation. In its series on a typical suburban neighborhood, Philadelphia used five to eight pictures every day in its non-public journalism series, all were of real people and none were from photo opportunities. In its election coverage, the public journalism Charlotte paper used mug shots or photo collages of candidates on nearly every cover, plus cutout photos of candidates in its full-page graphic of candidates' answers to voters' questions. In addition, Charlotte used four conventional campaign trail photos over the course of the series, in traditional political photojournalism style.

The only real-people photos Charlotte used were approximately three to five photos daily of the citizens who asked questions of the candidates or whose opinions were quoted. The Charlotte design director indicated in a telephone interview that the amount of campaign-trail photographs shot were "not nearly as many as five years ago... An effort was made to take photos of real people, but that makes things harder." The convention of candidate photographs for election coverage apparently remains strong, even at papers that have embraced public journalism principles. The design director's acknowledgment that finding photos of real people is harder than attending photo opportunities is a candid admission that goes to the root of the difficulty of altering established conventions.

Comments by designers at the public journalism papers in Binghamton, Madison, and San Francisco, all indicated their photographers tried to avoid photo opportunities in favour of real people; however, photo ops could not be entirely eliminated. The former graphics editor at the Madison paper provided some background on the thinking:

The photo staff hates dull pictures, first of all. There is nothing worse than a talking head (politician) or a grip-and-grin. They do try and look for action or images from the issue they are addressing. It is a combination of public journalism and aesthetics.

He also attributed the lack of photos (one photo over seven issues) to aesthetics:

With 'We the People,' the premiere events are these town meetings. They don't make particularly good photos. They are often held in the capitol, which has miserable lighting, and it's a sea of people sitting around. The marching orders are we will shoot that, but we would probably try to limit that to one. Otherwise, we would have photos and stories about journalists from different media getting together to organize 'We the People'."

The idea of using photos of real people that are not the result of photo ops orchestrated by people seeking to manipulate publicity goes to the heart of public journalism philosophy and reflects a conscious effort to avoid agenda-setting effects.

The use of this type of photo would be a sign that public journalism's goals are beginning to be translated into practice. Helping citizens participate in civic life. Of the two remaining hypotheses, neither showed any significant differences between public and non-public journalism. One was the hypothesis that public journalism would visually convey more mobilizing information to help citizens participate in their communities than non-public journalism (H1). There were no significant differences between the sampled public and non-public journalism issues' use of mobilizing information.

However, when comparisons were made within public journalism between large and small papers' issues, there was a highly significant difference in the visual communication of mobilizing information, with small papers scoring better. Only 14 per cent of large papers' stories used visual elements to convey mobilizing information, whereas 71 per cent of small papers' stories used one visual element, and 7 per cent used two.

In the public journalism genre, issues from both large papers sampled used no mobilizing information in visual format. However, both small public journalism papers sampled visually conveyed mobilizing information.

The topics—the Charlotte Observer's election coverage — cannot be the reason, however, since the two other papers which carried election coverage, including one non-public journalism paper (Omaha), listed mobilizing information. The other large public journalism paper, San Francisco, gave almost no mobilizing information on its transportation series. Both small public journalism papers listed mobilizing information frequently; Wisconsin had the most and most regular mobilizing information with its boxes for forum broadcasts, call-in lines and registration information for upcoming town meetings. Wisconsin even developed regular graphic devices its designers called democracy boxes. Perhaps the convention of having these boxes to fill kept mobilizing information in the forefront for Wisconsin designers. Binghamton usually publicized an upcoming priority setting conference or results of the economic teams' reports.

One reason for these results could be that mobilizing information is not new or unique to public journalism the way other variables can be. For this study, mobilizing information consisted of news citizens could use to participate in community life. However, the importance of information which allows people to take action has been discussed in scholarly and trade publications since at least the 1970s.

Well before the advent of public journalism, traditional journalism has offered dates of neighborhood watch meetings, names and addresses of redevelopment agencies that offer grant money, etc. Because of the length of time over which journalists have been aware of the importance of mobilizing information, and the ubiquitous nature of such information, it may not be surprising that there are no significant differences in the amount of mobilizing information conveyed visually in public and non-public journalism.

The greater resources at larger papers cannot help explain why small papers used more visual devices for mobilizing information than large papers. Mobilizing information should be quite familiar and top-of-mind to designers at both small and large papers, public journalism and non-public journalism. Perhaps another explanation for the highly significant difference between small circulation and large circulation public journalism designs that visually convey mobilizing information can be found in James Lemert and colleague's findings.

Because small papers may better reflect their small communities, there is more awareness of readers' desire for visual display of mobilizing information. If large public journalism papers are not providing mobilizing information, this supports Lemert's theory that mobilizing information is regularly missing when issues are located outside of town, where audiences ordinarily can't look up addresses and phone numbers. This may be the case for large newspapers that cover many different communities.

## VIEWS OF REAL PEOPLE

The other hypothesis that was not significant was that public journalism would use more visual devices to convey views of real people (H5). This non-significant finding between the public and non-public journalism issues sampled is interesting because views of real people rather than experts or politicians are one of the central tenets of public journalism. Although all designers interviewed said they tried to include views of real people, two said it was a copy desk decision and would be done mainly through pullquotes. However, textual analysis revealed that not all public journalism papers visually displayed views of real people. Both Wisconsin and San Francisco used no graphics or design elements for views of real people, although these views were carried within the text.

A lack of significant difference between public and non-public journalism's use of views of real people may signify that visual journalists do not fully understand or embrace this idea. If a significant difference were found to exist in the written communication of views of real people, but not in the visual communication, this would have implications for the integration of the designers and copy editors with the reporters and editors. It may indicate that designers have not been included in sessions devoted to explaining the philosophies of public journalism and do not understand its principles fully, or, they are aware of the importance of views of real people but are leaving it to reporters to include in stories rather than employing content-driven design to convey this visually. There was also no difference in the sampled issues between small and large public journalism's use of visual devices to convey views of real people, but this would be expected if all papers practiced public journalism the same way.

## THE IMPORTANCE OF UNDERSTANDING

Two final points of interest were revealed in the interviews when designers were asked whether they designed differently for public journalism than for non-public journalism. Designers at two papers said yes, public journalism design was different from non-public journalism design, and designers at the other two papers replied no, there was no difference. Interestingly, the no difference responses came from designers whose papers did not have training sessions on the concepts and techniques of public journalism, or who did not include visual journalists in those sessions.

Both affirmative responses came from newspapers whose designers did participate in public journalism education sessions. Understanding of public journalism principles was one of the explanations offered for some of the findings in this study, and the perception of designers regarding the difference in designing for public journalism reinforces such an explanation. Visual journalists who did not attend sessions aimed at explaining public journalism's goal and principles may not understand it as well as those who did and, therefore, may not consider ways to visually communicate those goals and principles.

Also, one of the designers interviewed complained that too many journalists at the paper felt like they had been ordered to do public journalism with no opportunity for discussion or input. This chapter did not offer training sessions in public journalism. "If they're really going to get people on board to do this and do this well, there has to be that discussion," said the designer, who asked to remain anonymous. "There are numerous ethical challenges in doing this, and they need to at least be explored, as do the possible pitfalls." Both these insights have implications for managing editors contemplating introducing public journalism into their newsrooms.

This study has used the emerging theory of public journalism, which claims a significantly different content than non-public journalism, and the theory of content-driven design, which says that visual meaning must reflect the written content, to examine the question prompted by these theories: If the content of stories generated through public journalism methods is different, and design is driven by content, shouldn't design for public journalism be different than design for non-public journalism?

The results from this study are mixed. Of six hypotheses that speak to the question of whether public journalism is visually different from non-public journalism, two showed significant differences among the newspaper issues sampled. Public journalism stories in this study used more visual devices to convey common ground and solutions, and ways to contact the media than did non-public journalism stories.. Four hypotheses showed no significant differences between public journalism and non-public journalism, but two had means in the direction hypothesized.

The public journalism issues sampled were more likely than non-public journalism to use fewer managed photo opportunities and more photos of real people than candidates or experts, but the differences were not significant These are signs that some of public journalism's goals may be beginning to be translated into practice by visual journalists, but that there are other goals that are not being addressed visually, at least in these newspapers.

The fact that the public journalism issues sampled were not significantly different from the non-public journalism issues in how they visually conveyed views of real people — one of the central tenets of public journalism — should be of concern. That the public journalism issues sampled visually communicated no more mobilizing information than the non-public journalism issues is less cause for worry because mobilizing information is not unique to public journalism the way the other characteristics can be. This study has also found that, in some cases, public journalism papers that have established new conventions in place of the old have found it easier to adhere consistently to public journalism principles; for instance, the development of standing graphics such as democracy boxes for mobilizing information.

One problem in the consistent communication of public journalism characteristics seems to be with journalists' fundamental understanding of public journalism. Confusion over and even unawareness of public journalism principles seems to be a basic, underlying reason why the practice of public journalism is not significantly different from non-public journalism in terms of visual communication. In addition, it appears that not all designers are practicing content-driven design.

For instance, this research found stories which included views of real people in the text but not in the design. In conclusion, there appear to be some significant differences in this sample in the way public journalism is visually communicated compared with non-public journalism. However, there is not enough significance to say that it represents a radical departure from non-public journalism, at least in the issues studied here. It appears another researcher's conclusion regarding the content of public journalism may be correct for the visual display as well: "there is no overriding, core philosophy of public journalism at some of the papers practicing it; instead it has become a label used to name a variety of special projects."

## Chapter 3

# Civic Journalism in Practice

There is little doubt that people believe the media are out of touch with the lives of ordinary citizens. A 1994 Times Mirror poll indicated that 71 per cent of Americans believe that the news media hinder efforts to solve society's problems. Recent polls show little change in this public animosity toward the press. The continuing decline in newspaper readership, fewer viewers of television news and a significant drop in voter participation all create what some critics believe is a lethal brew that is threatening not only journalism but democracy.

Studies show that citizens feel that no one is sincerely listening when they express their views and concerns. People are growing more and more isolated from one another and from the public life of their communities. And, despite evidence that people are interested in policy decisions that affect their lives - they no longer know how to access the system or make themselves heard.

As the 50th anniversary of the Hutchins Commission's report draws near, journalists are expanding the commission's concept of social responsibility and enlarging the traditional community journalism paradigm. Civic, or public journalists at some newspapers are attempting to bridge this journalist-citizen communication gap by using a variety of creative methods to systematically listen to citizens - to talk with rather than talk at the people.

This research examines different group-listening endeavors used by four newspapers. These mini-case studies focus on specific listening techniques reporters used to seek information and insights from citizens as they began reporting projects. The newspapers and projects are:

- The Columbia Missourian's School-to-Work project and its Religion in Public Life project.
- The Akron Beacon Journal's - Coming Together, a follow-up project of the newspaper's race relation series A Question of Colour.
- The Wichita Eagle's April 1995 mayoral election coverage and its 1995 neighborhood conversations project.
- The Tallahassee Democrat's Living Room Conversations method in its Public Agenda Project.

Communication theorists contend that when people hold conversations about topics they believe are important to them and to their families, a number of things happen. First, they begin to feel that their opinions are valued. They gain new insights into the topic by listening to others' opinions, and as they process the information, they start to weigh options. They begin to take ownership of the issues and to assume some responsibility in addressing community concerns.

The media often depend on opinion polls, and while this method has its benefits, it allows for no group interaction. Indeed, some critics argue that polls appear to widen the gap between media and citizens and further distance the people from civic participation.

In Coming to Public Judgment: Making Democracy Work in a Complex World, pollster Daniel Yankelovich argues that polls lack depth and fail to promote public judgment, a deliberative process that leads to problem resolution. Polls tend to define public judgment by adding up the score rather than by the process of thoughtful deliberation.

One of the most important elements in group conversations is the interaction among group members. In fact, researchers gave found that just by participating in the group process itself, group members develop a sense of involvement in the project. Often, the interactive conversation reveals information about issues that had never even occurred to the reporters. One scholar observed that group communication dynamics may "lead us to change the very way that we think about the problems that interest us."

Davis Buzz Merritt, Jr. of the Wichita Eagle, argues that newspapers must find new and innovative ways to listen to citizens. In Public Journalism & Public Life: Why Telling the News is Not Enough, Merritt writes that three elements are necessary for democracy to function: shared, relevant information, a method or place for deliberation about the application of that information and shared values on which to evaluate information and base public decisions. Journalists in these case studies say they are attempting to find ways for citizens to share relevant information with each other and with a wider readership audience.

In each of these case studies, journalists had to confront the aspect of source confidentiality. The usual method is to grant all participants some level of confidentiality. The reporter listens for themes in the conversations and uses the information only as background for subsequent reports. Often the reporter will call the participants back later for more in-depth and on-the-record interviews, but the conversations themselves usually are not reported unless the views, but the reporting staff has decided, with the permission of the participants, to do otherwise.

Although the case studies reveal a variety of listening techniques, most fit into three general categories: Focus groups, resource panels and community conversations. The following is a brief description of each method.

**Focus Groups**

Focus groups solicit information about citizens' attitudes, beliefs and community concerns. The data then are used to develop news reports. The information received from these discussions helps reporters focus on the topic issues and provide them with new perspectives. Communication scholars argue that focus groups enable researchers to better understand people's views of reality.

It is important to keep in mind, however, that just any group is not a focus group. Traditional focus groups are highly structured and follow specific procedures and methodology. Also, focus groups are not the answer for every reporting project. For example, they are not used to debate or grapple with issues or to recommend solutions, such as in a public forum. Nor can they be used like a survey to generalize results to a larger population. A focus group yields qualitative, not quantitative data.

## RESOURCE PANELS

In some instances, when journalists need specialty information, they call upon experts in the community to share their knowledge with the reporting staff. The expert or resource panel is one of many ways in which journalists attempt to gain understanding and broaden their perspectives when writing about complex and unfamiliar topics. The resource panel is a less structured method than a focus group, and it has a different research purpose. Resource panelists are chosen for their knowledge and expertise relating to a defined topic. While both focus groups and resource panels assist the journalist in gaining new insights from people in the community, the information core is different. A focus group is used to refine the questions. A resource panel is used to define the questions themselves.

When journalists decide to convene focus groups, they have already investigated the topic. They have a good idea about general issues, problems or concerns within the topic area. On the other hand, resource panels are used as a primary information source to define the topic itself. A resource panel is convened when the topic is complex and reporters have such limited knowledge they are uncertain how to even approach the coverage.

Unlike focus groups or community conversations, resource panels are created for audience interaction as well as interaction among panelists. The audience has an opportunity to ask questions of the panelists, which in turn usually generates more conversation among the panelists and then sparks additional questions from the audience. This double-level interactivity is one of the benefits of resource panels, and is especially valuable for reporters, who have the opportunity to learn from experts.

## COMMUNITY CONVERSATIONS

This technique is the most fluid of the information newsgathering methods and allows a great deal of versatility and creativity. The process of creating a community conversation depends upon the target population and what the research question is: what information the journalist is seeking from the citizens. Reporters target specific groups, neighborhoods, or demographic characteristics. Participants are selected in a variety of ways, and meetings are arranged to suit the project, but they are usually held at comfortable and informal sites. The purpose of creating these community conversations is specifically to listen to citizens talk about an identified issue. Although it may seem similar to group interview techniques, there is one big difference. The focus is not on the reporter and his or her questions. The focus is on reporters listening to the citizens' conversations. While the reporter or the moderator leads the group and asks an opening question, the purpose of the community conversations is to listen, not to interview.

## CASE STUDIES

The purpose of these case studies is not to provide an in-depth examination of the newspapers' newsgathering processes or a fun description of the published product. Rather, the cases serve to identify the variety of methods newspapers are using in their newsgathering efforts, and to provide a glimpse into how reporters are using these listening techniques.

## CASE STUDY: THE COLUMBIA MISSOURIAN - FOCUS GROUPS

In May 1995, the University of Missouri School of journalism undertook a civic journalism project with its daily and Sunday newspaper. The paper created a series of four focus groups in a reporting project called School-to-Work, which investigated the problems high school graduates were experiencing in obtaining employment after graduation, and whether the public school system was addressing the needs of non-college bound students.

Four focus groups were convened targeting four populations: employers, teachers, students and parents. Jennifer LaFleur, a trained focus group moderator, served as the key resource person. Ideally, the reporting staff should be able to get initial story ideas from focus group conversations. In this case, the focus groups were held after the first series, Making Education Work, had been published April 30-June 4, 1995.

LaFleur cited several difficulties in this project. The first problem was in the timing. According to focus group methodology, the focus groups should have been held early in the planning stages of the project rather than after the series was published. Second, resources were limited, which forced the focus groups to be held in a classroom rather than in a neutral place. This gave participants the impression that the school had some stake in the results of the project. Also, there were no financial incentives offered, and some groups (students, parents) drew fewer than five participants. Third, only one set of focus groups was held with each of the four target populations. LaFleur prefers to hold at least two sets of focus groups, in this instance she would have preferred to hold eight, to elicit a wider spectrum of opinion.

Although LaFleur was no longer involved in the process, the taped focus group sessions were analysed later, and the Columbia Missourian staff did follow through in October 1995 with another series on the School-to-Work topic. Thus the focus group data was utilized as it should have been, as a source for story ideas prior to the reporting project. The second series, A Look Beyond the Classroom, was published November 11-16, 1995.

## CASE STUDY: THE COLUMBIA MISSOURIAN - RESOURCE PANELS

The Columbia Missourian staff first used the resource

panel concept during its 1994 reporting project on health care. Because of the complexity of the topic, reporters and editors knew they would need some help in understanding the issues.

Journalism techniques such as focus groups, polls or surveys, did not seem to fit the research need. The newspaper staff needed insights from experts in the field. It was decided to convene a panel of health care experts so that students could gain knowledge and ask questions about the proposed reporting assignment. George Kennedy, a faculty member overseeing the project, explained the process.

"In that project we were overwhelmed with the scope and complexity of the issue and the gap in the knowledge level we knew was needed. We put it (the resource panel) together out of desperation, and it turned out to be more useful than any of us had ever imagined it to be."

The resource panel served two purposes, Kennedy said. First, the panelists were able to raise the knowledge level of the reporting staff "so we at least knew what the questions were." Second, the panel presentation helped build the reporting team by creating a shared experience among the staff.

For its 1995-96 reporting project, the journalism school decided to focus on the topic of religion and its relationship to public fife, and again decided to use resource panels. Although the topic of religion is of growing interest within the media, studies have shown that journalists are ignorant about it and uncertain about how to cover it. Professors and editors saw resource panels as a way to confront this lack of knowledge among journalism students, editors and professors.

Three separate resource panels were convened in October and November 1995, with panelists grouped according to specific criteria. The first panel was composed of four religion scholars.

Members of the second panel were clergy, and the third panel was composed of four former or current politicians who spoke on religion and politics. These sessions were held in a conference-classroom, ran approximately two hours each and were videotaped. Student reporters attending were able to question the panelists during the final portion of the sessions.

The panels served to not only expose the students and faculty to new information about religion, but also provided students with new sources to tap for story information. The project had an additional, hidden benefit, as well. Panelists said the experience not only added to their own knowledge about other faith groups in the community, but also helped them better understand reporters' perspectives. Several panelists voiced interest in being kept informed about the project and suggested that more such discussions be held. In this sense the group process appeared to help promote good will between the newspaper and the panelists. It also created a learning environment for the panelists as well as for the students and faculty.

## CASE STUDY: THE COLUMBIA MISSOURIAN - COMMUNITY CONVERSATIONS

The community conversations experiment was a follow-up to the religion resource panels. To seek views about religion and public life from different faith traditions, the students and faculty decided to hold a series of community conversations. These were created within a two-week time frame during which the target communities were contacted, individuals found to participate and meeting places and times arranged. The specific groups included members from the Jewish faith, Evangelical churches, the Interfaith Council, the ecumenical youth group, Church Women United, the Catholic faith, African-American churches and clergy.

Each community conversation was attended by a reporter representing the school's three media: newspaper, television and radio. Their primary role was to listen to the group discuss their faith and how they saw it interacting with public life in the community. One of the reporters served as moderator of the discussion, while the others took notes. Other than the opening question, reporters asked few questions. Instead they listened to the conversation among group members. After the community conversations were held, the reporting team gathered to discuss and critique its experiences and to create common themes that would be used later for framing the stories. While most of the community conversations went well, some faltered. The most common problem was an insufficient number of participants. Too few participants discouraged interactive discussion.

From these community conversations, the reporting team developed six topic themes on how religion interacts with public life. These were: public policy, race relations among faiths, ecumenism, outreach, youth and the future, women, health. The reporters then used these themes to develop specific story ideas to plan the project. The series was published the first week of June 1996, and the circulation department reported that those issues sold out.

## CASE STUDY: THE AKRON BEACON JOURNAL - FOCUS GROUP

Of all the case studies, the Akron Beacon Journal most closely followed the standard focus group procedure in its 1993 Pulitzer-Prize winning race relations series A Question of Colour and its 1994 follow up Coming Together project. The paper has used focus groups for a number of years, said Bob Paynter, the paper's project editor. In this case, the problem confronting reporters was getting people to be candid about the race topic. Editors decided that focus groups, with assurance of confidentiality, would be the best method to use to coax candor about an issue many are unwilling to talk about.

The paper convened one group comprised of white participants and one of black participants for each of the five areas of concern that had been previously identified in a survey. These areas were: Racial attitudes, housing, education, economics and crime. The focus group participants were selected along targeted geographic areas hot bed neighborhoods as well as along economic and racial lines. The newspaper was able to define the exact population it wanted because it had up-to-date survey data.

Paynter called the focus groups a "wonderful tool" in

the 14-month project, but cautioned journalists to remember that "focus groups are not the story. They lead you to the story."

Another benefit of the focus group method in this instance was the creation of the level of trust among participants and toward the media. "The focus groups ended up being ice-breaker sessions about the race issue," Paynter said. "People began to be comfortable in talking about it. They ended up being very informative warm-up sessions for great interviews later."

The newspaper added another dimension in this project. In addition to the community focus groups, it also convened an in-staff focus group of reporters and copy editors to explore the staff's views on race relations. This session enhanced reporter sensitivity to the issue.

## CASE STUDY: THE WICHITA EAGLE - PSEUDO-FOCUS GROUP

This newspaper has been a leader in the use of polls, focus groups and public forums in civic journalism projects. its two most recent projects have used a variety of techniques to elicit community information, said Jon Roe, election team leader at the paper. While the first project was called a focus group, it was actually a variant of the stringent focus group methodology.

In March 1995, the newspaper ran a classified ad asking for people to contact the paper's research department if they wanted to be involved in a study concerning the city's mayoral election. Citizens' concerns had already been identified from a prior survey. Group participants were chosen from those responding to the classified ad. Attempts were made to create a mixed group composed of an equal number of males and females, blacks and whites, and those in favour of the incumbent and those in favour of the challenger. A dozen people were invited, 10 showed up, Roe said.

The session was held at the newspaper's research facility, and the plan was to have the two mayoral candidates view the discussion from behind the one-way mirror. Group participants would know they were being observed, but would not know who was observing them. The session was video-taped. However, one candidate did not show up, so only the incumbent viewed the session and later joined the group for further discussion. Roe said the process encouraged group participants to go beyond personal attacks on the candidates and to begin to address the issues of the campaign.

Mama Young, a researcher at an independent research centre housed in the newspaper building, noted that, in this situation, the Wichita Eagle did not follow usual focus group procedures. The sample was biased in that it used volunteers rather than a random sample of the population, and the moderator was a journalist who asked questions. When the format is changed, it is no longer a focus group.

## CASE STUDY: THE WICHITA EAGLE — NEIGHBORHOOD CONVERSATIONS

The newspaper worked with the Harwood Group on its neighborhood conversations project, which involved setting up a number of neighborhood meetings based on specific group criteria. Project editor Roe said the newspaper saw "five levels of democracy" in its community. It covered the top level, official government sources, and the last level of personal stories fairly well. It was the in-between levels that reporters were failing to tap. These other levels included places such as community civic clubs, churches, bars, restaurants, barber or beauty shops and incidental meeting places such as supermarkets, backyards, shopping centers.

In the first phase, to find out more about the people in these areas, 10 reporters in teams of two or three went out to map seven different neighborhoods. Offering a small monetary incentive to participants, the paper set up pseudo focus groups in these neighborhoods. Groups of about 10 people were convened in each of the seven neighborhoods. A reporter served as the moderator, or in this case, interviewer, and the group agreed to have their comments published, if they were identified only by their first names.

Roe said that, had just one person not agreed, no names would have been used.

In the second phase of the neighborhood conversations project, reporters were given an assignment "to find a group of people and go sit and listen to them." The only other requirement was that the group had to be talking about education.

"I ended up talking with ministers and asking them where to find these groups in Wichita, and I found out that the neighborhoods were the churches," Roe said. He sat in on an adult class at a church where the members' conversation focused on their children who were just starting school. "When you talk about public journalism, you talk about getting into neighborhoods, you invariably end up at a church. The church is the local activist in many, many ways," he said."

While these neighborhood conversations are not focus groups, neither are they group interviews. Instead, they illustrate another way in which the reporter seeks insights from people at all levels in the community. The advantages are twofold. The process brings reporters into neighborhoods and provides them with new perspectives about situations as well as new story ideas. The disadvantages of these efforts are that they are time consuming and use a great amount of staff time without immediate production of stories. "You have to have a whole new breed of editor as well as reporter to do this," Roe said.

## CASE STUDY: THE TALLAHASSEE DEMOCRAT – LIVING ROOM CONVERSATIONS

Other variants on the group phenomenon include the living room conversations held by the Harwood Group for the Tallahassee Democrat. These were conducted as part of the newspaper's Public Agenda civic journalism project, underwritten by the Pew Charitable Trust. For the Public Agenda project, the newspaper conducted a survey in 1994 to clarify the important public issues. Later, a public meeting was held to discuss the survey findings. As a follow-up, another survey was planned for 1995. Lou Heldman, executive editor and senior vice president of the paper, said the living room conversations were conducted to frame the questions for that public survey. Twelve groups were created according to standard demographic criteria. The groups were composed of from three to five people, and they met in participants' living rooms. The sessions were conducted by Richard Harwood or his associates within a two- or three-week period in 1995.

Heldman said this research method offered several advantages. The natural environment provided a better comfort level for participants, which encouraged conversation. As Heldman said, "It seemed stripped of techniques. It came across as a conversation, even though the moderator had a clear set of questions and goals. It was moderated without artificiality."

But this technique has its disadvantages as well. First, these groups do not lend themselves to observation. The natural setting means that there are no one-way mirrors to allow for observation, nor is there any video taping. The only documentation is an audio tape. Because there were no observers, there were no opportunities for journalists to ask follow-up questions of the participants, as is sometimes done after a focus group, he said. There were no reporters present in these groups, and the participants were assured of anonymity. In November 1995, the newspaper ran articles on the community concerns identified in these 11 living room conversations.

Virginia Fielder, vice president of research for Knight-Ridder Inc., one of the corporate leaders in the media's use of focus groups in civic journalism projects, cautions journalists not to lose sight of the purpose of these journalistic techniques. The primary purpose is not to define a structured research project as much as it is to encourage public deliberation about issues affecting people's lives. Just the existence of the group interaction and the involvement of the journalist in analyzing the discussion has great value, she said. Fielder said that, at the heart of every civic journalism project is citizen involvement. These mini-case studies serve to identify ways in which newspapers are seeking information from the people in their communities.

The study suggests that group listening techniques are serving as a catalyst for knowledge and discussion, not only among numerous citizen groups but among reporters, editors and students as well. Journalists are finding ways to actively engage citizens in conversations and to systematically listen to citizens' discussions on a number of topics. The journalists interviewed said they maintain their journalistic independence while broadening their own perspectives about the community on which they report, using these techniques to add greater depth to their news reports. In effect, these journalists seem to be creating new paradigms for newsgathering, using a citizen-based informational foundation.

Group processing studies show that group members often develop a sense of involvement in the project just by participating in the group process itself. Group dynamics can create new perspectives among all participants. These case studies suggest that these listening techniques not only may benefit the journalistic endeavor, but also may have positive effects on the citizens who participate. However, journalists interviewed cautioned that the techniques should not be viewed as ends in themselves, but instead as additional research tools when planning reporting projects.

# Chapter 4

# Views on Public and Traditional Journalism

What does the public need to know? What role should news play in local community life? What are the central characteristics of good journalism? Debates and discussions about these fundamental questions primarily have been limited to journalists and those who study journalism. But what about consumers of journalism? This study set out to discover what everyday citizens think about journalistic practice and the role of journalists in reporting local news.

For decades, a few journalists and many scholars have wondered how journalistic practice may affect the public. For a decade and a half, a smaller group has wondered whether journalistic practice has contributed to Americans' dwindling interest in news and declining participation in civic life. This concern led editors and reporters in Wichita, Kansas; Charlotte, North Carolina; Columbus, Georgia; Bremerton, Washington; Minneapolis, Minnesota; and Portland, Maine, to introduce new journalistic techniques to re-engage the public in news and civic life.

Davis "Buzz" Merritt, then editor of the Knight-Ridder-owned Wichita Eagle, spearheaded one of the first journalistic projects to reengage the public in local news and civic life. Concurrently, New York University journalism scholar Jay Rosen, then director of the Project on Public Life and the Press, began asking pointed questions about the role of journalists and journalism in public life. Eventually these efforts led to a new journalistic movement and scholarly area called civic or public journalism that connected journalistic practice, the public, and the fabric of civic life in new ways.1

What does the public think of journalism practice in general and civic journalism in particular? What does the public expect of local news? By gaining greater insight into the public's expectations of local news, it may be possible to identify key issues that could, in the long run, increase the public's interest in news and civic life.

A review of forty-seven public journalism studies conducted from 1995 through 2001 revealed that public journalism has primarily been studied in three areas: content, journalists, and effects of public journalism on the audience.

## CONTENT AND PUBLIC JOURNALISM

Studies have found that public journalism content has distinct characteristics. For example, McGregor, Comrie, and Fontaine studied coverage of a New Zealand election campaign, comparing papers that endorsed public journalism and papers that did not, and found the public journalism papers covered the race more constructively.

By comparing the Seattle Times Front Porch Forum Project coverage with the coverage by the Times in earlier years as well as content in the Seattle Post-Intelligencer, Blazier and Lemert found that among eleven public journalism traits, providing mobilizing information was the most distinguishing factor between the public journalism project and earlier coverage by the paper and coverage by the competition. Moscowitz also found mobilizing information in a study comparing coverage of homelessness in the Knight-Ridder-owned, civic journalism-oriented Charlotte Observer with the Gannett-owned, traditional journalism-oriented Indianapolis Star.

The Charlotte Observer was also less likely to use official sources and more likely to include solutions to problems in its coverage. seeking out citizen sources rather than relying solely on official sources has been identified as a characteristic of public journalism. By comparing two papers, one civic, the other not, Kennamer and South found the civic-affiliated paper had a much greater number of unaffiliated sources than the other. Kurpius also studied sources and found that local television news stories, employing public journalism techniques, used a larger percentage of African American sources than represented in the general population. Furthermore African American, Latino, and female journalists were more likely to use minority and female sources in their stories.

Rather than focus on the text of a story, Coleman compared the visual elements in public journalism and traditional journalism content. Although for the most part, visual elements did not distinguish public journalism and traditional journalism, Coleman did find that public journalism storie's were significantly more likely than traditional journalism stories to include visual elements that facilitated contact of the media by the public.

Because interactivity lends itself to citizen involvement and public journalism principles, Choi compared public journalism and traditional journalism newspapers in an online environment, expecting that online public journalism newspapers would exhibit more public journalism characteristics. Content analyses of online stories from the Rochester Democrat, Charlotte Observer, Orlando Sentinel, online versions of public journalism-oriented newspapers, and the Buffalo News, Winston-Salem Journal, Florida Times Union, online versions of traditional journalism-oriented newspapers, found little difference in the content of online newspapers that represented public journalism and traditional journalism newspapers.

Journalists and Public Journalism. Because a decision to practice public journalism usually rests with a senior editor or producer, Kurpius examined the relationship between management and content. In two separate examinations of local television news, Kurpius found that visionary managers were the key for the civic-model of successful issues coverage at local television stations, but he also discovered that market forces may hinder civic reporting efforts in local media in the long run.

Factors that may influence journalists' attitudes toward public journalism were studied by scholars in New Mexico. After journalists at the Albuquerque Journal and Albuquerque Tribune and journalism students at the University of New Mexico completed self-administered questionnaires as part of a convenience sample, the results showed "a progression of socialization that begins with students supporting civic journalism."

Journalism students without newsroom experience appeared to be more supportive of civic journalism than practicing journalists and journalism students with newsroom experience. The authors suggested that civic journalism appeared to be inconsistent with autonomy, an attribute greatly valued by practicing journalists and journalism students with newsroom experience.

Indiana University scholars asked journalists directly about civic journalism in their most recent national survey. Although their previous national surveys of journalists, which were conducted in 1982 and 1992, had documented the backgrounds, attitudes, and values of journalists, the latest national study represented the first time that specific questions about public or civic journalism practices were asked. According to "The American Journalist in the 21st Century," 72% of journalists approved of giving ordinary people a chance to express their views on public affairs and 58% endorsed providing possible solutions to society's problems. Only 32% approved of convening meetings to discuss public issues.

Effects of Public Journalism on the Audience. The sixteen audience-centered studies identified in the Massey and Haas review examined the effects of civic journalism on the public rather than the public's expectations of journalism." For example, one study reviewed by Massey and Haas found evidence that public journalism produced positive results. In a study of broadcast and print media that included Wisconsin Public Television and Radio, WISC-TV, the Wisconsin State Journal, and the Wood Communications Group and their collaborative effort to provide a more civic-oriented approach toward election coverage, Denton and Thorson found respondents in Madison said the project made them more knowledgeable about the election, encouraged them to vote, and gave them useful tools to assess campaign information.

Although the literature found civic journalism practices improved public attitudes and increased knowledge of election issues, overall, the Massey and Haas review of public journalism studies found mixed audience effects. Public journalism was found to both increase and suppress voter turnout, to both increase participation in civic projects and have no impact on civic participation, and to produce both strong and weak agenda-setting effects.

After reviewing forty-seven empirical studies, Massey and Haas criticized the public journalism literature for its lack of methodological rigor and for narrowly focusing on "jewel box" civic journalism projects that were conducted at the Wichita Eagle, Charlotte Observer, and Wisconsin State Journal. Only one of the authors' six recommendations for future research involved the public and that was to conduct laboratory experiments that "could prove more useful for more convincingly identifying whatever causal factors may be behind any public-journalism influence on news audiences."

Surprisingly, none of the recommendations that resulted from this comprehensive review of public journalism studies focused on the public as an independent, active, and integral component of the communication process with opinions and expectations about a new type of journalism that ventures to re-engage the audience in the civic arena.

Although civic journalism has been discussed, practiced, debated, and studied for over a decade and a half, the public's perspective on civic journalism has not been studied empirically. Understanding the public's view of local news and civic journalism is important for the practice and business of journalism as well as society as a whole. Without an assessment of what the public expects of local news, it will be virtually impossible to identify journalism practices that may help reverse declining attention to news, restore dwindling public trust in news as a whole and journalists in particular, and bring back the vanishing participant in civic affairs. Unlike much of the research on public journalism, which has focused on the effects of specific public journalism projects on voting rates and other measures of civic participation, this study explores the public's views about journalism as well as the public's expectations of local news and the underlying dimensions of those expectations.

*Specifically, the following research questions will be answered:*

*RQ1:* What do survey respondents regard as the important attributes and roles of journalism and how does that compare with the norms of traditional and public journalism?

*RQ2:* How do survey respondents compare with journalists on the importance of practices and norms associated with traditional and civic journalism?

*RQ3:* What segments of survey respondents as defined by race or ethnicity, age, income, education, and gender are more likely to endorse civic journalism and traditional journalism norms?

*RQ4:* What are the underlying dimensions of survey respondents' expectations of local news?

As part of a research project for a local newspaper and local NPRaffiliated public radio station that was starting up a local news division to complement the national news broadcast from NPR, the authors worked with the radio station managers to design a research study that would ascertain public opinion about local news. A Pew Centre for Civic Journalism grant provided funding for the audience study. The radio station manager believed that understanding the public's expectations of local news was a prerequisite to building a radio news division that would report local news of importance and meet the public's needs.

The spring 2001 survey, conducted in a southwestern metropolitan area by a professional telephone survey unit, used random digit dialing to select the sample. Interviews were completed with 600 adults, representing a response rate of 62.2%. Calculation of the response rate was based upon the number of completed interviews (n=600) relative to the number of completed interviews plus refusals (n=286), incomplete interviews (n=37), and persons contacted but not interviewed due to illness, language barriers, or other impairments (n=36).

Answers to the four research questions were based on survey respondents' ratings of roles of local news media and characteristics of news coverage. Respondents were asked: What do you think is the most important role of local news media? Rate each on whether you think it's "extremely important," "somewhat important," or "not very important." The roles were (1) report the widest range of news; (2) concentrate on certain topics; (3) provide a forum for community views; (4) be a watchdog of powerful people and the government; (5) highlight interesting people and groups in the community; and (6) offer solutions to community problems. Respondents were also asked the following: What is the most important characteristic of news coverage you want? Rate each on whether you think it's "extremely important," "somewhat important," or "not very important." The characteristics were (1) accuracy; (2) rapid reporting; (3) understand the local community; (4) unbiased reporting; (5) care about your community; (6) be inclusive of different points of view; and (7) provide explanation of issues and trends.

To determine how survey respondents compare with journalists, the survey respondents' opinions about practices and norms associated with traditional and civic journalism were matched with journalists' opinions from "The American Journalist in the 21st Century" national survey. Specifically, the opinions of survey respondents and journalists were compared in four areas: offering solutions, providing a community forum, being a watchdog, and rapid reporting. Although both studies used random sampling and "extremely" on the measurement scale, there were several methodological differences.

The question wording in the national survey of journalists differed on the four opinions that were compared. For offering solutions, the national survey asked journalists how important it was "to point people toward possible solutions to society's problems." For providing a community forum, the national survey asked journalists how important it was "to convene meetings of citizens and community leaders to discuss public issues." For being a watchdog, the national survey asked how important it was to "investigate claims and statements made by the government." For rapid reporting, the national survey asked journalists how important it was to " get information to the public quickly."

In addition to the difference in wording, the present study relied on a three-point scale to measure opinions about journalistic norms while the national survey of journalists relied on a four-point scale of "extremely," "quite," "somewhat," and "not really important." The difference in question wording and the number of points on the measurement may have affected the number of respondents that chose "extremely" as an option. The final methodological difference was that the present study was conducted in spring 2001 in one southwestern metropolitan area while the national survey of 1,149 journalists was conducted summer and fall of 2002.

The survey questionnaire also included questions about socio-economic backgrounds and media use. Standard survey questions were asked to ascertain number of years lived in the area, marital status, level of education, income, age, and race or ethnicity. Respondents were also asked if they had children living at home and their gender was recorded.

To establish media use, respondents were asked if they read the primary daily newspaper 4-6 times a week, 1-3 times a week, less frequently, or never. Similarly, respondents were asked if they read the primary Sunday newspaper 3-4 times a month, 1-2 times a month, less frequently, or never. Respondents were also asked how often they heard news on the radio, which TV stations they watched for local news, and how often they obtained local news from the Internet.

Bivariate analyses with appropriate statistics were used to determine if opinions about public and traditional journalism practices and norms differed by race or ethnicity, age, income, education, or gender. A factor analysis was used to identify underlying dimensions of survey respondents' attitudes about the roles and characteristics of public and traditional journalism.

## SOCIO-ECONOMIC BACKGROUND AND MEDIA USE

Survey participants had established roots in this southwestern metropolitan area. The median number of years lived in the area was twelve; 55% were married and 42% had children at home. Although education was high, different educational levels were represented: 21% had a high school degree or less, 27% had some college, 28% were college graduates, and 24% completed at least some graduate school. Different income groups were also represented: 34% had a household income of less than $40,000; 31% had incomes between $40,000 and $69,000, and 35% had incomes of $70,000 or higher. Slightly more than one-third of the respondents were ages 18 to 39; 31% were ages 40 to 69; 35% were 70 years or older. Respondents were fairly diverse: 68% were white, 19%; were Latino, 7% were African American, and 5% were Asian American or other. The remaining 1% did not specify race or ethnicity.

When asked how many times a week they read the primary local newspaper, 30% said never or less frequently than 1-3 times a week, 25% said 1-3 times a week, and 44% said 4-6 times a week. Survey participants were more devoted to the Sunday newspaper with 64% reporting they read it 3-4 times a month. In addition to the newspaper, survey participants relied on other local news sources: 80% watched one of the five local TV news outlets, 59% often heard news on the radio, and 18% often turned to the Internet.

## THE PUBLIC'S VIEWS ON JOURNALISTIC NORMS

The ratings of thirteen characteristics and roles of news coverage were examined to answer RQl (What do survey respondents regard as the important attributes and roles of journalism and how that compare with the norms of traditional and public journalism does?). The overwhelming majorities said that accuracy (94%) and unbiased reporting (84%) are extremely important, but two major tenets of traditional journalism did not receive strong endorsements. The traditional journalistic norm of being a watchdog of powerful people and the government was supported by only 49% of survey respondents and rapid reporting was endorsed by only 35%.

## THE PUBLIC'S VIEWS ON THE ROLE OF LOCAL NEWS

Slightly more than half (51%) said offering solutions to community problems was extremely important, and 49% said providing a forum for community views was extremely important. To answer RQ2, these views were compared with journalists' views about civic journalism practices.

## COMPARING THE PUBLIC AND JOURNALISTS

Although the survey of the public was conducted in a southwestern metropolitan area and the survey of journalists was conducted nationally, results from the two surveys were compared because both studies used random sampling techniques, included similar questions about characteristics of traditional and public journalism, and incorporated "extremely important" on the measurement scale. A difference in proportions test on independent random samples was used to determine if survey respondents were significantly different from journalists in their endorsement of two civic journalism norms and two traditional journalistic norms.

Even though the majority of survey respondents strongly endorsed the fundamental characteristics of journalism, accuracy and unbiased reporting, there was a statistically significant gap between survey respondents and journalists on two roles that are an integral part of traditional journalism: watchdog and rapid reporting. Only 49% of survey respondents said being a watchdog of powerful people and the government is extremely important, but 70% of journalists said that traditional journalism role is extremely important.

Survey respondents were also significantly less likely than journalists to say that rapid reporting was extremely important (35% vs. 59%).

The roles and characteristics of traditional and civic journalism were analysed by five socio-economic characteristics (race or ethnicity, age, income, education, and gender) to better understand survey respondents' opinions about traditional and civic journalism roles and characteristics. Although there was no statistically significant difference between survey respondents and journalists in their endorsement of the civic journalism role of providing solutions to problems, there were significant differences when this civic journalism role was analysed by sub-segments of survey respondents.

## SOLUTIONS

African Americans and Hispanics were significantly more likely than whites and Asian Americans to say that the civic journalism role of offering solutions to community problems was extremely important. Almost three quarters (72%) of African Americans and 64% of Hispanics said offering solutions was extremely important, but only 45% of whites and 47% of Asian Americans said this civic journalism role was extremely important.

Segments of survey respondents that made less money and had less education were more likely than wealthier and more educated segments to say offering solutions to community problems was extremely important. Almost three-fifths (59%) of adults who had incomes of less than $50,000 compared to 44% of adults with incomes of $50,000 or more said offering solutions was extremely important. This inverse relationship was also apparent when offering solutions to community problems was analysed by education. Adults with a high school education or less (68%) were more likely than adults with some college (54%) and adults with a college degree or higher (42%) to say offering solutions was extremely important.

Females were also more likely than males to attach

greater value to the public journalism role of offering solutions with 56% of females compared to 44% of males saying it was extremely important for local news to offer solutions to community problems.

## WATCHDOG AND RAPID REPORTING

The traditional journalism characteristics of watchdog and rapid reporting were also analysed by the five socio-economic variables and three were significantly related. The oldest age group (55+) was more likely than the youngest age groups to value the watchdog role of traditional journalism, with 62% of adults 55 or older compared to 47% of adults 35 to 54 and 45% of adults 18 to 34 saying being a watchdog of powerful people and the government was extremely important.

An inverse relationship emerged when the traditional journalistic characteristic of rapid reporting was analysed by education. Among adults with a high school degree or less, 47% said rapid reporting was extremely important; 30% of adults with a college degree or higher said rapid reporting was extremely important. Females attached greater value to rapid reporting than males. Among females, 40% said rapid reporting was extremely important but only 30% of males said this traditional journalistic practice was extremely important.

## THE UNDERLYING DIMENSIONS OF THE PUBLIC'S EXPECTATIONS OF LOCAL NEWS

To better understand the underlying dimensions of survey respondents' expectations of local news reporting, researchers factor analysed the six roles of local news and seven characteristics of journalism. The good neighbour dimension that emerged included attributes of public journalism: caring about your community, highlighting interesting people and groups in the community, understanding the local community, and offering solutions to community problems.

The watchdog dimension was represented by four roles of local news including being a watchdog of powerful people and the government, concentrating on certain topics, providing a forum for community views, and providing explanations of issues and trends. The unbiased and accurate reporting dimension was defined by those two traditional characteristics of news; the fast dimension was represented by the traditional news characteristic, rapid reporting. Providing a wide range of news and being inclusive of different points of view did not load high on any one dimension. In fact, the inclusive factor loading was similar for the good neighbour, watchdog, and unbiased and accurate dimensions.

Although more than fifty empirical studies have been conducted on public or civic journalism, none of the studies has tried to gauge public opinion about this new approach to journalism practice. This study provided insight into a journalistic practice that developed over the past decade and a half in response to the vanishing newspaper reader and disappearing participant in civic affairs. Furthermore, this study provided insight into the public's views on traditional journalistic characteristics. At a time when newspaper readership, participation in civic life, and the credibility of journalism are at all-time lows, this study helped answer broader questions about journalism: Is traditional journalism meeting the public's expectations? Is the civic journalism movement on the right track? The results of this survey suggest that, in many cases, the public and the press, including traditional journalism and the civic journalism movement, are on separate tracks headed in different directions and unless something is done to better meet the public's expectations, civic participation, newspaper readership, and the credibility of the press may continue to decline.

While it is reassuring to know that the survey respondents overwhelmingly endorse accuracy and unbiased reporting, it is important to recognize that these same expectations can cause the public to turn away from the news. When Jayson Blair fabricates the news at the New York Times or star foreign correspondent Jack Kelley is accused of inventing parts of stories reported by USA Today, the public's trust in the news media is shaken and the reasons for reading the news are threatened.

It is also important to note that long-held norms of traditional journalism, being a watchdog and rapid reporting, are not strongly valued by a majority of the survey respondents. Only 49% said being a watchdog of powerful people and the government was extremely important, and 35% said rapid reporting was extremely important. But when the survey respondents were analysed by age, the press as watchdog was popular in the oldest age group. Over three-fifths of adults 55 years or older said the news media's traditional role of being a watchdog was extremely important.

Offering solutions to community problems, a characteristic of civic journalism, was strongly endorsed by only half of the survey participants as a whole, but when different segments were analysed, this public journalism practice was found to be more popular than first thought. The popularity of offering solutions is most evident among those who have traditionally been disenfranchised from the power sources of government and business: African Americans, Hispanics, adults with less income and education, and women. Perhaps these groups are looking to news media as a source for help.

Do the public's expectations of local news fit the traditional journalism model, the civic journalism movement, or some other ideal? The factor analysis of thirteen roles and characteristics of journalism revealed four dimensions with being a good neighbour-not watchdog, unbiased and accurate, or fast-representing the dominant expectation. Being a good neighbour included caring about your community, highlighting interesting people and groups in the community, understanding the local community, and offering solutions to community problems.

The expectation that the press should be a good neighbour may be related to declining trust in the news media and declining attention to news. If the public expects the press to be a good neighbour but the press fails in that role because it sees its professional responsibility as a watchdog, there is clearly a disconnect between the public's expectations and the press' expectations which civic journalism practices may not be able to fix.

Buzz Merritt and Maxwell McCombs argue for an expanded watchdog role of the press that is consonant with the good neighbour perspective:

News media need to be creative watchdogs and agenda setters scanning the horizon for the gaps in current public life. Part of this larger watchdog role is functioning as social radar, not just a chronicler of what government and other institutions are doing right now, whether good or bad. This means discovering the concerns of citizens and defining what the public needs to know in very expansive terms.

But for this expanded watchdog role to resonate with the public, the news media must educate the public and even persuade the public that in the role of watchdog, they are looking out for the public in the same way that a good neighbour would.

According to Andrew Kohut, director of the Pew Research Centre for the People and the Press, a decade and a half ago, which was about the time of the first civic journalism projects, the public thought the press was "too sensational, too pushy, too rude, too uncaring about people and the public." But most people saw journalists as moral, professional and caring about the interests of the country. Today, the public considers the news media even less professional, less accurate, less moral, less helpful to democracy, more sensational, more likely to cover up mistakes and more biased.

These are not exactly attributes of a good neighbour. Because this study represents only one metropolitan area in the Southwest, additional studies should be conducted in other parts of the country. Because different communities have different characteristics and needs, it is possible that they have different expectations of their local news. It is also possible that even with different community characteristics and needs, the public's expectations of local news are similar, regardless of community size or geographic location. Only by replicating this study in other communities can the public's expectations of local news be determined.

According to a 3 May 2005 New York Times article, the 1.9% drop in daily circulation and 2.5% decline in Sunday circulation reported by the Audit Bureau of Circulations represented the "largest circulation losses for the industry in more than a decade, and indicate an acceleration of the decline."

The magnitude of the circulation decline for 814 daily newspapers suggests that it is imperative that future studies determine how the public's expectations of local news relate to readership of newspapers and use of other news media. Future studies should also determine how participation in civic life is related to the public's expectations of local news. Finally, it is important for future studies to focus on the public's expectations of news with special attention paid to the concept of the press as a good neighbour. By gaining greater insight into the public's expectations of local news, it may be possible to initiate a dialogue between the public and the press. This dialogue may lead to a closing of the gap between the expectations of the public and the press that could, in the long run, reverse declining attention to news and waning participation in civic life.

## Chapter 5

# Newspaper Journalists Views on Public Journalism

There seems to be a shared wisdom among observers of civic (or public) journalism that the most vociferous critics of this emerging movement are the journalists themselves. While public journalism ultimately depends on the "publics" it is attempting to engage, journalists' attitudes are obviously critical to the fate of this movement. Jay Rosen and Davis Merritt, the two principal founders and leading evangelists of civic journalism, have each stated that this new approach to covering communities can succeed only if journalists internalize its values and participate in its evolving definition. Anderson, Dardenne, and Killenberg add that this will require substantial rethinking of traditional journalistic values and the learning of new skills such as listening and mediating.

How can journalists take on such responsibilities if they're opposed to the idea of civic journalism in the first place? Perhaps they're not. This study takes a systematic look at the assumption that most journalists reject the practice of civic journalism. These are the results of a 1996 survey of more than 1,000 newspaper journalists. The study's purpose is to offer a fully explicated definition of the concept of civic journalism, to gauge journalists' support for practices associated with this concept, and to explore possible antecedents of acceptance of these practices.

One reason for the contention over the merits of civic journalism is the absence of a universally accepted definition. In a published debate with Merritt, Paul McMasters rhetorically asked for guidance as to whether civic journalism is "a technique, a theory, a practice, or a philosophy, a new method or a new order, an elaboration on what already exists, or a radical revolution." The most appropriate response would be that civic journalism is some quantity of all of the above. Even Rosen has acknowledged that the term's definition is still in development. Fouhy and Schaffer, fortunately, have offered a simple working definition: It is a set of journalistic "initiatives which make a deliberate attempt to reach out to citizens, to listen to them, and to have citizens listen and talk to each other."

"Initiatives," of course, could refer to intellectual or philosophical innovation or to a pragmatic plan of activity in conjunction with a short-term news project. Merritt and Rosen argue for the former understanding; in fact, Merritt claims that many of those who deride civic journalism are observing only its most superficial manifestations, without attempting to understand its philosophical roots. The two fundamental axioms of civic journalism (in Merritt's conception) are that journalism is inextricably bound up with the public life of a community, whether its practitioners acknowledge it or not, and whether its practitioners like it or not; and that journalists have an obligation to engage citizens with their communities.

Rosen adds that because most American citizens have become disengaged from the public life (which includes political decision making), some institution or institutions must step forward to reconnect people to the public processes that can revitalize democracy. Civic journalists see journalism as an appropriate institution. In this conception, however, the successful public life extends beyond specific political events, such as informing the electorate before an election in order to improve voter turnout. Rosen often cites John Dewey's formulation of democracy not as a form of government but as a way of life.

In order for journalists to serve as the catalyst for such invigoration, Merritt warns, they must set aside a few of the "journalistic reflexes" that traditional journalism has instilled. Such reflexes include placing a premium on conflict; framing issues at their extreme positions (rather than also reporting complex "gray" areas or areas of agreement); adopting "adversary" positions toward those in authority; conceiving of readers and viewers as spectators and not potential participants; and assuming that an attitude of "detached objectivity" will lead to credibility for the journalism. Merritt proposes instead that journalists seek out the concerns of a wide variety of citizens and, through their journalistic practice, motivate them to become involved in solving civic problems.

This notion emerged in the form of experiments at a few different newspapers in the late 1980s, and it attained some national notice when Merritt's own Wichita Eagle and its parent company, Knight-Ridden embraced civic journalism in the early 1990s. But it began to resemble a national movement in journalism in 1993, when the Pew Charitable Trusts hired a staff to develop public-journalism strategies and began funding projects in several cities across the country. Since that time Pew has funded dozens of projects, many of them joint ventures involving newspapers, radio stations, and television stations in the same community.

As Merritt could have predicted, journalists have often framed the controversy over civic journalism in accordance with extreme positions, and those who harbor serious objections to the movement have been given ample voice in the trade press. Consequently, tales of failed attempts at civic journalism have traveled widely. For example, after a project in North Carolina in which several media revised their political campaign coverage in ways that focused on issues of citizen concern, several politicians observed that the new approach had not improved the electoral process.

Editors in the elite media accused their North Carolina colleagues of abdicating their news judgment in order to follow an agenda set by public opinion polls. In California, a paper hosted a town meeting involving an ongoing dispute over building codes, which turned into a brawl. The editors of the paper reportedly recast the originally embarrassing story into a positive account. A Connecticut paper sent reporters out in vans on weekends to give away merchandise and to engage citizens in public conversation on community issues, but the reporters said the citizenry, in a hurry to finish shopping, were not interested in conversing.

Merritt's general response to such stories of misguided efforts, or disingenuous reporting of efforts, is twofold: Many newspaper editors attempt public journalism without understanding its underlying philosophy, and those who understand its philosophy should realise that the results of any one project are unimportant. Civic journalism is not a marketing device or a commitment to report only "positive" news. It is a partnership between journalists and their community, and if it is not undertaken as a long-term commitment it is likely to fail.

The stories of civic-journalism-gone-wrong have also raised deeper concerns, about the movement's philosophy. Some critics worry about its self-conscious rejection of the notion of detachment. McMasters argues that journalists must be dispassionate and detached in their coverage of news in the same way physicians are detached in dealing with patients' medical problems. Too much involvement in community issues compromises their professional competence. Friedland responds that a rejection of detachment does not imply taking sides or reporting with a bias toward a particular group or position. If there is bias, civic journalists assert, it is bias in favour of a smoothly functioning democratic process. Kruh states that the civic journalist's bias should be no more offensive to traditional journalism than the medical writer's bias toward the eradication of disease.

Another concern is a perceived loss of the "watchdog" role of journalism that is strongly implied in the First Amendment. Stepp notes that when journalism commits itself so fully to solutions it inevitably associates itself with the public policymakers who are leading the planning and implementation of a solution. This constricts the journalists' time-honored (though much debated in academic circles) freedom to criticize governmental officials and policy. Some practitioners respond that they publicly monitor officials' responsiveness to public concerns in a manner resembling traditional "watchdog" journalism.

Some say they have experienced quite the opposite of boosterism. Editors at the Charlotte Observer have reported that during their civic journalism projects they were publicly monitoring local officials' responsiveness to citizens' concerns and that "we told the community hard truths about itself."

A third undercurrent of philosophical discomfort involves journalistic pandering. Critics worry that in responding too eagerly to citizens' views, journalism will become little more than market research. Polls and focus groups will replace professional news judgment; that is, news media content will reflect what audience members want to consume, rather than what journalists think their audiences need to know.

Merritt has responded that public journalism is ultimately more concerned with public Life than it is with journalism.23 Journalists who are intent on improving public discourse will not be content to feed their audience inane (but popular) pabulum, regardless of what a focus group may indicate.

As his responses in the foregoing paragraphs indicate, Merritt seems to believe that much of the criticism of civic journalism is rooted in misunderstanding. He readily acknowledges his critics' "angry dismisiveness." It is entirely possible, however, that if civic journalism were defined in a way that reflected its philosophical tenets (as put forth by Merritt, Rosen, and other early advocates of the movement), journalists might react differently than with dismissive heuristics such as "boosterism," "focus-group pandering," "loss of objectivity" and "same old same old." This study's empirical inquiry, therefore, begins with an explication of civic journalism.

## DIMENSIONS OF CIVIC JOURNALISM

The foregoing review of the literature and controversy concerning civic journalism displays recurrent themes that can be aptly transferred into dimensions of the variable concept "approval of civic journalism."

As we have seen, civic journalism involves journalistic initiative rather than reactive coverage; it involves an interest in moving toward solutions to community problems that takes journalism far beyond the detached reporting of the problems; it involves ongoing, long-term commitment to the betterment of the public life; and it involves not only the reporting of important public issues but also nonpublished efforts to probe citizens' concerns and engage them in the public life.

With the help of Ed Fouhy, former executive director of the Pew Centre for Civic Journalism, the research team for this project developed the following dimensions and indicators of civic journalism.

1. Enterprise. In the view of Merritt, Rosen, and others, civic journalism starts with the initiative of the journalists in reinvigorating the public life. It is rooted in the belief that journalists have a stake in the health of a community's public life, and that journalism stands uniquely poised to engage citizens. This enterprise not only discovers problems of common concern but continues to motivate citizens to seek out solutions. This is one of the aspects of civic journalism that has prompted the observation that it is no different from traditional enterprise reporting. That is true to some extent, but it is different in two basic ways: It begins with a consideration of what will improve the public life, rather than what will make a good story, and it implies a commitment to solving community problems beyond the publication of one story or series.
2. Information for Decision Making. This dimension speaks to the development of what Charity has termed "public judgment. A principal role for the civic journalist is to enable citizens not only to communicate in a public arena but to be able to work toward solutions without necessarily being led by institutional policymakers. It requires journalists not

only to listen to and synthesize public commentary but to present independent research on alternative public views, so that citizens can be informed in their public judgment. This also involves the journalists' close monitoring of official responses to the various alternatives. The effect, Charity states, is that the reporting can "foster a sense of drama and possibility" in the community.

Merritt also sees in this dimension an obligation of the civic journalist to identify shared ideas he calls "core values," to which all participants in the public discussion would adhere. The recognition of core values is often the critical first step in the assessment of alternative solutions.

3. Facilitation of Discourse. Critical to the success of public deliberation is that citizens feel they have an opportunity to discuss issues and concerns themselves in a public forum -not merely to read about them in the news media. The civic journalist does what is necessary to begin and sustain this public deliberation, even if it means taking nontraditional steps to convene participants. The most common practice in this dimension is the news media's hosting a "town meeting," usually to discuss a particular issue. Anderson, Dardenne, and Killenberg and Charity have written extensively about the news media's suitability for such a role, as they comprise one of the few institutions in American communities that regularly address a wide range of issues across economic, racial, and social boundaries. Public agencies and other private organizations have convened innumerable meetings, of course, but civic-journalism proponents cite the failure of current public life generally as an indication of the more traditional institutions' inability to kindle true public discourse.
4. Attention to Citizens' Concerns. This dimension of civic journalism refers to the rejection of agendas set by those in political and economic authority and the

> substitution of a citizens' agenda. Charity believes this aspect to be so strange to traditional journalists that retraining is needed, to enable them to elicit, understand, and represent the concerns of ordinary, unaffiliated speakers and to accord those concerns at least as much credulity as they do the concerns of those wielding power.

This dimension is the source of the critique that civic journalism relies mindlessly on focus groups and market research. Merritt and others respond that if such research is truly oriented toward news-consuming preferences, then it is indeed inappropriate as a tool of civic journalism. The value of seeking out public opinion is in setting an agenda for public discourse that reflects popular concerns regardless of political leaders' priorities. This understanding of public opinion resonates with the recent work of political scientist James Fishkin, who urges that public opinion research take place among small, representative groups of citizens who have been carefully informed of the issues under discussion.

The results would represent not an aggregation of individual Americans' uninformed hunches and heuristics but instead the "considered judgments of the public," which would elevate the utility of public opinion. Fishkin observes that this idea "builds on the movement toward public journalism."

As the final stage of the explication, indicators of each dimension were written for inclusion in the survey instrument. Respondents were asked "How do you feel about the following approaches to journalism?" The dimensions were represented by the following sentences:

1. (Enterprise) "A newspaper develops enterprise stories, supported with editorials, to focus public attention on a community problem and tries to help the community move toward a solution."
2. (Information for Decision Making) "A newspaper reports on alternative solutions to community problems, pointing out trade-offs that may be involved."

3. (Facilitation of Discourse) "A newspaper conducts town meetings to discover key issues in the community and follows up with stories focusing on these issues and some possible solutions."
4. (Attention to Citizens' Concerns) A newspaper polls the public to determine the most pressing community issues, then tries to get the candidates to focus on these issues."

While all four dimensions are meant to reflect basic conceptual changes in the way a news organization covers a community, the indicators represent two distinct degrees of departure from current norms. The Enterprise and Information dimensions' indicators represent modest departures from current reporting and editing practices, while the Discourse and Citizens' Concerns indicators represent bolder departures. The indicators were grouped as such in part of the data analysis.

**Empirical Research on Civic Journalism**

Because civic journalism is a relatively recent phenomenon, what little scholarly work has been done on the movement has been mostly evaluative and prescriptive, rather than empirical. Most of the empirical work has been concerned with the impact of civic journalism projects on political participation and community awareness.

For example, in a comprehensive, Pew— funded study of civic-journalism projects in four cities in 1996, Thorson et al. found that awareness of civic journalism projects was positively associated with citizens' attitudes that are known to bring about political participation.

Their overall conclusion was that civic journalism helps reconnect citizens to public life. In Pew's own report of the same study, 40 per cent of those surveyed in the four cities said the project had made them think more positively about their community.

Less work has been done about the journalists' attitudes and reactions to civic journalism. In a content analysis of the coverage of "The People Project" at Merritt's Wichita Eagle,

Riede found that the journalists broke away from only a few traditional routines. He saw a reduction in the political reporting that focuses on personality and political strategy and an increase in substantive reporting of issues. He also noted an increase in stories that encouraged readers to become involved in community organizations and debates. He noted a tone of increased "engagement" and activism, as distinct from detached objectivity.

But he still saw widespread allegiance to experts and politically important people as sources for stories. Voices of "the people" were published more often, but usually superficially and episodically, in ways that could not facilitate discourse. "In fact, the project's doggedly nonadversarial stance, its avoidance of negativism and conflict and its faith in the efficacy of compromise and orderly voluntarism gave it a profoundly conservative tone."

In the Pew Center's own report of the four-city research project in 1996, reporters at the conclusion of the projects were portrayed generally as unimpressed with what they had done. Some thought their stories had been boring and had been read by only a few; others thought their work, focusing in-depth on a single issue, quickly had become repetitive. The Pew evaluators seemed to think that newsroom executives and middle managers were most supportive of the projects, and rank-and-file newsroom employees least supportive.

Webster University researchers surveyed editors and journalism educators to gauge levels of support for various aspects of civic journalism. They found that about half the editors approved the use of polls and focus groups to determine what stories the press should cover.

Majorities of the sample of editors also approved of the notions that journalists should see people not as news consumers but as players in the democratic process; that journalists should devote more attention to what affects ordinary citizens and less on the "major news events of the day;" and that political coverage should include more issue analysis and less "horse race" analysis.

The Webster project does offer a strong indication,

however, that civic journalism is not as reviled as the popular, anecdotal accounts would have us believe. But the project surveyed only editors and educators, not rank-and file reporters, photographers, or copy editors-the foot soldiers of this campaign.

The most theoretically provocative finding is found in the most recent study of American journalists by Weaver and Wilhoit. In a replication of earlier analyses, the researchers used factor analysis to identify three "ideal types" of roles for journalism in society. In the analysis of their 1992 survey data, they found renewed evidence of identification with the roles of "disseminator" (whose priority is to deliver information factually and quickly); "interpreter" (whose priority is to provide analysis of complex problems), and "watchdog" (whose priority is to serve as adversary of government and business).

The analysis, however, also revealed a fourth, puzzling factor: journalists who identified with developing the cultural interests of the public, providing entertainment and relaxation, setting the political agenda, and letting ordinary people express their views.

The last item suggested a dimension of civic journalism to the extent that Weaver and Wilhoit labeled this factor "populist mobilizer." Unfortunately, the "ordinary people" item had the weakest loading in the factor, but it obviously intrigued the researchers: "If our analysis is right, the new role ('populist mobilizer') is tantalizing evidence that the spirit of the 'public journalism' movement may have established a foothold among the core values of a tiny minority of journalists."

What sorts of journalists might embrace civic journalism? Another important goal of the current study was to develop a rough profile of the journalist who seems supportive of the indicators of civic journalism, based on a host of independent variables. In this regard the recent research literature provides some guidance. The Pew project's authors found qualitative evidence that younger journalists were less enthusiastic about what they were involved in, which the authors attributed to a sense of professional transience and a lack of commitment to the communities in which they worked.

The size and type of the news organization also may be a factor. In their investigation of the "populist mobilizer factor, Weaver and Wilhoit cautiously suggested that small-market journalists may have more favorable attitudes toward civic journalism than their metro-market counterparts. They found greater resonance for that factor-especially for the item "allowing ordinary people to express their views"-among journalists at radio stations, weekly newspapers, and small-sized dailies.

This is hardly surprising if civic journalism involves a commitment to local issues and community discourse-which are more likely staples in the news diet of small-market media.

From the explication of the term civic journalism and from the suggestions of previous research, a set of hypotheses was developed:

H1: Majorities of the newspaper journalists will approve of each of the four indicators of civic journalism.

One goal of this project was to gauge journalists' approval of civic journalism without explicitly introducing the terms civic journalism or public journalism, thus keeping at bay the generally negative reaction that those terms seems to elicit, and thus keeping the focus of the survey on the concepts and practices of civic journalism rather than on labels. The expectation of approval stems from the findings of the Webster and Pew studies (in which editors, at least, approved of many aspects of civic journalism).

H2a: The smaller the journalist's newspaper, the more accepting he or she will be of these civic-journalism approaches.

This would verify the finding of Weaver and Wilhoit that the "populist mobilizers," few though they were, were more often in small-market media.

H2b: Newsroom managers will be more accepting of civic journalism approaches than will rank-and-file journalists such as reporters, copy editors, and photographers.

This would reflect the general sense of the Pew

investigators who detailed the complaints of some of the reporters involved in civic journalism projects. It would also reflect Merritt's contention that support of civic journalism results from an understanding of its philosophical underpinnings. Because top editors are the most likely staff members to introduce and assign a civic journalism project, they are the journalists also most likely to have read and thought about civic journalism's purpose.

H2c: The younger the newspaper journalist the less accepting he or she will be of civic journalism approaches.

This last control variable would reflect the Pew authors' impression that younger journalists were less sympathetic to their projects' goals and practices.

H3: The association between identification with the "interpreter role of the media and approval of civic journalism will be stronger than the association between civic journalism and the "disseminator" and "watchdog" roles.

The disseminator and watchdog roles represent two traditional attitudes that Merritt and Rosen find somewhat incompatible with civic journalism.

The disseminator role implies a telling of the news without context or understanding, but rather a detached forwarding of information. The watchdog role implies a state of "adversariness" that delights in conflict and news that splits groups apart in a community. Rosen maintains that civic journalists constantly challenge elected leaders to heed the public discourse, but that bringing down public officials is not a goal of civic journalism.

H4: The stronger the feeling of the importance of neighborhood and community news, the stronger the approval of civic journalism.

Civic journalism focuses on the concept of community, and because community in journalism is often defined as a geographic community, it seems likely that civic journalism-friendly news people will also be highly interested in issues of local communities. Respondents were asked to rate the importance of "a number of things that newspapers the size of the one you work for do, or try to do, today," which included the item, "Cover community and neighborhood news." Respondents could choose a response from a fourpart scale ranging from "Extremely Important" to "Not Very Important."

H5a: Journalists who approve of a top editor's involvement in local civic organizations will be more likely to accept civic journalism than will journalists who disapprove of such activity.

H5b: Journalists who approve of rank-and-file staff members' joining civic organizations will be more likely to approve of civic journalism than will journalists who disapprove of such activity.

This set of hypotheses attempts to bring to a personal level the civic journalism tenet of involvement in one's community. One measure of a journalist's rejection of the traditional detachment from the people and issues that one covers would be the attitude toward personal involvement of the journalist in the community-not involvement in a particular faction or political cause, but in a nonpolitical civic organization.

If a journalist feels favorable toward making at least that modest personal connection to the community, he or she will endorse the connection for both the top editors and for rank-and-file staff members.

In the same vein, we might also expect journalists who themselves felt involved in their local communities-actually, not hypothetically-to share that attitude.

H5c: Journalists who describe themselves as involved in their local communities will be more likely to approve of civic journalism than will journalists who describe themselves as uninvolved.

The final set of hypotheses examines attitudes about the current state of journalism at one's newspaper. Proponents and observers alike seem to agree that civic journalism has grown out of a dissatisfaction with the role journalism has played lately, especially with journalism's inability to connect to citizens, and its inability to connect citizens to one another.

H6a: Journalists who feel their own papers do not connect

well with readers will be more likely to approve of civic journalism than will those who feel well connected with readers.

H6b: Journalists who feel their own papers are getting worse in quality will be more likely to approve of civic journalism than will those who feel their paper is improving.

## THE SURVEY METHOD

The survey was conducted in the fall of 1996 under the auspices of the Human Resources Committee of the American Society of Newspaper Editors. A stratified probability sample of newspaper employees was constructed. From a list of the 1,487 newspapers in the United States, 61 were randomly selected, after measures had been taken to ensure proportionate representation from eight circulation categories. Three of the newspapers in the original group of 61 declined to participate; in these cases the research team randomly chose substitute newspapers from the same circulation groups.

The directing editor of each selected paper was asked to select randomly a sample of journalists from his or her staff. Only full-time employees who fit the categories of reporter, copy editor, photographer, artist, supervisor, or editorial writer were to be included. The number of participating employees depended on the size of the paper, again in order to maintain the validity of the stratified probability sampling procedure.

Each employee participating received a survey packet, which included the questionnaire with instructions and a computer-scannable answer sheet. Participants were assured, both in the written instructions and by the on-site survey coordinator, that responses would be entirely confidential. If an employee declined to participate, a substitute was to be chosen by use of the same "nth name" random process. Editors were asked to give the employees three days in which to complete and return the questionnaire, which in a pre-test in August 1996 had taken respondents about 30 minutes to complete.

Of the 61 newspapers that eventually agreed to

participate, only 3 failed to return their questionnaires by the 15 October 1996 deadline. All 3 of these were below 25,000 in circulation. Thus of the 1,191 questionnaires sent, 1,037 were returned, for a response rate of 87.1%.

The four indicators resulting from the explication of civic journalism appeared as closed-ended items in the survey; respondents could choose the degree to which they approved or disapproved of each.

The two "modest" approaches to civic journalism appear first, and more than 90% of the respondents expressed some level of approval. The two "bolder" approaches, involving the polling of readers and the town meeting, appear next, each garnering more than 70% approval. The mean approval for all four measures is 81%, with only 19% on average expressing some degree of disapproval.

It cannot be known what the approval ratings would have been if this section of the instrument had been labeled "civic journalism," but clearly without the labeling these journalists seem to be comfortable with the approaches described in the four items.

It should also be noted that none of the four items cited any of the more controversial or radical examples of civic journalism, such as training editorial employees in mediation and conflict resolution, or having staff members register citizens to vote. This, of course, was in keeping with the explication of the concept, which was based in large measure on the work of the movement's two theoretical founders, Merritt and Rosen.

The "strongly approve" rating for the modest approaches was, predictably, different from the "strongly approve" results for the two bolder measures: a mean of 60% compared to a mean of 28%. The results for "somewhat approve" were 10 percentage points higher for the bolder approaches, however.

The journalists seem to be implying support for town meetings and polling the public for agenda issues, but not as enthusiastically as doing enterprise stories and providing information on alternative solutions.

Survey respondents were asked to attach comments

whenever they felt moved to supplement their closed-ended responses, and a few of these were directed to the items on civic journalism.

A staff member at a large East Coast paper wrote, again without using terms like "civic journalism," an eloquent explanation of the movement's rejection of detached objectivity: "Many papers, while remaining objective, led in some way the struggle for civil rights. Now, we do not lead as much as we try simply to report... Unless newspapers make people in their communities feel a part of them, as if they have a stake in them, they will disappear. Papers cannot be observers and reporters of a community. People no longer want to be merely observed. People want to be cared about."

A few others, however, voiced caution about the direction civic journalism may be taking. A journalist at a small paper in New England stated that there is only one place to be a catalyst for community discourse: "A newspaper and the stories it reports should reflect its surrounding communities and should always seek out the input of its readers. It is not a paper's role to 'lead' its readers, but to listen to its readers. There is plenty of room for our own agenda and suggestions of alternative solutions via the editorial and op-ed pages."

To test the remaining hypotheses, an index was created with the four civic journalism measures (Cronbach's alpha =.61) that enabled correlation and regression analysis using "civic journalism approval" as a dependent variable 46.

H2a is supported: the smaller the newspaper, the greater the support for the index of the four civic-journalism approaches. This association was especially pronounced for the two "bolder" forms of civic journalism. The influence of newspaper size remains significant throughout a multiple regression involving the variables with the strongest bivariate associations with the dependent variable.

Newsroom managers did indeed seem more receptive to civic journalism approaches than rank-and-file employees did (H2b), but the strength of this factor pales in the course of the regression. Age appears not to be a predictor of support for civic journalism. While it is likely that older, higher-ranking journalists may be the initiators of a civic journalism project at a paper, a three-way crosstab analysis also revealed that older reporters and copy editors are among the most skeptical about civic journalism.

A few other personal variables were examined for possible correlations with support for civic journalism. Education seemed to make no difference, and while women seemed to approve of civic journalism more often than men do, the difference was never statistically significant.

The third hypothesis sought to learn whether conceptions of journalism's roles have any influence on attitudes toward civic journalism. But the connections seem flimsy.

The "interpreters" were neither less nor more supportive of civic journalism than others; the "watchdogs" and "disseminators" held no significant association with civic journalism either. H3 thus gets no support. It is worth noting, however, that "watchdogs" and "interpreters" both significantly influence approval of the "modest" approaches to civic journalism, but not the "bolder" approaches. Even that influence, however, lost its significance in a regression.

H4 predicted that journalists who accord respect to neighborhood and community news would applaud civic journalism approaches, and the data support the hypothesis. The influence is particularly strong when the two bolder approaches are considered.

Neighborhood and community news is one of the few independent variables to hold its influence throughout the regression. In a regression on only the bolder approaches, this variable had a higher beta coefficient than any other variable in the equation.

It was also predicted that journalists who were comfortable with their bosses' and colleagues' involvement with civic organizations would approve of civic journalism techniques, as would journalists who themselves felt "more involved than others" in the community. H5a and H5b, posing the hypothetical questions about staff involvement, both enjoyed strong positive correlations with civic-journalism support. The data suggest that those who approve of these civic-journalism approaches are also likely to approve of journalists at any level becoming personally involved in community organizations.

That approval does not extend to the respondents' personal lives, apparently. H5c enjoyed no support. Whether the respondents were involved in community activities themselves seemed not to make a difference in the attitude on civic journalism. This may suggest that journalists are more open to the personal dynamics of civic journalism in theory, but that there is no connection, at least not yet, between their own actual community involvement and their support for civic journalism. Perhaps they see journalists' personal lives as simply detached from whatever professional values they espouse.

The sixth set of hypotheses examined measures of dissatisfaction with the current state of journalism, but the data did not support either H6a or H6b. Whether the journalist felt his or her paper was connecting with readers was irrelevant to his or her feelings about civic journalism. The evaluation of the journalist's own paper, in fact, was significant in the direction opposite that of the hypothesis. It was expected that those who feel their own papers are deteriorating in quality would look to civic journalism as a means of rescue.

However, the data indicate that the higher the journalist's rating of his or her own paper, the more positive the reaction to civic journalism. And this influence held its significance throughout the regression. Apparently those who see their newspapers' quality eroding have no faith that civic journalism is the answer, and those who embrace civic journalism are journalists who think their paper is improving. Perhaps civic journalism will require a sense of collective confidence in the enterprise before it can win newsroom adherents.

Thus only a few independent variables remained, after a four-step regression, as significant influences on a journalist's approval of these four approaches to civic journalism: The smaller the newspaper, the greater the attention to neighborhood and community news, the greater the approval of journalists' joining community organizations, and the greater the sense that one's own paper is improving, then the more likely the approval of civic journalism.

It must be noted, however, that the regression equation accounted for only 14% of the variance of the dependent variable. Clearly other factors, not explored in this survey, also influence support for civic journalism.

One final piece of analysis was conducted: a factor analysis to follow up on Weaver and Wilhoit's earlier discovery of the "populist mobilizer." The data in the present study were gathered more than four years after the Weaver-Wilhoit survey.

Weaver and Wilhoit had included only one item that could be clearly identified as an indicator of civic journalism ("letting ordinary people express their views"). In a factor analysis of the present data, with a full mix of professional-role items including disseminator, interpreter and watchdog, the four civic-journalism items loaded onto their own separate factor (eigenvalue 1.88).

As the discussion above indicated, approval of civic journalism is correlated with some of the other, older role conceptions, but not robustly so. It could very well be that a new understanding of journalism's role in society has indeed begun to emerge, as Weaver and Wilhoit speculated in 1996, in which a newspaper's commitment to the public life, for at least some journalists in some situations, takes precedence over obligations of disseminating information quickly, analyzing events, or serving as adversary to powerful institutions.

Whether or not newspaper journalists scoff at the term "civic journalism," this much is clear: Many of them seem to approve of four specific manifestations of the movement's guiding principles. It would be inappropriate, however, to draw overarching conclusions about the future of civic journalism on the basis of this study alone. The survey's four approaches to civic journalism were referents of pillars of the movement's philosophical foundation, and while they represented a fundamentally different approach to journalism, not even the two "bolder" approaches seem revolutionary in form.

In fact, it might be argued that the two "modest" items are quite similar to longstanding normative understandings of strong local news coverage. Further research on journalists' conceptions of civic journalism is warranted, and it might begin with a broader selection of approaches and strategies, to see where journalists might finally "draw the line" and begin objecting to certain approaches. Because civic journalism projects increasingly involve broadcast and online media, further studies should include more than newspaper journalists.

Rosen has stated that the definition of civic journalism is phenomenological: Ultimately, it will be whatever journalists say it is.

For this reason it is important to measure not only what journalists think of a Merritt-Rosen— derived definition of civic journalism, as this study has done, but also to measure how journalists themselves would define the term.

If their definition emerges as similar to the explication of this study, then the future of civic journalism is more promising than even this study suggests. If, however, journalists define it in ways that cause Merritt, Rosen, Charity and others to howl with exasperation, it's more likely that the journalists will also disapprove. Then proponents of civic journalism will truly have their evangelistic work cut out for them.

The most influential independent variables have created a profile of sorts of the pro-civic-journalism practitioner. It suggests that civic journalism may enjoy greater success in smaller communities and in media outlets that are seen by their employees as improving.

But here, too, further inquiry is needed. In carefully steering away from respondents' preconceived notions of civic journalism, the survey instrument did not measure whether the respondent had read or discussed any materials regarding civic journalism, or had participated personally in a civic journalism project. These factors could be expected to influence a journalist's opinion of the movement and its practices.

Even with this early indication that a large proportion of the newspaper work force seems poised to approve of (at least this conception of) civic journalism, it is still unclear whether this will create any deep changes in journalism, or in the quality of civic life.

Riede's study of Merritt's own paper suggested that journalistic routines are extremely difficult to alter even in one of the pantheons of the movement.

Some scholars question whether civic journalism can survive within a liberal-economic media model like the United States'. Glasser and Craft, for example, suggest that civic journalism, if implemented consistently and seriously, might either risk losing its ratings appeal among advertisers or would challenge power structures in a way that would anger advertisers.

Rosen and Merritt, predictably, have pondered this concern and responded, but with different views. Rosen asserts that civic journalism, properly executed, can draw in a large audience of citizen— participants and thus more advertising revenue.

Merritt acknowledges that civic-journalism content may not compete for audience with the crossword puzzle or "Seinfeld" but that it doesn't have to. As long as it enjoys a permanent place in the mix of programming or editorial features that maximize an audience, it can continue to uplift the public life.

Judgment on the viability and desirability of civic journalism is beyond the scope of this study. Such considerations assume, of course, that civic journalism will indeed catch on among the majority of journalists.

This study suggests that at least one aspect of Weaver and Wilhoit's earlier notion of a "populist mobilizer" attitude toward journalism has taken hold among newspaper journalists.

There may still be only a few journalists actually waving

"civic journalism" banners, but in terms of four specific activities that stem directly from the movement's philosophical roots, the movement is quietly finding acceptability. Civic journalism's ultimate reformative power—especially its ability to challenge powerful institutions on behalf of the public and "the public life"-will only be as strong as its support among its practitioners. That support seems to have made important initial strides.

## Chapter 6

# Changing Patterns of Reporting

Journalists reflect a pattern of access, credibility, and news practices across media content through the people they choose to quote or use in a television sound bite. Media scholars, journalists, and the communities they serve continue to debate the lack of source diversity, the level of expected diversity (which varies), and the path to achieving greater diversity since research on this subject began in the early 1970s. Source representation is a type of diversity most frequently studied by researchers who address this issue in ways that range from media channels and news structures to the diversity and affiliations of people represented in the news. If journalism is a reflection of the community, the quality of that reflected reality depends to some extent upon sources used.

During the past quarter century, only enterprise stories have shown promise for improving source diversity. Hansen found that such stories contained a greater diversity of sources. However, enterprise reporting is not common today, and there are no signs of improvement. One potential answer is civic journalism which assumes a stronger connection to non-traditional sources, leading to greater diversity of sources in news stories. This study tests a major assumption underlying civic journalism by asking whether civic journalism succeeds in moving television journalists toward more diverse sourcing patterns for race and gender.

Voakes, Kapfer, Kurpius, and Chern wrote: "Source diversity is a dispersion of the representation of affiliations and status position of sources to create a news product. The more even the dispersion of the representation among source affiliations, status, and proximity in a given story or medium, the greater the diversity." This study expands this definition to include the dispersion of representation of race and gender.

Reporters select sources for what they know, their position in an organization, and/or their status in society. Some selections are dependent on the form of media used. Newspaper and magazine stories reflect material through direct quotations or paraphrased statements by the reporter. For broadcast, it is the "direct voice of the quotee" or the quotee's words-restated by the reporter. This study uses these definitions.

Journalists gather information for their stories according to the norms and practices of their news organizations. Historically, the sources journalists turned to for information reflected a narrow section of society. Research shows sources are predominately white, male officials who are situated in proximity to the media organization and are easily regarded by journalists as providing credible information.

Some researchers focus on the governmental, business, and organizational affiliation and status of sources used. Others look at women and minorities as news sources. Still others analyse the structural elements that potentially alter source-selection patterns, including channels of news coverage, length and types of stories, and use of technological advances.

People of colour are generally missing from news coverage, unless it is coverage of crime or festivals. Grabe and Barnett found that 86 per cent of news sources in newsmagazine programs were Caucasians. Campell found underrepresentation of journalists and sources of colour in television news. "While news is not entirely white," he wrote, "the infrequent presence of journalists of colour and of minority news sources dictates an otherness that is compounded when the coverage that does exist perpetuates traditional racistnotions about minority life." Entman found that TV news used fewer black sources than white sources. Entman said, "The blacks received much less opportunity to convey their perspectives in their own voices and were much more likely than whites to be discussed by a police official not of their race."

Smith found that in both newspapers and television coverage of the San Francisco area, about 80 per cent of the sources used were white people. In television, black sources were used only 12 per cent of the time, and minority sources accounted for 19 per cent.

Several researchers found low gender diversity and a heavy reliance on elite male sources. Zoch and Turk found that 68 per cent of sources were male compared to 21 per cent female sources, but they attributed part of this to the heavy reliance on official sources who tended to be male. McShane found that women are underrepresented as sources in business magazines compared to their numbers in the labour force. Liebler and Smith's study of 159 network television news stories found journalists are more likely to choose males as sources and to present them in a professional capacity. Smith found that white men dominate news sourcing, but noted that minority women and men are used as sources in almost equal proportions.

Sigal argued in 1973 that routine news channels created efficiencies for journalists, who commonly rely on government officials and business leaders as primary sources. Today, marketplace forces dictate television journalistic practice more than beat routines. The FCC no longer requires television stations to assess their coverage of the communities in the local area of dominant influence. The lifting of this requirement, combined with the consolidation of ownership, has shifted the focus to demographically driven news based on advertisers' target audiences. Such marketplace emphasis creates a structure ripe for sponsor interference and these pressures are likely to continue or increase as larger ownership groups consolidate stations.

The federally mandated move to digital transmission standards also increased the financial burden stations face, resulting in increased airtime for news and therefore in journalists' workloads. Workload increases result in a greater reliance on non-local (feed) material and reapportionment of material (using the same story in multiple news programs). Sigal and others demonstrate that this leads to greater reliance on government officials as primary sources.

What works to improve source diversity? The answer is not much. Crisis coverage included much higher numbers of unaffiliated sources, but it is limited to a narrow type of coverage. One promising solution is enterprise reporting, a process through which journalists tend to use more diverse sources and fewer official sources than traditional news coverage, Hanson writes. However, enterprise reporting is costly because it takes time and effort to develop story angles and sources, and it is declining in use at television stations.

Civic journalism is an attempt by media organizations, print and broadcast, to link journalism and democracy to help public life go well. Friedland noted that the term "public" denotes three important associations: "public as government," "public as a collection of private opinions," and "citizens who argue and deliberate." Civic journalism is an effort to alter journalistic practices to improve the connection between journalists and the communities in news coverage.

Civic journalism, in theory and practice, is a public discussion; thus there is no universally accepted definition. Jay Rosen, one of the founders of civic journalism, wrote that defining civic (or public) journalism "is something you're always doing as you try to figure out the shape the thing has." In his book, Rosen offered this definition:

Public journalism is an approach to the daily business of the craft that calls on journalists to (1) address people as citizens, potential participants in public affairs, rather than victims or spectators; (2) help the political community act upon, rather than just learn about, its problems; (3) improve the climate of public discussion, rather than simply watch it deteriorate; (4) help make public life go well, so that it earns its claim on our attention.

Civic journalism is designed to improve journalists' understanding of the community, its citizens, values, problems, issues, and aspirations. This deeper and more contextual understanding of the community is assumed to show through reporting as journalists identify alternative frames or angles for stories and focus more on developing enterprise reporting.

The definitions of civic journalism tend to avoid ties to the norms and routines of journalistic practice. Civic journalism specifically aims to improve connections to public life through development of new listening posts in non-traditional places (outside of government offices).

Civic journalists, therefore, must think differently about source choices. They identify people in the community who act as catalysts, connectors, and experts. Community catalysts are individuals who help initiate change and problem solving. Connectors are community members with a vantage point to see across community boundaries. Community experts are those people who hold the institutional memory for the community. Civic journalism also encourages reporting in five key layers of public life: official, quasi-official, third-place, incidental, and private. This is very different from the traditional conceptualization of source diversity, and while this would seem to dictate improved source diversity, no evidence exists that source diversity has in fact been altered at television stations where civic journalism is practiced.

In traditional journalistic practices, the value of a citizen source is often questioned. Charity wrote, "Many newspapers treat the printing of citizen voices as a kind of welfare system for the news-space impoverished-a service aimed much more at good community relations than at forwarding the debate on public issues-but public journalists think differently. They are perfectly comfortable drawing on citizens for ideas." Television journalists also tend to view citizen sources as simply storytelling elements that add emotion to the expert source's ideas.

While many newspapers have embraced civic journalism, the development of television forms of civic journalism has been less successful. Still, several shining examples of television attempts exist, including KRON's "About Race" project that spanned almost three years. But television civic journalism may be starting to develop. In the past two years, the number of entries to the Pew Centre for Civic Journalism Batten Awards has increased steadily, indicating a growing willingness to attempt this type of work.

Some evidence also exists that civic journalism improves source diversity in newspaper coverage. Kennamer and South compared election coverage in two newspapers, one civic and one traditional.

They found the civic journalism paper used a much greater percentage of unaffiliated sources (43 per cent vs. 12 per cent). Boynton found increased use of female sources in civic journalism work in her study of the Charlotte Observer, although female sources tended to be used less prominently. Boynton also found that male reporters were more likely to use female sources, but that many of these female sources were from the unaffiliated ranks.

Massey also found increased use of female sources in civic journalism newspaper stories. However, in his study the gender of the reporter was a confounding variable, because only female reporters increased their use of female sources.

This study builds on the previous research on source diversity. It asks whether a new form of journalistic practice that includes an emphasis on enterprise reporting and digging deep into community life does in fact improve diversity of source race and gender. Improved diversity might provide additional proof of the value of television forms of civic journalism. Lack of improvement will provide evidence of the limitations organizational norms and routines place on the practice of television journalism.

This study focuses on the diversity of sources presented in civic journalism television news reports. Because the number of television stations that practice civic journalism is limited, this study assumes that any station attempting civic journalism would be likely to submit a tape to the James K. Batten Awards contest. The Pew Centre for Civic Journalism has a history of encouraging stations to submit entries. Of primary interest is whether television civic journalists used greater diversity of sources-race and gender-compared to proportions in the 2000 U.S. Census. This leads to the following hypotheses for television coverage:

*H1:* Civic journalism will use minority sources in proportions equal to the U.S. Census.

*H2:* As part of an expected increase in minority sources in civic journalism stories, minority reporters will use a greater percentage of minority sources than non-minority reporters do.

*H3:* Civic journalism will use female sources in proportions equal to the U.S. Census.

*H4:* As part of an expected increase in female sources in civic journalism stories, female reporters will use a greater percentage of female sources than male reporters.

The data consist of a content analysis of all the television news stories on 184 entry tapes submitted for the James K. Batten Award from 1996 through 2001. This award is the premier recognition for civic journalism work in the United States. A total of 1,071 news sources was coded by three trained coders. The stations ranged in market size from the second largest to number 156. Stations were from all parts of the country. All the reports were original content created for the station by station employees. The Scott's pi intercoder reliability coefficient for each variable ranged from.84 to 1.0.41

News sources were defined as any person or group to which information was attributed. If a source appeared more than one time in a single story, the source was coded only once and the times for both appearances combined. The sources were coded for affiliation, race, and gender.

The first hypothesis predicted proportional use of minority sources when comparing civic journalism to U.S. Census data. This hypothesis was supported with some qualifications. Civic journalism used a higher percentage of minority sources (35.5%) than the actual population in the United States (24.9%). African-American sources (23%) were presented at a rate almost twice that of the population (12.3%). Asian-American sources (3.4%) were presented at a level almost equal to the Census (3.6%). Latinos were underrepresented compared to the Census (77% vs. 12.5%).

The second hypothesis, predicting that reporter race would be related to minority source selection, was also supported. African-American reporters were more likely to use African-American sources (38.2%) in their stories than non-minority (17.9%) or Latino reporters (18.6%). Latino reporters also were more likely to use Latino sources (33.9%) than non-minority (7.2%) or African-American reporters (2%). Minority reporters might simply hold a greater affinity for using minority sources, or they may be more likely to cover beats and communities with disproportionately more minorities.

The third hypothesis predicted parity use of female sources compared to U.S. Census data. In the civic journalism stories studied, women represented little more than 40% of the sources. Civic journalism did not reach the 50.9% census level. Thus the hypothesis was not supported. The fourth hypothesis predicted that female civic journalists would use a greater percentage of female sources. This hypothesis was supported. In fact, female reporters were significantly more likely than their male counterparts to include female sources in their stories. However, even in this case, female source representation does not rise to Census levels.

This study provides evidence that civic journalism alters the routines of coverage in a positive manner. While this research did not look at the nature of the portrayal of the sources, positive or negative, it does indicate that groups disproportionately left out of news coverage do gain access and an opportunity to express their views in a television civic journalism model.

Based on these results, it is possible to say that civic journalism produces a positive effect on the diversity of sources presented on television news. When compared to the literature on television sourcing, the difference is even more pronounced. Women and minorities are portrayed more often in civic journalism than in traditional journalism.

Civic journalism minority source use (35.5%) more than doubled Grabe and Barnett's findings of 13.6% minority source use in television magazine shows.43 In contrast with

Smith's study of television news in one of the most diverse communities in the country, San Francisco, civic journalism was still higher than the 19% of minority sources reported. Minority sources in civic journalism exceed their proportion in the population. This is primarily explained by the high level of African— American sources used in civic journalism (23%) compared to the African-American population reported in the Census (12.3%). However, both this study's and Smith's findings are significantly lower for Latinos compared to the Census data. People of Asian descent were reported at parity levels in all three versions.

At a basic level, it makes sense that journalists find it easier to locate sources most like themselves. Journalistic norms push journalists to cross racial and gender boundaries in search of diverse representations for their stories. Civic journalism tools help journalists effectively cross boundaries and understand unfamiliar communities in deeper and more meaningful ways. The findings in this study certainly indicate more work is needed, even within television civic journalism. African— American reporters over-compensated in their presentations of African— American sources compared to the Census. This is likely a response to less-than-equitable source use in stories covered by journalists of other races. Two important points maybe made here. One is that non-minority civic journalism reporters made progress in covering minority communities. The other is that civic journalism appears to give minority reporters the opportunity to draw minority sources into coverage. More research is needed to investigate how minority journalists use civic journalism tools within organizational routines to improve source diversity.

Television civic journalism's female sourcing is higher than the best gender diversity reported in the literature. For example, Zoch and Turk's study of 2,998 sources in the front and metro sections of daily newspapers found only 20.8% of sources were women. Liebler and Smith's analysis of 448 sources in 159 network television stories found even lower levels; women made up only 16.3% of all sources. Because the civic journalism entries studied here came from both networks and local stations, the percentages are not entirely comparable.

Unlike the sourcing by reporters of colour, female source use by female reporters did not reach the Census benchmark of 50.9%. Some might argue that a more fair comparison is with the level of female workers in the U.S. workforce. However, civic journalism is not simply covering the workforce. Also of note is that male civic journalists easily topped the best reported level of female source use in the literature (20.8%) by using 37.4% female sources in their work.

This replicates Boynton's finding that a civic journalism newspaper included a "significantly higher number of female sources than found in other studies where women comprise one-third or less of the identifiable sources." Grabe, Zhou, and Barnett's study of television news magazines found that "female reporters seek out more female sources (38.3%) than male reporters do (27.6%)." The current study replicates this finding but at higher levels. Of the sources selected by female television civic journalists, 44.5% were female. For male civic journalists, female sources accounted for 37.4% of all sources used. The enterprise nature of news magazines studied by Grabe, Zhou, and Barnett likely improved source diversity on these programs.

Improved source diversity in civic journalism should not be surprising because it relies heavily on an enterprise model of coverage. In 1991, Hansen found that enterprise reporting improved source diversity. However, the civic journalism model goes well beyond simply developing an enterprise report. Civic journalism dictates that reporters spend time in communities gaining a greater depth and context of understanding. If it is true that reporters tend to use people they know and trust as primary sources, and if civic journalism creates a routine of getting to know and trust people in diverse communities, then it makes sense that civic journalism practices would improve the diversity of sources in race, gender, and affiliation.

The adoption rate of civic journalism among television stations remains low. While KRON-TV in San Francisco provided proof that television news is capable of doing high-quality civic journalism, Kurpius found that television forms of civic journalism were generally not sustainable in the current market-driven news model. While managers and journalists indicated a desire and a willingness to use a civic model for coverage, marketplace forces limited the potential for development without the now commonplace foundation financial support for this type of work.

The need for improved source diversity remains, even in civic journalism. Women and Latinos are still underrepresented. While the benchmark for improving gender diversity is a stable target, the Latino population is one of the fastest growing in the country. This will challenge journalists who make good faith efforts to accurately and effectively represent the communities they cover.

Another concern is that television stations are unlikely to see the gains found in this study because of the limited adoption of civic journalism techniques at stations across the country. This limits the potential for finally correcting an almost half-century-old problem in television's coverage: the lack of inclusion and accurate representation of minorities and women in news content. However, more work is needed. For instance, because there are differing levels of adoption of civic journalism practices among television stations, it is unclear at what level the tools start to produce improved diversity. In addition, a qualitative study of news workers within civic journalism television organizations might provide a better understanding of exactly how they altered their routines to improve diversity.

# Chapter 7

# Investigative Reporting

Undercover techniques used by journalists are increasingly coming under public scrutiny. Those targeted by investigative news operations are challenging the methods rather than the accuracy of the reporting - and often winning sympathy from the public. It is a trend that came into sharp focus in January 1997 when a twelve-member jury in North Carolina decided that ABC News should pay $5.5 million in damages to the Food Lion supermarket chain because ABC's reporters posed as employees and used hidden cameras to uncover alleged sales of spoiled meat at some of its stores. The jury found that network producers had trespassed and committed fraud when researching a Primetime Live segment in 1992 that accused the company of selling spoiled meat. Although Food Lion officials disputed the accuracy of the ABC report, they did not sue for libel. Rather, they accused ABC of fraud because it used techniques such as having producers submit fake resumes to get jobs in the meat department of company stores, and then used hidden cameras to film there.

Many journalists argue that hidden cameras and other undercover reporting techniques have long been necessary tools for exposing vital issues of public policy and health. The type of hidden-camera reporting ABC used to investigate Food Lion has become a staple of national and local TV news in recent years as cameras have become increasingly miniaturized. But some media critics say that TV producers have overused them in recent years in a push to create splashy shows and bolster ratings. In fact, the verdict against ABC may reflect a growing public sentiment against news organizations that are perceived as undisciplined and overly aggressive. Several jurors in the Food Lion case said, for example, that although they supported investigative reporting, they took issue with ABC's reporting methods.

In particular, they pointed to the use by producers of false resumes to gain jobs in Food Lion stores in South and North Carolina. In addition, the Food Lion case nicely illustrates the public's "schizophrenic" attitude toward the use of investigative reporting techniques such as hidden cameras. While many viewers seem to be uncomfortable with the growing amount of surreptitious taping, investigative TV shows have attracted a growing number of loyal viewers.

Despite the great public attention the Food Lion case attracted and the widespread speculations by the media about a possible backlash of this verdict on the future of investigative reporting, the overall impact of this particular case might have been overstated. A representative telephone survey of 1,001 American adults ages 18 and older conducted by the Roper Research Centre shortly after the verdict against ABC found that the majority (80 per cent) of those who had heard about the case said they thought ABC was not doing anything out of the ordinary in employing the reporting techniques. Of the 51 per cent who said they heard about the court case, half said they sided with ABC News, 21 per cent said they sided with the supermarket, and 27 per cent said they didn't know.

In view of these recent developments in public attitudes toward investigative reporting, this study compares past findings on perceived public importance of investigative reporting and the acceptability of different reporting methods with findings from a national telephone survey of 1,211 respondents conducted in February 1997 by Princeton Survey Research Associates for the Pew Research Centre for The People & The Press. In particular, results from five polls conducted between 1980 and 1997 are compared to track possible changes in public approval of investigative reporting techniques.

Additionally, the 1997 poll data is analysed for possible predictors of respondents' approval of investigative reporting techniques such as age, gender, education, income, and media use. While past studies have found only weak relationships between approval of investigative reporting and respondents' individual-level characteristics, the increased use of these techniques in popular TV shows and local evening news during the 1990s may have changed the previously found weak relationships, especially as more targeting of specific demographic groups by these programs has occurred. One goal of this study is to see if demographics are better predictors of opinions about investigative reporting in the late 1990s than in the 1980s.

## RELATED STUDIES

Hidden cameras and other undercover reporting techniques have long been necessary tools for exposing vital issues of public policy and health. But despite the rising popularity of stories based on investigative reporting techniques and their more frequent use by TV shows such as 60 Minutes or Primetime Live, only scant attention has been paid to the question of how the audience perceives investigative reporting by the media. While some critics argue that the Food Lion verdict reflects overt hostility toward sensational TV news magazine reporting, others argue that Americans generally respect and are interested in the information generated by investigative reporting, including undercover techniques.

Both viewpoints might be only partially right. Two previous studies that analysed public attitudes toward investigative reporting found fairly consistent evidence for the hypothesis that people approve of investigative reporting in general, but are much less likely to support specific investigative reporting techniques such as the use of hidden cameras or microphones.

The first study, based on a representative telephone survey conducted by the Chicago Sun-Times in 1980, found strong support for the general concept of investigative reporting among 603 Chicago residents. More than three fourths of the respondents in this survey considered it "very important" for newspapers to do investigative reporting, and almost 78 per cent said that investigative reporting is worthwhile for a "problem to be exposed, no matter what happens later."

Specific investigative reporting techniques, however, received much less support, especially the so-called "checkbook journalism," which tolerates reporters paying for information or interviews (45 per cent approved). The study also found that the approval of investigative reporting was largely independent from respondents' demographic characteristics and media use habits, but interest in an ongoing investigative reporting series, "The Accident Swindlers," did predict perceived importance of investigative reporting (beta =.32).

Ten years later, a study by Daniels and Weaver9 compared the results of three opinion surveys that included questions on investigative reporting and were conducted throughout the 1980s with the results of the 1980 Chicago survey. Overall, compared to 1980, the level of public support for investigative reporting was found to be lower on a national and statewide level. However, throughout the 1980s, a large majority in all three surveys still thought that such reporting was at least "somewhat important." Daniels and Weaver also found that specific investigative reporting techniques received lower levels of public support than was found in the 1980 Chicago survey.

While a majority of respondents in the 1980 Chicago survey approved of most investigative reporting techniques ("hidden cameras & microphones," "reporters not identifying themselves," "use of anonymous sources," "paying for information" and "reporters paying for information"), the nationwide and statewide polls conducted later failed to find majority support for any of these techniques. The authors concluded that this might have been a result of the frequent use of such journalistic techniques over time in Chicago.

Similar to the findings obtained in the 1980 Chicago

study, none of the respondents' demographic characteristics was significantly linked to the perceived importance of investigative reporting in the 1984/85 ASNE poll or the 1989 Indiana survey. However, weak relationships between support for investigative reporting and frequency of newspaper reading were found in the ASNE poll and the Indiana survey.

The purpose of this chapter is to update the findings of the two previous studies with data from the 1997 Pew Research Centre National Survey, which included a number of questions about the public's perception of investigative reporting originally used in the 1981 Gallup poll.

Such an update is important because, during the past ten years, significant changes have taken place in the public perception of the press. While surveys conducted a decade ago showed that many Americans criticized the press as inaccurate, unfair, and biased, these flaws have been traditionally overlooked by those who recognized the media's contributions to society as a political "watchdog" and information disseminator.

Today, those Americans who value the function of the press in society still judge the media more favorably than those who do not, but fewer Americans like the news product and many are less interested in the news in general. Moreover, while most people still trust the news, a growing minority "believes little or nothing of what they hear or read or has little or no trust in major news organizations."

Overall, public attitudes toward the press have worsened during the past decade, a trend which might eventually undermine the crucial support the media still receive as a democratic forum.

It is therefore imperative to identify the possible reasons for this negative trend in public perceptions of the media, especially as they relate to peoples' trust in the media. This study analyses one potential cause by comparing the public approval of investigative reporting in general with the approval of specific investigative reporting techniques.

To expand on previous studies, the analysis of possible

predictors for approval of investigative reporting will be broadened to a series of questions that tap people's attitudes toward the function or role of the press in society, thus allowing a fresh look at why people like investigative reporting but dislike its journalistic techniques.

This most recent study is based on a representative telephone survey conducted by Princeton Research Survey Associates among a nationwide sample of 1,211 adults, 18 years of age or older, during the period of 20-23 February 1997.

Telephone numbers were selected by random digit dialing techniques, proportionally stratified by each county's share of telephone households in the United States. Within each contacted household, interviewers asked to speak either with the "youngest male 18 or older" or "the oldest woman 18 or older." The sampling error for this survey is plus or minus 3 percentage points at the 95% confidence level.

To evaluate the potential changes in public opinion about investigative reporting during the past years, the 1997 survey is compared with four national and state polls containing questions on investigative reporting that have been conducted between 1980 and 1989.

All five surveys include a series of identically worded questions that ask respondents whether they approve or disapprove of specific investigative reporting techniques such as "using hidden cameras and microphones," "having reporters not identify themselves as reporters," "running stories that quote an unnamed source," or "paying informers for their information or testimony."

In addition, the 1981 Gallup survey and the 1997 Pew survey contain two questions that assess whether respondents "approve or disapprove of investigative reporting by the news media," and whether they would "like to see more of this type of reporting or less."

The findings of the most recent 1997 survey are discussed in light of respondents' demographic characteristics, media use patterns, and attitudes toward the press, and, where possible, compared to previous results. Demographic variables used from the 1997 survey are gender, age, education, race, party identification, and place of residence.

## FINDINGS

### OVERALL APPROVAL OF INVESTIGATIVE REPORTING

A comparison of results from the 1997 Pew survey with results from the 1981 Gallup survey shows that the overall approval of investigative reporting has slightly increased during the past sixteen years. Even though the 1997 survey was conducted in the wake of the Food Lion case, which raised questions about news gathering techniques used by ABC News reporters, almost 84% of the respondents in 1997 said that they approved of the news media's practice of uncovering and reporting corruption and fraud in business, government agencies, and other organizations.

This compares to a similar, but smaller, majority of 79% that expressed support for investigative reporting in the 1981 Gallup survey. While support for investigative reporting in general has risen between 1981 and 1997, no difference is found in the level of demand for more investigative reporting stories. In 1997,64% of Americans said that they would like to see more of this type of reporting rather than less (29%), as compared to 66% who said they would like to see more of these stories in 1981 (19% less). Nevertheless, the data clearly show that most Americans still not only approve of investigative reporting in general, but that they would also like to see more investigative reporting by the news media.

### APPROVAL OF INVESTIGATIVE REPORTING TECHNIQUES

Similar to previous findings, the 1997 survey shows that general approval of investigative reporting does not necessarily translate into approval of specific investigative reporting techniques. Approval of most investigative reporting techniques is only weakly correlated with approval of investigative reporting in general. Only about one-third of all respondents approve of reporters concealing their identity (33%) or paying informers for information (31%), while slightly more approve of news organizations' use of hidden cameras and microphones (46%), or running stories that quote unnamed sources (53%).

Thus, while an overwhelming majority of respondents approve of investigative reporting in general, almost as many respondents also disapprove of concrete investigative reporting practices. In fact, among those respondents who approve of investigative reporting in general, more than 15% do not approve of any of the four tested investigative reporting techniques, and only about 7% approve of all the techniques.

A comparison of national poll results between 1981 and 1997, indicates a moderate, national-level increase in approval for using hidden microphones and cameras (up 8%) and quoting unnamed sources (up 11%), but no increase in approval for reporters concealing their identity or paying for information. The observed increase in approval for the use of hidden cameras and microphones is notable in light of the fact that both techniques were used in ABC's Food Lion story.

## IMPACT OF DEMOGRAPHICS

Results from the 1997 survey closely mirror the findings of previous studies that analysed the demographic profile of those people who are more likely to approve of investigative reporting in general. Consistently over the past sixteen years, it appears that especially the younger, more affluent, and better-educated respondents have a more positive view of investigative reporting by the media, although these relationships have been weak in strength.

To evaluate the potential impact of respondents' demographic characteristics on overall approval of investigative reporting and the specific reporting techniques, provides a demographic breakdown for both types of approval (general and specific) together with results from the question that asks whether respondents would like to see more or fewer investigative reporting stories.

In general, demographic characteristics do seem to have a distinct but weak influence on who approves of investigative reporting and whether someone is likely to want more investigative reporting stories. While respondents who are more educated are more likely to approve of investigative reporting and most of the investigative reporting techniques (except for quoting unnamed sources and paying informers), they are less likely to want more investigative reporting stories. The greatest support for investigative reporting is found among the 30- to 49-year-old respondents, but specific investigative reporting techniques find the most support among those under the age of 30.

Older respondents are especially skeptical of investigative reporting in general and tend to disapprove in particular of quoting unnamed sources and reporters paying for information. They are also less likely to want more investigative reporting stories. Familiar patterns are also observed for the relationship between income and approval of investigative reporting. The poorest respondents (less than $20,000 yearly income) are less likely to approve of investigative reporting, especially the use of hidden cameras and microphones and reporters concealing their identities, and these poorer people are also more likely to want fewer such stories.

Previous studies that looked at the rate of approval of investigative reporting in relation to place of residence found that rural respondents are less likely to approve of investigative reporting. The 1981 Gallup survey, for example, found that respondents from cities of more than 500,000 were more likely to approve (84%) than those from smaller cities. Results from the Pew survey indicate that this difference still exists in 1997. While the highest levels of approval for investigative reporting in 1997 can be found in the suburbs (88%), significantly less support is found in rural areas (78%). Rural residents, however, do not vary much from people living in suburbs or cities on whether there should be more or less investigative reporting.

In line with previous findings, party identification does

not seem to influence whether respondents approve or disapprove of investigative reporting, although Republicans are less likely to approve of quoting unnamed sources. There is also little difference between African-American and white Americans in their approval of investigative reporting. However, the relatively few people of other races (predominantly Asians) are more likely to favour investigative reporting, especially the use of hidden cameras and microphones, concealing identity (going undercover), and, to a lesser extent, quoting unnamed sources.

These minorities are also more likely to ask for more investigative news stories. Somewhat more distinct differences are found between men and women. While men are less likely to approve of quoting unnamed sources (possibly because more men are Republicans than women), women are more likely to disapprove of the use of hidden cameras and microphones and paying for information, but are more likely than men to want more investigative reporting stories.

Statistical Analysis: Logistic Regression Analysis. In order to evaluate the individual contributions of respondents' demographic characteristics, media use, and attitudes toward the media on approval of investigative reporting, a series of logistic regression analyses are used. The logistic regression procedure allows us to examine the influence of multiple independent variables on dichotomous dependent variables. Compared to ordinary least squares (OLS) regression, which presents coefficients that result in the smallest squared distances between the observed and the predicted values of the dependent variables, in logistic regression those coefficients which make the model results most "likely" are selected.

However, because the logistic regression model is nonlinear, the interpretation of regression coefficients is not as straightforward as in OLS regression. Logistic regression coefficients (B) can be interpreted as the change in the ratio of approval versus disapproval of investigative reporting associated with a one-unit change in an independent variable while holding other independent variables constant. Thus a positive B indicates that an increase in the independent variable predicts an increase in the support for investigative reporting, whereas a negative B suggests that an increase in the independent variable predicts a decrease in support controlling for other independent variables. To assess the statistical significance of these coefficients, this study uses the Wald statistic.

Overall, six logistic regression models are used for the analysis of approval of investigative reporting. The first model predicts overall "approval of investigative reporting" in general, while the following models predict the approval of four investigative reporting techniques discussed above ("using hidden microphones and cameras," "reporters not identifying themselves," "quoting unnamed sources," "paying for information"). In line with the requirements for logistic regression models, all five dependent variables provide binominal answer categories (approve = 1; disapprove = 0; don't know = missing). The last regression model predicts whether people are more likely to want more or fewer investigative reporting stories (more = 1; fewer = 0; don't know = missing).

Respondents' media use is assessed by a series of questions asking respondents to state on a 4-point scale (regularly = 4; never = 1) how often they watched or read the following types of media products: the "nightly network news," the "local evening news," "CNN," "60 Minutes," "Dateline NBC," "TV news shows," "daily newspaper," and "tabloid papers."

Another important block of variables included in this study are measures of respondents' attitudes toward the role of the press in society. According to recent polls, the public's assessment of press performance has grown increasingly negative in recent years. A majority (56%) now say news stories and reports are often inaccurate, up more than 20 percentage points from 1985, when a similar majority (55%) said news organizations get the facts straight. The press is also attacked for its lack of fairness. Two-thirds (67%) say that in presenting news on political and social issues, news organizations tend to favour one side rather than dealing fairly with all sides. This negative view of the press is more prevalent now than it was twelve years ago, when a much smaller majority (53%) criticized news organizations for biased coverage of political and social news.

Attitudes toward media are measured with five dummy variables that assess respondents' attitudes toward the press by asking whether they believe that (1) "criticism by the press keeps political leaders from doing their job"; (2) "press coverage of the personal and ethical behaviour of political leaders is excessive"; (3) "press criticism of the policies and proposals of political leaders is excessive"; (4) "news stories are often inaccurate"; and (5) "news organizations tend to favour one side when reporting about political and social issues" (all coded: yes = 1, no = 0).

Control variables include measures of gender (male = 1; female = 0), age, education, race (two dummy variables: White and Black), party identification (two dummy variables: Republican and Democrat), income, and place of residence (rural = 1; small city, suburb, large city = 0).

## FINDINGS FOR LOGISTIC REGRESSION MODELS

In line with previous findings, no significant links are observed between income, education, race, or political party identification on approval of investigative reporting. Older respondents, however, are less likely to approve of the use of hidden cameras and microphones (B = -.02) and of reporters not identifying themselves as reporters (B = -.02). Similar to the findings reported in 1982 and 1992, respondents living in rural areas of the country are less likely to approve of investigative reporting in general (B = -.50) and reporters not identifying themselves (B = -.44). Interestingly, male respondents are less likely to approve of quoting unnamed sources (B =-.30), but more likely to approve of paying for information (B =.35).

Media exposure to CNN is positively related to approval of quoting unnamed sources (B =.15), while those respondents who regularly watch Dateline NBC are more likely to approve of the use of hidden cameras and microphones (B =.25). Interestingly, those people who regularly watch tabloid-style TV shows such as Hard Copy or Inside Edition are less likely to approve of reporters not identifying themselves. None of the standard media exposure variables, such as frequency of reading the newspaper or watching TV news, was significantly related to any of the dependent approval measures, reinforcing the findings from the earlier studies that frequency of media use is less important than what one reads or views.

The most consistent predictors of respondents' approval of investigative reporting are attitudes toward the function of the press in society. Respondents are less likely to approve of investigative reporting when they believe that criticism by the press keeps political leaders from doing their job (B between -.34 and -1.01) or when they think that reports and stories by news organizations are often inaccurate (B between -.35 and -.89). Thus, those who are dubious about the media's watchdog role are more likely than others to say they want less, not more, investigative reporting.

The best predictors for respondents' willingness to see more investigative reporting stories in the media are age, place of residence, media exposure, and attitudes toward the media. Exposure to CNN (B =.15) and 60 Minutes (B =.20), on the other hand, boosts the likelihood of asking for more investigative news stories. Additionally, those who believe that the media are keeping politicians from doing their jobs are less likely to ask for more investigative news stories (B = -.47).

Overall, the findings reported here indicate that public opinion about investigative reporting did not change much during the past sixteen years. Similar to previous findings, a majority of respondents in the 1997 survey approve of investigative reporting in general, independent from such demographic factors as age, education, gender, or party identification. Compared to the findings reported in the 1981 Gallup survey, the percentage of respondents who approve of investigative reporting in 1997 has slightly increased to

84%. This indicates that a vast majority of people still favour a press that uncovers and reports on corruption and fraud in business and government, and that this support is increasing rather than diminishing over time.

Another important observation of this study is that the approval for investigative reporting remains much higher than the approval for specific investigative reporting techniques. Only about one-third of the respondents in 1981 and 1997, for example, approve of reporters working undercover or paying for information. Evidently, Americans do expect the media to take their role as a public watchdog seriously, but they also expect that the media do so with the greatest degree of openness possible.

Interestingly, during the past eight years, the public approval of hidden cameras or microphones and the use of anonymous sources in the news media also has slightly increased. This might possibly be a reflection of the more frequent employment of hidden cameras in news shows such as 60 Minutes and the increasingly routine use of anonymous news sources in political reporting. It is reasonable to assume that the repeated exposure to undercover news stories and source identifiers such as "a high-ranking government official" in regular news stories reinforces the impression that these techniques are standard journalistic practice. Asking respondents whether they approve of reporters not identifying themselves or actually paying for information, on the other hand, might create images of ethical misconduct on an individual level and thus could help to explain the lower approval ratings.

Overall, findings indicate that the best predictor for whether people approve or disapprove of investigative reporting is their general attitude toward the media's role in society. Those respondents who see the media as a force that undermines the work of politicians and those who believe that news stories are often inaccurate, are less likely to approve of investigative reporting in general and of most investigative reporting techniques.

Compared to the other observed relationships in the

various logistic regression models which were tested here, attitudes toward the press proved to be the strongest and most consistent predictor for approval of investigative reporting. In light of the mostly insignificant relationships observed between media exposure and approval of investigative reporting, it appears that approval is primarily a function of attitudes toward the media, rather than increased exposure to investigative news stories.

It is somewhat alarming, though, that especially those who have a very negative view of the media's function in society are also more likely to disapprove of the very techniques that allow the media to operate as a political and social watchdog.

Because a vast majority of the people approve of investigative reporting in general, the explanation of this schizophrenic attitude is likely to be found in negative perceptions of specific investigative reporting techniques among most respondents, but especially among those who are critical of the press.

While the six regression models are fairly similar in total amount of variation predicted in approval of investigative reporting, it should be noted that the unexplained variance in all models is high, especially for the four models predicting approval of specific investigative reporting techniques (89 - 94%, based on Nagelkerke R2 estimates). This suggests that opinions about investigative reporting are related to other, unknown factors that were not included in this study or that they are fairly idiosyncratic, or both. The logistic regression model predicting approval of investigative reporting in general produced the highest Nagelkerke R^sup 2^, but most of the explained variance here is related to the above mentioned attitudes toward the role of the press in society and place of residence.

Future studies should search for other possible predictors to better explain why people are so much in favour of investigative reporting but, at the same time, disapprove of most techniques that make this kind of journalism possible. The findings of this study suggest that the focus at the individual level should be on attitudes and values rather than on respondents' demographic characteristics or their media use patterns. There are some hints here, however, that community-level characteristics, such as rural residence, may also play an important role in the formation of attitudes and opinions about investigative reporting, as suggested by the comparison of Chicago residents' opinions with those from national and Indiana samples in the 1980s.

More frequent exposure to investigative reporting projects that seem to be worthwhile revelations of wrongdoing is likely to influence public opinion about such reporting in general, as well as the specific methods used to carry it out. The key, though, seems to be whether the public perceives the use of ethically questionable reporting practices as justifying the exposure of wrongdoing, as in Chicago in 1980. And even there, levels of support for specific reporting methods were lower than support for investigative reporting in general, suggesting that such techniques should be used sparingly by news organizations that value public support, as Weaver and Daniels concluded in 1992.

## Chapter 8

# Unmaking of Civic Journalists

Perhaps more than any other profession, journalism grapples with an apparent contradiction between autonomy and public service. Sociologists define professional autonomy as wide latitude of judgment in executing occupational duties.[1] Autonomy provides discretion in the application of techniques and separation from influences that threaten a professional's ability to apply expertise in service to the public. Thus, practitioners adhere to norms of public service even as the lay public itself is excluded from formal decision making. This conception of autonomy becomes problematic when applied to the press, according to advocates of civic (or public) journalism.

This reform movement is based on the premise that news media should go beyond the mere reporting of information to act as a catalyst and as a forum for the revitalization of democracy. But according to civic journalism opponents, these goals threaten the institutional independence of the press and thereby jeopardize journalistic autonomy. Under the traditional view of journalism, autonomy allows the press to cover public affairs with some protection against partisan bias and other corrupting influences.

If civic journalism is to succeed in the long run as a reform movement, it must meet head on the tension between the profession's autonomous identity and its role in democracy. Civic journalism has focused on the implementation and consequences of professional values, but it has been less concerned about understanding the origins of these values as a function of professional socialization. The purpose of this study is to model the process by which professional socialization predisposes college students to reject or embrace civic journalism.

We will first assess the extent of support for various dimensions of civic journalism within two groups: journalism students and professional journalists living in the same community. Our general expectation is that students will be relatively supportive of civic journalism while professionals will express reservations in light of their commitment to autonomy. We will then consider college experiences that might help to explain when and why this gap emerges.'

Our intent is not to argue for the merits of civic journalism, but to provide insight into why support for it might erode as a consequence of professional socialization. For those who do support civic journalism, this line of inquiry could suggest implications for curriculum reform geared toward enhancing-or preventing the erosion of-civic journalism support.

This approach will also allow us to make an empirical contribution to the ongoing debate as to whether civic and traditional journalism principles coexist in harmony, or whether the two perspectives necessarily conflict as values take shape during professional socialization.

Why Autonomy Is Important to Journalists. While autonomy for all professions is ostensibly a mechanism of public service, it also accommodates the psychological needs of the practitioners. Autonomy contributes to group identification-the perception of belonging to a particular human group. Cheney and Tompkins observed that identification helps to sustain "an individual's or a group's 'sameness' or 'substance' against a backdrop of change and 'out side' elements." Prior research shows autonomy strongly correlated with both professional identification of journalists and job satisfaction.

Management trends in news media have increased the need for autonomy in recent decades. Comparison of the findings of Johnstone, Slawski, and Bowman in 1976 with those of Weaver and Wilhoit for 1986 and 1996 reveals that perceived autonomy declined. As Johnstone, Slawski, and Bowman surmised, the bureaucratization of media organizations diminishes the sense of autonomy among rank-and-file reporters. In the first two surveys, 60 per cent of respondents reported they were almost entirely free to select the material on which they worked; this dropped to 51 per cent in the third study.

Potential threats to autonomy include increased corporate chain ownership, the crumbling of the metaphorical wall between business and editorial, competition from Internet sources of news and entertainment, and the blurring of editorial and business functions in news organizations. With an erosion of perceived autonomy, and without the organizational protection and academic credentials of other professions, journalists are likely to feel vulnerable in the face of structural changes.

This probably accounts for some of the defensiveness, if not outright hostility, many prominent journalists express toward civic journalism, a reform movement that is itself an explicit challenge to traditional notions of autonomy.

## CIVIC JOURNALISM AS A MULTI-DIMENSIONAL CONCEPT

In efforts to document the amount of support among reporters and editors, researchers have sought to isolate specific values associated with civic journalism. Bare developed a "personal public journalism" scale that formed a continuum from general goals to specific practices. Support decreased along the scale in the movement from abstract goals to practices that violate professional detachment.

One purpose of this study is to identify where students and professionals might depart in their evaluations of specific goals and practices. We will consider first the possible reactions to a questionnaire item that explicitly mentions "civic journalism" as a reform movement.

## "CIVIC JOURNALISM" AS A POLITICIZED TERM

Several proponents of civic journalism have lamented

that the term itself has become politicized in that it evokes disdain in professional circles instead of contemplation. Consequently, we expect that the professional respondents, and perhaps some students, will react negatively to a question that merely mentions "civic journalism." Analysis of responses to this item could help us to evaluate responses to the other questionnaire items: if respondents express support for specific goals and practices, yet object to "civic journalism" itself, this would suggest that they are responding to something not captured by the other attitudinal items.

Given the lack of prior research on differences between professionals and students in support for civic journalism, we propose a research question rather than a formal hypothesis:

RQ1: In comparison with professionals, will students express stronger support for "civic journalism" as a general description of the reform movement?

## CIVIC JOURNALISM GOALS

The press traditionally understands its role as a disseminator of accurate information that allows individuals to participate as competent citizens. This requires neutrality in the coverage of political actors, institutions, and issues. By contrast, civic journalists argue that news media should not be neutral about the quality of civic participation in their communities. We asked respondents to assess their support for two goals associated with civic journalism: going beyond the mere transmission of information to increase political participation, and focusing on news that helps a community to solve problems. While these goals are potentially problematic in light of the norm of detachment, they are described at a fairly abstract level, with the threat to autonomy more implicit than explicit. Thus, we again propose a research question instead of a hypothesis:

RQ2: In comparison with professionals, will students express stronger support for civic journalism goals?

## CIVIC JOURNALISM PRACTICES

We do anticipate differences between professionals and

students in the evaluation of practices that might jeopardize autonomy. For example, we asked respondents to assess their support for news media sponsoring meetings to address local problems. According to professional critics, such events cripple the ability of journalists to remain critical of the favored policies.

We also asked respondents to evaluate the use of polls to help journalists decide what should be covered. Critics have dismissed this technique as another manifestation of how marketing has intruded into the newsroom. Handing news judgment over to the public directly violates the profession's traditional understanding of autonomy.

H1: In comparison with professionals, students will express stronger support for practices associated with civic journalism.

## ANTECEDENTS OF SUPPORT FOR CIVIC JOURNALISM

A review of prior literature suggests that college experiences and attitudes adopted during professional socialization will influence students' acceptance of civic journalism. Potential predictors of civic journalism support include the amount of college instruction, anticipatory socialization as a psychological construct, working for a campus paper, and support for traditional roles of the press.

## FORMAL INSTRUCTION

Participation in a college journalism curriculum should influence the likelihood of students adopting values similar to those of professionals. Weaver and Wilhoit reported that alumni of journalism programs expressed a connection between their formal education and their current news values. Students are likely to adopt a commitment to professional autonomy-and consequently a reticence about civic journalism-to the extent that instruction emphasizes the conventional understanding of professional detachment and neutrality. Prior participation in a civic journalism project should also predict support, but we did not include this variable because of the minimal presence of civic journalism in the journalism programme where we recruited respondents. The programme had provided only one civic journalism class (in 1998), with an enrollment of eleven students.

## ANTICIPATORY SOCIALIZATION

Individuals typically view themselves as members of a profession long before they join a specific organization. "Anticipatory professional socialization" represents the extent to which an individual has thought seriously about a particular career. An important dimension of this process is "identification," or the perception of belonging to a particular group. This need for professional membership and acceptance might predispose students to reject civic journalism.

A central argument of civic journalism is that news media should display their inner workings, thereby becoming more accountable to the public. But if students begin to value an insider's perspective on newsroom culture, this group identification could evoke an aversion to the civic journalism critique.

## WORKING FOR A COLLEGE NEWSPAPER

While these two factors should facilitate the adoption of traditional values, neither duplicates the degree of autonomy experienced by professionals. Working for an independent college newspaper, however, might represent an indelible socializing experience that produces a resistance to civic journalism. Campus newspapers vary in their degree of independence from journalism departments and university administrations, but a tradition of American universities is that student newspapers should maintain substantial institutional independence.

The experience of working for a campus newspaper- including the sense of empowerment gained from reporting and editing with little or no instructor supervision— should instill an appreciation for autonomy that cannot be duplicated in the classroom.

Theorists of human development have observed that a young person's identification with an occupation or profession facilitates a realization of self identity, and thus many students might become attracted to journalism precisely because it allows them to express independence and personal identity through their writing and news judgment.

*H2:* Students with campus newspaper experience will be less supportive of civic journalism compared to other students.

## SUPPORT FOR TRADITIONAL ROLES

Civic journalism opponents argue that its goals and practices are not compatible with the traditional mission of the press as an institution that relies on autonomy to provide accurate and balanced information. In the case of journalism training, the question is whether the formation of a professional identity will allow for not only multiple role conceptions among students, but for acceptance of roles that are potentially incompatible. Prior surveys of professionals provide evidence that journalists do identify with more than one role.

Weaver and Wilhoit identified three highly correlated but distinct attitudes about professional purpose: interpretation, dissemination, and adversary orientations." The interpretive function resonates with a recommendation of the Commission on Freedom of the Press-that journalists should investigate the truth about facts while providing a context that gives them meaning.

The disseminator function highlights the need for the press to transmit information that is useful to a large audience, while the adversary function reflects the importance of acting as a "watchdog" of government.

In a survey of newspaper staff members, Arant and Meyer concluded that the majority of journalists do not support practices that violate professional autonomy, but those who did also supported traditional roles of news media. In the context of this study, we anticipate that students would support the traditional roles. But with relatively little concern about journalistic autonomy, measures of traditional values might correlate strongly with civic journalism support among the students, given that the overarching commitment to public service is reflected in all of these role conceptions. We propose the following research question:

*RQ3:* Will support for the dissemination, interpretive, and adversary roles predict students' support for civic journalism?

The student respondents attended the University of New Mexico (Albuquerque), and the professional journalists were recruited from two daily newspapers published in the same city. While the restriction of respondents to one community in the Southwest limits the external validity of findings, the design eliminates regional factors as alternative explanations for possible differences between students and professionals.

## SAMPLING

We used a purposive sample of students in courses taught within the university's Communication & Journalism Department. The intent was to include a large percentage of students who identified to some degree with journalism as a profession. During April of 1999, we administered questionnaires to classes that contained students in four undergraduate major tracks: print journalism, broadcast journalism, public relations, and advertising. We would expect that some students would be sharply focused on journalism, with some fully involved in internships and writing for the campus paper (the Daily Lobo).

Other students, however, would have little or no interest in journalism as a career, but they would have at least some knowledge of news media as an academic topic. This diversity of student background creates the possibility for variance within the variables used to predict civic journalism support.

The sampling frame for the professional journalists was defined as all reporters and editors on the staffs of the Albuquerque Journal and the Albuquerque Tribune. The family-owned Journal represents the largest newspaper in New Mexico with a circulation of approximately 121,000. The Tribune is delivered in the afternoon to about 16,000 subscribers, the vast majority of whom live in Albuquerque. It is owned by Scripps Howard.

We were given permission to distribute questionnaires during the same time period in which we sought responses from the students. The staff list for the Journal included 144 reporters and editors while the list for the Tribune totaled 56.

Interviewing. Questionnaire items for students and professional journalists were identical in every respect practical.

We used paper-andpencil, self-administered questionnaires for both groups. The availability of students in classroom settings allowed us to directly distribute and administer their questionnaires (N=317 respondents), but this degree of supervision was not practical for the professionals' questionnaires.

In both newsrooms, we requested that an administrative assistant place a questionnaire, cover letter, and return envelope in the mail slots of all reporters and editors. Two weeks after the questionnaires were distributed, we distributed a reminder letter to coax potential respondents who had failed to complete a questionnaire.

This procedure produced a response rate of 59% for the Journal and 57% for the Tribune. These can be considered relatively high response rates given that the interviews were voluntary and unsupervised. The final sample consists of N=117 professional journalists.

## DESCRIPTION OF SAMPLES

Descriptive statistics reveal a range of interest within the student sample regarding journalism as a career goal. When asked if they plan to pursue a career in journalism, 55% disagreed or strongly disagreed, 16% indicated they were not sure, and 29% agreed or strongly agreed.

For the sample of professional journalists, we sought to gather data reflecting variance in newsroom status among reporters and editors.

When asked how many years they had worked in

journalism, 42% indicated 1 to 10 years, 26% indicated 11-20 years, and 32% reported more than 20 years.

## CIVIC JOURNALISM MEASURES

One question asked explicitly about civic journalism:

"Several newspapers in recent years have initiated projects known as 'civic journalism.' Indicate the extent to which you agree with the goals of civic journalism."

Respondents were asked to answer using a 1-5 scale for each question, with 1 meaning "strongly disagree" and 5 indicating "strongly agree." No answer (NA) was coded as 3.

*Two items described goals:*

"Local media should focus on news that directly helps a community solve its problems."

"Local media should go beyond simply reporting news in efforts to increase public participation."

Two items described practices:

"Local media should sponsor community meetings to help citizens solve problems."

"Reader or viewer interest polls should be used to help journalists decide what should be covered."

Predictors of Support for Civic Journalism. Variables used to predict students' support for civic journalism include journalism experiences in college and support for traditional media roles.

College Journalism Instruction. A summed two-item scale (r=.40) assessed the extent of formal instruction:

"Are you a major in the UNM Department of Communication & Journalism?"

"How many news writing courses have you taken at the college level? Include any courses taken this semester." Career Anticipation. A summed 6-item scale (alpha=.85) measured the extent to which students had anticipated a career in journalism. Responses to the first two questions were coded as yes=2; no, NA=1.

"Do you plan to write news for the Daily Lobo?"

"Do you plan to undertake a news writing or editing internship?"

For the remaining questions, respondents used a 1-5 scale with 1 meaning "strongly disagree" and 5 "strongly agree."

"I plan to pursue a career in journalism."

"I hope to work in a newsroom."

"My interest in a news-related career is growing stronger.

"I have always wanted to be a journalist."

College Newsroom Experience. A summed two-item scale (r=.38) assessed the extent of involvement with the university newspaper.

"Have you been a news writer for the Daily Lobo?"

"Have you worked as an editor for the Daily Lobo?"

Dissemination Role. A single item measured support for the role of news media in disseminating information. Respondents used a 1-5 scale, with 1 meaning "not important" and 5 indicating "extremely important."

"How important is it for the media to concentrate on news that is of interest to the widest possible public?"

Interpretive Role. A single item scale measured support for the interpretive role of news media in covering public affairs.

"How important is it for the media to provide analysis and interpretation of complex problems?"

Adversary Role. A summed two-item scale (r=.18) measured support for the role of the media in acting as an adversary of government.

"How important is it for the media to be an adversary of public officials by being constantly skeptical of their decisions?"

"How important is it for the media to investigate claims and statements made by government?"

The five civic journalism measures were first entered together in a one-way repeated-measures multivariate analysis of variance (MANOVA), with journalism experience (student without newsroom experience, student with newsroom experience, professional) as the independent variable. Using all four algorithms, the analysis showed a significant effect for the dependent variables considered together.

When the civic journalism measures were subjected to

separate one-way ANOVAs, significant effects were obtained for the following items: local media should go beyond reporting news to increase participation, local media should sponsor meetings, and polls should be used to help journalists decide on news coverage.

With respect to the premise that news media should attempt to increase participation, there was not a significant difference between students with newsroom experience and professionals-both expressed significantly less support for this goal compared to the students without newsroom experience. The same pattern occurred with the practice of local media sponsoring meetings. These results suggest that students with newsroom experience were becoming more like professionals and less like their fellow students in their evaluations of civic journalism.

Finally, the professionals expressed significantly less support, in comparison to both groups of students, for the use of polls to help journalists decide on coverage. Collectively, the three cases show a clear pattern of decreasing support for civic journalism as the respondents gain experience via newsroom participation.

The first research question asks whether college students, in comparison to professionals, express stronger support for the attitudinal item that explicitly mentions "civic journalism" as a reform movement. No significant difference was found.

RQ2 addresses whether college students express stronger support for civic journalism goals. The means for students and professionals are nearly identical with respect to the premise that local media should focus on news that helps a community to solve problems. But in the comparison between students without newsroom experience and professionals, a statistically significant difference exists for the item that concerns media going beyond reporting to increase public participation.

While the first goal describes an agenda-setting function that facilitates a community response to a problem, it apparently does not evoke suspicion among the professionals to the extent of the second goal. To "go beyond" the reporting of news might have suggested a kind of advocacy journalism to the professional respondents.

Hi states that the students will express stronger support for practices associated with civic journalism. Both measures generated significant differences between the student and professional respondents, in support of Hl. The second practice in particular (use of polls) would challenge autonomy if respondents interpreted it as diminishing the importance of professional expertise.

In the interpretation of these results, it is useful to consider that civic journalism has existed for only about ten years, and consequently the older professional respondents would not have been exposed to it while in college. Meanwhile, neither of the Albuquerque papers had conducted projects identified as civic journalism. As for the students' exposure, their journalism programme had not adopted civic journalism as a regular component of the curriculum. Thus, we urge caution in making inferences that would generalize these results.

For example, Arant and Meyer found that the amount of civic journalism support was related to whether a newspaper had previously conducted a project.

H2 proposes that students with campus newspaper experience will be less supportive of civic journalism compared to other students. Lending support to H2, students with newsroom experience were less supportive of the goal in which media go beyond reporting to increase participation. This is also the case for the practice of news media sponsoring meetings.

We consider next the importance of campus newspaper experience in relation to other experiences that might explain the erosion of civic journalism support. We decided to examine this deterioration of support with respect to a civic journalism practice in light of our theoretical argument that specific techniques, rather than abstract goals, would more likely generate opposition as professional socialization proceeds.

The largest variance in student responses occurred with

the item that advocates media sponsorship of meetings. This variable was used as the dependent variable in a multiple regression model in which the three indicators of educational experiences are entered as an initial block of independent variables. The second block includes the measures of support for traditional media roles.

In the first equation, only newspaper experience accounted for a significant amount of variance. The beta is negative, demonstrating that writing and editing for a campus newspaper diminish potential support for civic journalism. The second equation addresses RQ3: Will support for traditional media roles predict support for civic journalism?

The attitudinal measure for the interpretive role did account for significant incremental variance, but support for the dissemination and adversary roles did not. All of the betas were positive, however. While these results do not provide overwhelming support in favour of RQ3, they certainly do not suggest a scenario in which the adoption of civic journalism values is accompanied by a rejection of the traditional roles for news media.

This study represents the first empirical effort to model the origins of civic journalism values as a function of professional socialization during the college years. The results confirmed that students tended to be more supportive of civic journalism in comparison to professionals who work in the same community. Gaps between the student and professional respondents emerged when questionnaire items described specific practices that violate the norm of detachment, such as news media promotion of town hall meetings.

A subsequent analysis of factors that might explain these results suggests a scenario of professional socialization that begins with students predisposed to support civic journalism. Acquisition of these values during the college years, meanwhile, is not associated with an erosion of commitment to traditional roles. However, in leaving the classroom for the newsroom, the unmaking of civic journalists might occur as reporters and editors develop a stronger sense of autonomy. One experience in particular— working for the campus paper-appears to instill a sense of autonomy that diminishes acceptance of civic journalism.

## A BROADER VIEW OF AUTONOMY

College instruction would ideally promote an open-minded orientation to journalistic roles and an appreciation for both the limitations of routine reporting and the potential for innovation. But those who would reform the curriculum to promote civic journalism must acknowledge the inherent need for increased autonomy during the beginning stages of professional socialization. The desire for autonomy is an inevitable outcome of the process by which students identify with the profession. Journalistic autonomy, consequently, should be appreciated not as a fixed disposition but as a developmental process.

From the perspective of civic journalism advocates, the results of this study highlight the need for college instruction to encourage a broader conception of journalistic autonomy. However, would-be reformers should acknowledge the importance of autonomy for students and for professionals rather than issuing a wholesale attack on editorial detachment. The irony of professional autonomy is that it is the best hope for implementing reform even as editorial detachment appears to preclude civic journalism. Civic journalism can challenge students and professionals to reconceptualize autonomy as the independence to transcend conventional practices that would otherwise limit the contribution of the press to democratic life.

The results of this chapter are based on a single study in one community, thus restricting any inferential claims based on an assumption of external validity. But the findings reflect a certain degree of construct validity given our emphasis on autonomy as a professional value that should dampen support for civic journalism. Students who work for a campus newspaper should be moving closer to professionals and away from fellow students; the data consistently fit this pattern across various measures of civic journalism support.

Future research would ideally incorporate a panel design

of at least two years' duration, with a larger and broader sample of respondents, to track the development of journalistic values as students enter the initial stage of their professional careers. Studies should also incorporate direct attitudinal measures of autonomy as a professional value to supplement the attitudinal and experiential measures used in this study.

We suggest a framework for field research based on the development of operational measures that represent the twentieth-century ethos of professional journalism (e.g., detachment, free press, watchdog role, people's right to know, criticizing institutions) alongside the civic journalism approach (e.g., social responsibility, community building, self-criticizing press institutions, problem-solving). This approach might generate insight that can be used for the reform of journalism instruction as educators promote autonomy in service to democracy.

In the first equation, only newspaper experience accounted for a significant amount of variance. The beta is negative, demonstrating that writing and editing for a campus newspaper diminish potential support for civic journalism. The second equation addresses RQ3: Will support for traditional media roles predict support for civic journalism?

The attitudinal measure for the interpretive role did account for significant incremental variance, but support for the dissemination and adversary roles did not. All of the betas were positive, however. While these results do not provide overwhelming support in favour of RQ3, they certainly do not suggest a scenario in which the adoption of civic journalism values is accompanied by a rejection of the traditional roles for news media.

This study represents the first empirical effort to model the origins of civic journalism values as a function of professional socialization during the college years. The results confirmed that students tended to be more supportive of civic journalism in comparThis debate has been fueled by the lack of a clear definition. Although respected academics and editors have thrown their support behind the movement,

Rosen conceded in 1994 that "we're still inventing it. And because we're still inventing it, we don't really know what `it' is." In more recent writings, Rosen has distinguished civic journalism from traditional journalism, suggesting that informing the public and acting as a watchdog are not enough. "The times demand something additional: Journalists should try to strengthen the political community's capacity to recognize itself, converse well, and make choices" (Rosen's italics).

Scholar Philip Meyer writes the failure of civic journalists to define what they are doing has caused two problems: critics can build straw men to attack instead of finding fault with the real thing; and supporters have an automatic defence to critics by claiming the civic journalism that is drawing criticism is not the same civic journalism that supporters embrace.

Merritt writes mat me media's attempt to actively help citizens participate in the political process is a departure from traditional journalistic detachment. It is this departure that has critics of the movement worried that civic journalism is embarking on a slippery slope into advocacy journalism, a move they perceive threatens to destroy objectivity, and in the process, credibility. Some critics, such as Max Frankel of the New York Times and Leonard Downie of the Washington Post, argue that journalism must remain detached.

To focus on "solutions and [community] connections will inevitably distort the news agenda, devalue problems for which no easy remedy is apparent, and end up compromising the paper's independence." Other critics charge that civic journalism panders to the public and advertisers, becoming more a marketing ploy than a journalistic endeavor. Merritt has voiced his frustration that the substance of the civic journalism debate is being lost in a firestorm of "angry dismissiveness" that is based on faulty assumptions.

In a theoretical sense, some scholars believe civic journalism's activism extends social responsibility beyond the recommendations of the Hutchins Commission, calling for a communitarian media that rejects the libertarian ideals espoused by the Enlightenment thinkers who shaped the Constitution and First Amendment. Thomas Jefferson and James Madison, among others, borrowed from the ideas of John Milton and John Locke to create a form of governance that maximized individual freedom, placing the press outside the realm of government with the famous words "Congress shall make no law...."

Contemporary scholar John C. Merrill writes that under this libertarian model freedom was focused on the rights of the press, not on its social or democratic responsibilities. The Hutchins Commission report of 1947 was in response to the media's excessive and irresponsible use of freedom, and it shifted the focus of press freedom from the rights of the press to what the press should do.

Much of the research about how journalists envision their roles in society is framed within the libertarian and social responsibility theories. John Johnstone, Edward Slawski and William Bowman found in the mid-1970s that journalists identified their roles as neutral or participant. Those who adhered to the neutral "nothing-but-the-truth" perspective saw themselves as objective and detached, guided by libertarian principles. The participant perspective was attractive to journalists who saw an obligation to go beyond reporting factual information by providing the interpretation and context necessary to give events meaning. This "whole-truth" perspective parallels social responsibility as defined by the Hutchins Commission.

David H. Weaver and G. Cleveland Wilhoit, using many of the same survey items as Johnstone, Slawski and Bowman, identified three belief systems in 1983 that represent the roles journalists conceive for themselves: interpretive/investigative, information disseminator and adversarial. The interpretive role, which was the most dominant, closely resembles that of the participant in the Johnstone, Slawski and Bowman model; the disseminator role was adopted by Weaver and Wilhoit to represent the neutral perspective; and the adversarial role emerged after the researchers added questions to probe the depth of the participant role.

John Bare, in a 1994 survey of news staffs at the (Raleigh, N.C.) News and Observer, Omaha World-Herald and Wichita Eagle, expanded the work of Weaver and Wilhoit by adding three types of civic journalism measures: personal public journalism (journalists' attitudes regarding their personal duty to solve community problems); community trust (journalists' faith in community leaders to solve local problems); and institutional public journalism (journalists' attitudes regarding their newspaper's duty to solve community problems).

Bare found that the investigative/interpretive was dominant at the News and Observer and World-Herald, but at the Wichita Eagle, a paper that under Merritt's leadership practiced civic journalism from its inception, the institutional public journalism role was dominant. He concluded that the traditional and civic journalism belief systems coexist; however, because civic journalism at the Eagle had become the dominant institutional belief, when two belief systems are in conflict, the more traditional belief system is less important.

Critics and theorists have voiced their thoughts on civic journalism, but beyond Bare's work very little is known about journalists' attitudes toward this potentially profound change in the role of the media. This research is a step toward addressing this issue by asking journalists at two similarly sized newspapers, the Mobile (Ala.) Register and the Wichita Eagle, to react to a series of statements about the role of the media in society and civic journalism. By examining these journalists' attitudes and beliefs, the researchers hope to clarify what civic journalism means to practitioners and identify how its tenets relate to traditional journalism theory and practice.

The 40 subjects in this Q methodology study sorted opinion statements in January 1997 about the role of journalism in society and civic journalism. The statements were selected from the literature to represent various views about civic journalism and more traditional roles of the news media. Because a variety of definitions of civic journalism exist, participants were left to define the term for themselves. In this way, researchers could explore each journalist's attitudes and beliefs about civic journalism and journalism's societal roles.

The journalists sorted 48 statements according to their degree of agreement or disagreement into a forced distribution grid that resembles a normal bell-shaped curve. Because a vast majority of the statements are created to stimulate a response (they are not neutral), respondents are forced to make subtle differentiations between their extent of agreement and disagreement on the statements. The Q sorts are factor analysed to reveal clusters of opinions. The resulting Q factors are representative of types of people who share similar attitudes and beliefs. The numbers reported parenthetically in this chapter represent the type's overall feeling toward a specific statement along an 11-point intensity scale; a +5 indicates the strongest agreement, -5 indicates the strongest disagreement and 0 indicates neutrality.

Q studies are not intended to indicate how many people in a general population fit within a specific factor or type, rather they present a picture of the types of thinking that exist in relation to a specific issue. The intent of this research was to draw a sample that represents a cross-section of journalists with different levels of exposure to civic journalism. To this end, journalists from two newspapers with different civic journalism experience — the Mobile Register, a mid-size daily that practices mostly traditional journalism, and the Wichita Eagle, a mid-size daily that has practiced civic journalism since its inception — were asked to participate. A researcher administered the study to 20 volunteers from each newspaper during a one-day newsroom visit.

*The demographic spectrum of the journalists in this study includes:*

- 23 females and 17 males;
- A range in age from 22 to 60, with 60 per cent of the respondents between the ages of 36 and 55;
- 4 African-Americans, 2 Asian-Americans, 32 Caucasians, 1 Hispanic, 1 other;
- All have some college, 26 have bachelor's degrees, 7 have master's, 1 has a Ph.D.

Because a factor analysis of the Q sorts yields groups of like individuals who share attitudes and beliefs, it is appropriate to think of each group or type as an individual and helpful for the purposes of understanding and clarity to give each type a name. The four types that emerged in this study are Civic Journalist, Concerned Traditionalist, Neutral Observer and Responsible Liberal. Throughout this analysis, the pronoun he or she is used in accordance with the gender composition of each type.

The four factors extracted had eigenvalues greater than 1.7. These factors together explain 57 per cent of the variance, with the Responsible Liberal accounting for 18 per cent; the Neutral Observer, 15 per cent; the Civic Journalist, 13 per cent; and the Concerned Traditionalist, 11 per cent.

## THE CIVIC JOURNALIST

The Concerned Traditionalist thinks it is acceptable for journalists to involve themselves in community activities, and seems to consider advocacy when he disagrees with the statement that "mobilizing support for public projects is not the business of journalists" (-3).

It is the role of the media to create forums for dialogue, and the Concerned Traditionalist believes that this includes the media sometimes using their resources as a civic partner. "It is difficult to report on a community you don't love or respect," a respondent writes.

Some activism is approved, but the Concerned Traditionalist strongly disagrees that journalists are responsible for making sure public life goes well (-4). In a traditional sense, he believes the media should be the agenda setters, disagreeing even more strongly with the statement that journalists should set a public agenda based on public demands (-5). "We can't write or not write about something because of anyone's demands," one contends. "The public can't always get what it thinks it wants."

However, the Concerned Traditionalist sees the public as playing a vital role in journalism. He supports the idea that good reporters have always listened to citizens (+4), and wishes journalists were closer to the attitudes and opinions of the public.

The Concerned Traditionalist agrees that journalists need to distance themselves from government leaders and get closer to the people they are writing for (+3). "Citizens are still the most important part of journalism. We are not here to serve politicians," one writes. Reporters should develop a sense of what it is like to be poor or a member of a minority group that is severely discriminated against. "Many of the problems we write about as journalists have to do with poor people's issues," another writes. "We need to be closer to those people to accurately reflect their difficulties."

The Concerned Traditionalist is somewhat cynical, though, about some techniques used to reconnect journalists to the public. He does not think public opinion polls, for example, are a good way to find out what the public thinks. "I have seen, time and again, my own newspaper fall on stories when it is too easily influenced by unscientifically conducted polls and anonymous call-in opinion lines. Such features may entertain and sell but are not serious journalism," one writes. Although a closer relationship with the public is desirable, the Concerned Traditionalist also agrees with the statement that the motive behind the recent "get back to the people" trends at some newsrooms is little more than a commercial response to the declining circulation in the business (+2).

Six of the seven Concerned Traditionalists are male, ranging in age from 26 to 47. The only female has the highest factor loading (.718) of all the members of this type. Two of the four African-Americans in the sample are in this type. Four members say they practice civic journalism and three say they do not. Each paper is about equally represented on this type, with four journalists from Mobile and three from Wichita.

## THE NEUTRAL OBSERVER

The Neutral Observer believes that journalists should remain objective, even detached from what they report. She is the only type in this study who is ambivalent about the media's commitment to social responsibility. The Neutral Observer is most skeptical of the ideals and practices of civic journalism, and she believes the democracy will survive whether or not reporters change the way they practice journalism.

The Neutral Observer sees the journalist's central mission as reporting and analyzing the news, not shaping it or directing its outcomes. She agrees with the idea that it is not the journalist's responsibility to fix what's wrong in a community (+4), and strongly disagrees with the statement that the role of journalism is to ensure that public life goes well (-5). "Civic journalism is social engineering. Newspapers have somehow accepted this idea that they have need to shape their communities," one writes. Rather than attempting to solve social problems, the Neutral Observer sees the media's role as revealing them, with the media acting as windows to the world, pointing things out and holding problems up for scrutiny.

The Neutral Observer is more comfortable than any other type when the media serve as independent watchdogs over society's institutions. "Civic journalism is vastly different because it dilutes media independence and integrity, assuming a community consensus as opposed to a separate voice," one writes. She believes the media should provide factual information and let the public decide the truth. She disagrees with the idea that journalists have failed to live up to their responsibilities to inform people about the challenges around them (-2).

For the Neutral Observer, the concept of independence is closely linked with journalistic neutrality and a freedom from social responsibility. She is the only journalist to disagree with the statement that "the media are too powerful to pretend they have nothing to do with social well-being" (-2). Furthermore, the Neutral Observer is the only type that thinks mobilizing support for public projects is not the business of journalists and that subsidizing and promoting events to get citizens involved in civic affairs is not the job of newspapers.

And she is the only type in the study to think that the media should refrain from sometimes using their own resources as a civic partner.

The Neutral Observer believes journalists should be able to separate their work from the political process. She disagrees with the statement that journalists should work to improve the way in which they participate in politics instead of denying that such participation exists (-3). The media provide a method in which people in the democracy can share and discuss information, but the Neutral Observer does not think it is the media's responsibility to get people to participate in a democracy. It is, rather, the media's job to provide people with the information they need to take part in one. The Neutral Observer disagrees strongly with the statement that reporters need to change the way they do journalism in order for democracy to survive (-4).

The Neutral Observer sees civic journalism more in economic terms than the other types. She agrees most strongly that the need to "get back to the people" trend in some newsrooms amounts to little more than a commercial response to newspapers' declining market penetration (+5). "If journalists really focused on news rather than wasting resources on "civic" things, newspapers would be better, tighter and more real," one writes. The Neutral Observer is the only group in this study that thinks civic journalism is public relations – what the promotions department does, only with a different name and a fancy evangelistic fervor.

Journalists should not let the public's demands set the news agenda. The Neutral Observer thinks it's lazy journalism when reporters rely on citizen groups to tell them what to write about. She disagrees with the idea that opinion polls are a good way to find out what people think (-3), and with the suggestion that focus groups, town meetings and phone surveys are tools journalists should use regularly (-3). However, her reluctance to follow a public agenda does not mean discounting the value of ordinary citizens as news sources. The Neutral Observer, more than any other type in this study, supports the belief that it is a journalist's responsibility to cover the news from the citizen up, and not from the expert down (+3).

Of the 10 journalists that factor on this type, eight are women. Only one person is from Wichita, the rest from Mobile. Their ages range from 23 to 53. There are seven Caucasians, two African-Americans, and one person who responded "other." Not surprisingly, only one person in this type practices civic journalism.

## THE RESPONSIBLE LIBERAL

The Responsible Liberal thinks the ideals of objectivity and social responsibility serve journalism well, but she is open-minded toward civic journalism. She likes the civic journalism ideals of getting closer to the citizens, but is not an activist calling for a new press system. The Responsible Liberal thinks journalists should remain detached, reporting on issues of importance in a healthy democracy to an intelligent, rational audience. The Responsible Liberal also acknowledges that the media's freedom belongs to the people and should be used for the welfare of society. The Responsible Liberal is a practitioner of civic journalism, but she is not a strong supporter of some of movement's core concepts and remains much less pessimistic about the current state of journalism than reformers.

The Responsible Liberal sees the media's role as one of providing a window to the world, pointing out issues and problems for public scrutiny. She agrees that average citizens are intelligent and capable of rational choice if given the opportunity (+4), so the journalist's job is not so much solving social problems as revealing them. A proponent of objectivity, the Responsible Liberal agrees that the journalist's central mission is to report and analyse news, not to shape it or direct outcomes (+3).

One Responsible Liberal writes, "A journalist who thinks it's his or her role to solve problems is a journalist with an agenda. Let's focus on showing the way to solutions." The Responsible Liberal believes good reporters have always listened to citizens. But this does not mean it's the media's responsibility to get people to participate in democracy; providing people with the information to participate is enough. The Responsible Liberal does not see the need for major changes in the practice of journalism, disagreeing with the statement that reporters must change the way they do journalism if democracy is to survive (-3). "(Civic Journalism) is not so new, it's a change in emphasis," one writes. "The goal — to get people talking — has always been the goal."

The media should be responsible, and generally they are, the Responsible Liberal believes. Freedom of the press does not belong to editors and publishers, but to the people (+3), and the media play a role in democracy by sharing information and providing a forum for discussion. The Responsible Liberal believes the media should provide more than just facts, but the media should not be blamed for a lack of public knowledge or interest in civic affairs.

According to one, "Journalism and journalists have not failed — they are doing incredible work every day in communities, large and small. I do not believe the overriding goal of journalism is to make sure "public" life goes well. Sometimes it does not go well — we should not cover that up." The Responsible Liberal disagrees with the ideas that journalists have failed in living up to their responsibilities to inform people about the challenges around them (-4), and that a new kind of press system is needed to refocus the political debate (-3).

Responsible Liberals seem intrigued by some of the ideas behind civic journalism, but are not ready to embrace many of the practices. The Responsible Liberal thinks it's all right for the media to sometimes use their own resources as a civic partner (+2).

Similarly, focus groups, town meetings and surveys are tools journalists should use regularly. The Responsible Liberal implies seeing merit in civic journalism by disagreeing strongly with the idea that civic journalism is public relations (-4). But she is ambivalent toward some civic journalism concepts. She disagrees slightly with the ideas that journalists too often present public life as a depressing spectacle (-2), and that journalism needs a stronger guiding ethical or moral philosophy (-1).

The Responsible Liberal is not attracted at all to some key concepts of the civic journalism movement: the journalist's role is to enrich the civic life of the community (0), and it is the media's role to bring people together to solve society's problems (0). "If they aren't careful, newspapers can get caught up in the gimmicks of civic journalism and unduly shift their focus from excellent day-to-day work to `project journalism,'" one writes. Perhaps most telling is the Responsible Liberal's strong disagreement with the statement that it is journalism's responsibility to make sure public life goes well (-5).

xnàúnons department does, only with a different name and a fancy evangelistic fervor.

Journalists should not let the public's demands set the news agenda. The Neutral Observer thinks it's lazy journalism when reporters rely on citizen groups to tell them what to write about. She disagrees with the idea that opinion polls are a good way to find out what people think (-3), and with the suggestion that focus groups, town meetings and phone surveys are tools journalists should use regularly (-3). However, her reluctance to follow a public agenda does not mean discounting the value of ordinary citizens as news sources. The Neutral Observer, more than any other type in this study, supports the belief that it is a journalist's responsibility to cover the news from the citizen up, and not from the expert down (+3).

Of the 10 journalists that factor on this type, eight are women. Only one person is from Wichita, the rest from Mobile. Their ages range from 23 to 53. There are seven Caucasians, two African-Americans, and one person who responded "other." Not surprisingly, only one person in this type practices civic journalism.

## THE RESPONSIBLE LIBERAL

The Responsible Liberal thinks the ideals of objectivity and social responsibility serve journalism well, but she is open-minded toward civic journalism. She likes the civic journalism ideals of getting closer to the citizens, but is not an activist calling for a new press system. The Responsible Liberal thinks journalists should remain detached, reporting on issues of importance in a healthy democracy to an intelligent, rational audience.

The Responsible Liberal also acknowledges that the media's freedom belongs to the people and should be used for the welfare of society. The Responsible Liberal is a practitioner of civic journalism, but she is not a strong supporter of some of movement's core concepts and remains much less pessimistic about the current state of journalism than reformers.

The Responsible Liberal sees the media's role as one of providing a window to the world, pointing out issues and problems for public scrutiny. She agrees that average citizens are intelligent and capable of rational choice if given the opportunity (+4), so the journalist's job is not so much solving social problems as revealing them.

Journalists should not let the public's demands set the news agenda. The Neutral Observer thinks it's lazy journalism when reporters rely on citizen groups to tell them what to write about. She disagrees with the idea that opinion polls are a good way to find out what people think (-3), and with the suggestion that focus groups, town meetings and phone surveys are tools journalists should use regularly (-3). However, her reluctance to follow a public agenda does not mean discounting the value of ordinary citizens as news sources. The Neutral Observer, more than any other type in this study, supports the belief that it is a journalist's responsibility to cover the news from the citizen up, and not from the expert down (+3).

Of the 10 journalists that factor on this type, eight are women. Only one person is from Wichita, the rest from Mobile. Their ages range from 23 to 53. There are seven Caucasians, two African-Americans, and one person who responded "other." Not surprisingly, only one person in this type practices civic journalism.

## THE RESPONSIBLE LIBERAL

The Responsible Liberal thinks the ideals of objectivity and social responsibility serve journalism well, but she is open-minded toward civic journalism. She likes the civic journalism ideals of getting closer to the citizens, but is not an activist calling for a new press system. The Responsible Liberal thinks journalists should remain detached, reporting on issues of importance in a healthy democracy to an intelligent, rational audience.

The Responsible Liberal also acknowledges that the media's freedom belongs to the people and should be used for the welfare of society. The Responsible Liberal is a practitioner of civic journalism, but she is not a strong supporter of some of movement's core concepts and remains much less pessimistic about the current state of journalism than reformers.

The Responsible Liberal sees the media's role as one of providing a window to the world, pointing out issues and problems for public scrutiny. She agrees that average citizens are intelligent and capable of rational choice if given the opportunity (+4), so the journalist's job is not so much solving social problems as revealing them.

Journalists should not let the public's demands set the news agenda. The Neutral Observer thinks it's lazy journalism when reporters rely on citizen groups to tell them what to write about. She disagrees with the idea that opinion polls are a good way to find out what people think (-3), and with the suggestion that focus groups, town meetings and phone surveys are tools journalists should use regularly (-3). However, her reluctance to follow a public agenda does not mean discounting the value of ordinary citizens as news sources. The Neutral Observer, more than any other type in this study, supports the belief that it is a journalist's responsibility to cover the news from the citizen up, and not from the expert down (+3).

Of the 10 journalists that factor on this type, eight are women. Only one person is from Wichita, the rest from Mobile. Their ages range from 23 to 53. There are seven

Caucasians, two African-Americans, and one person who responded "other." Not surprisingly, only one person in this type practices civic journalism.

## THE RESPONSIBLE LIBERAL

The Responsible Liberal thinks the ideals of objectivity and social responsibility serve journalism well, but she is open-minded toward civic journalism. She likes the civic journalism ideals of getting closer to the citizens, but is not an activist calling for a new press system. The Responsible Liberal thinks journalists should remain detached, reporting on issues of importance in a healthy democracy to an intelligent, rational audience.

The Responsible Liberal also acknowledges that the media's freedom belongs to the people and should be used for the welfare of society. The Responsible Liberal is a practitioner of civic journalism, but she is not a strong supporter of some of movement's core concepts and remains much less pessimistic about the current state of journalism than reformers.

The Responsible Liberal sees the media's role as one of providing a window to the world, pointing out issues and problems for public scrutiny. She agrees that average citizens are intelligent and capable of rational choice if given the opportunity (+4), so the journalist's job is not so much solving social problems as revealing them. But she is ambivalent toward some civic journalism concepts. She disagrees slightly with the ideas that journalists too often present public life as a depressing spectacle (-2), and that journalism needs a stronger guiding ethical or moral philosophy (-1).

The Responsible Liberal is not attracted at all to some key concepts of the civic journalism movement: the journalist's role is to enrich the civic life of the community (0), and it is the media's role to bring people together to solve society'Most previous research on journalists' perceptions of their roles in society has defined these roles within the framework of libertarian and social responsibility theories. Civic journalism has extended the boundaries of social responsibility, and the movement's reliance on some new techniques has sparked debate among journalists and scholars.

The journalists in this study, however, generally do not see civic journalism as a drastic departure from past practice and are open to experimenting with new ways that allow the media to respond to a changing society. The beliefs of most journalists in this sample are not anchored to either libertarianism or social responsibility, but rather a synthesis, with nearly all journalists willing to accept, if not embrace, more than one role for the news media.

These findings support previous research that indicates journalists are pluralistic in their conceptions of media roles. Civic journalists want change to come more quickly to the practice of journalism, with the citizen having a greater say in shaping media content. Yet they do not appear willing to walk too far from the free press model and can be seen as trying to assert many of the ideals the Hutchins Commission recommended 50 years ago.

Civic journalism's lack of a clear definition contributes a great deal to the term's semantic baggage. For many journalists and scholars, civic journalism is a catalytic term drawing immediate praise or rejection. However, given the opportunity to sort a series of statements about the media's role in society that contained many civic journalism ideals but few direct references to the term, the journalists in this study exhibited thoughtful, coherent visions.

Most of these journalists accept the idea that there is more than one legitimate, ethical approach to journalism and do not think that civic journalism should be considered, as one journal stated, either "the death or savior" of journalism. Merritt has lamented that journalists and scholars are "missing the point" about civic journalism's commitment and goals, but this study suggests something different. Journalists in this sample are attempting to integrate their traditional practices with new civic-minded approaches to advance their understanding of journalism and journalism's role in the American democracy.

# Chapter 9

# Evaluative Research on Public Journalism

The movement's ultimate goal is to help revitalize civic life. To achieve that, it would seemingly need to succeed at two broad objectives. First, journalists must be convinced to use public journalism's practices to repair the damage that traditional journalism has been accused of causing to the public's interest and participation in the civic life of their communities and the nation. Second, public journalism must make a difference among news audiences. Because of it, more "average citizens" should be convinced to think about and participate in civic affairs more often.

However, much of the "empirical evidence about whether civic journalism actually is achieving its objectives is fragmentary and impressionistic." Success often is claimed on the basis of "`look what we did... look how we did it" anecdotes. This study offers a fuller assessment of what is known and what more should be known about public journalism's capacity to modify the attitudes, beliefs, and behaviours of journalists and news audiences.

## PUBLIC JOURNALISM RESEARCH

Evaluative studies on public journalism were identified primarily from Communication Abstracts and the AEJMC convention paper databases. To be included in the analysis, a study had to focus explicitly on public journalism's attitudinal or behavioural effects on journalists or news audiences. It had to use quantitative or qualitative social-scientific research methods, and to include data not already published. This excluded re-analyses, review articles, and anecdotal narratives.

We located forty-seven evaluative studies that fit the selection criteria. A quarter of them included national-sample surveys of newsmedia executives or journalists. Three-fifths looked at newspapers and five looked at television news departments. Nine focused on both print and broadcast news media, mostly as public-journalism project partners.

There was a tendency among these works to concentrate on a handful of early-adopter "public" news organizations. The Wichita Eagle (Kansas) or the Charlotte Observer (North Carolina), or both, were included in more than one-third of the thirty-nine studies that looked at specific news-media organizations. Fifteen per cent featured the Wisconsin State Journal of Madison. The Journal also was a partner in the multiple-media "We the People/Wisconsin" project that was the sole or partial focus of four media-specific studies. "We the People" partner WISC-TV of Madison and KRON-TV of San Francisco were included in five studies each, making them the most researched public-journalism broadcasters.

The majority of the studies focused solely on one of the following research concerns: journalists' attitudes and beliefs about public journalism, their "public" newswork behaviours, and public journalism's effects on news audiences. The continuum that this tripartite division suggests reflects the widely held assumption that journalists' favorable attitudes and beliefs about public journalism may influence their newswork behaviours, and that their newly "public" news-reporting practices may produce measurable attitudinal and behavioural effects on news audiences.

Admittedly, the dynamic of causality likely is more complicated, if causation is even part of the equation. For our purposes, the distinction between journalistic attitudes, newswork behaviours, and audience effects provided a useful organizing heuristic. It also is a close fit with the framework that Chaffee and McDevitt suggested for evaluating public journalism's performance.

We modified the Chaffee and McDevitt scheme somewhat in adapting it to the present work. Evaluative studies of journalists' attitudes and beliefs about public journalism and their public-journalism newswork behaviours were taken to represent Chaffee and McDevitt's "news media" level of analysis.

Their "individual" and "community" levels of analysis were collapsed into a single category that we named "civic attitudes." It was represented by investigations of public journalism's potential to influence the attitudes and increase the knowledge of news audiences toward politics and civic affairs, including public-policy issues and solutions to community problems. We also made a single "civic participation" category of Chaffee and McDevitt's "primary group" and "civic organization" levels of analysis. It included studies of public journalism's potential to increase voter turnout, interpersonal discussions of civic affairs, and participation in civic groups. No study fit Chaffee and McDevitt's "policy maker" level of analysis, defined as government policy responses to the topics of public-journalism coverage.

## "NEWS MEDIA" LEVEL

## "NEWS MEDIA LEVEL OF ANALYSIS

A consistent finding of behaviour-change and persuasion research is that attitudes, beliefs, and behaviours are intertwined in a complex relationship. A common presumption is that a person may be more likely to change a behaviour if she first can be convinced to change her attitudes toward it. Public journalism could be defined as a behaviourchange movement whose intermediate goal is to persuade journalists to change their traditional ways by adopting certain civic-life-friendly newswork practices. How journalists feel and what they believe about public journalism's philosophy and practices could provide clues to whether they might agree to at least modify or supplement their traditional newswork behaviours.

## JOURNALISTS' ATTITUDES AND BELIEFS

We identified eleven studies that probed journalists' feelings toward public journalism as a primary focus or as part of wider-ranging analyses. The findings reported in ten of them can be usefully summarized into two categories. Studies in the first category analysed journalists' responses to attitude statements about public journalism. Studies in the second category arrayed responses into attitude and belief scales to develop typologies of journalists.

Taken together, the attitudinal-statement studies offer a somewhat mixed picture of journalists' affinity for public journalism. On the one hand, they collectively suggest that the surveyed journalists held a generally greater liking for the less activist-and, arguably, less nontraditional-shadings of public journalism's philosophy and practice. They were comfortable with the notion of using their reporting to help their communities move toward solutions to public problems, for example. On the other hand, a number of the studies suggested a degree of affinity for the more activist-and, arguably, more nontraditional— practices of public journalism, such as news-media-sponsored town meetings.

It appears, however, from the attitude- and belief-scale studies that journalists' affinity for a newswork philosophy or practice could be based more on their perceptions of its utility than on any absolutist notion of journalistic ideology. It may be that only the most vocal partisans on each side of the debate pay strict attention to "public" and "traditional" labels.

Gade et al. found that when public journalism was framed as a normative press role, it was not in full blossom even at such an icon of the public-journalism movement as the Wichita Eagle.

Instead, about half of their Wichita journalist-respondents were attitudinally more comfortable with press roles that represented a blend of public- and traditional-journalism philosophies.

Bare found a similar co-mingling of beliefs in his study of journalists at the Eagle, the traditional Omaha World-

Herald (Nebraska), and what he described as the quasi-"public" News and Observer of Raleigh, North Carolina.

A number of these works also looked for characteristics that could predict a journalist's affinity for public journalism. A consistent finding was that the most likely public-journalism supporters are to be found among editors and reporters at small-sized newspapers. Notable among the several less consistently found attributes were a belief in the importance of community news, and in public affairs reporting and journalistic ethics. It perhaps is no surprise that editors are more likely to say they like public journalism's values when they work at newspapers where public-journalism reporting projects have been done. Gade and colleagues made the unsurprising discovery that journalists pegged as "public journalists" by their attitudinal-scale responses also tend to identify strongly with the movement's rhetoric.

## JOURNALISTS' NEWSWORK BEHAVIOURS

It appears from the attitudeand-belief studies that public journalism resonates with some journalists. It appears, too, that the attitudes and beliefs of public and traditional journalism co-exist within many newsrooms and individual journalists. In one sense, the attitudes and beliefs expressed by the surveyed journalists are signifiers for the value they may place on "public" and traditional newswork practices. It could be that they see the two sets of practices as merely different tools for different journalistic jobs. If so, this suggests a kind of occupational pragmatism that could compel journalists to produce news content by whichever set of newswork practices they believe would work best in a given situation, "public" and "traditional" labels aside.

If this analysis is correct, the public-journalism movement has not fully convinced journalists of the presumably greater utility of "public" newswork, and of the risk that traditional practices supposedly pose to civic life and democracy. This suggests that journalists could reflect an equivalent "half-step" approach to public journalism's practice, presuming that their newswork behaviours follow from their attitudes and beliefs. Twenty-three of the forty-seven evaluative studies looked for a public-journalism effect on news content and journalistic practices.

Among them, eleven involved content analyses of public journalism's use, or its intended use, for elections reporting. Another six used content analysis, focus-group interviews, or self-administered questionnaires to look at some aspect of public journalism's use as a daily reporting tool for general news coverage.

Politics, particularly elections, hold a special place in public journalism's philosophy, which cites declining public participation in self-governance activities as evidence that civic life in the United States is in trouble. One of the movement's principal goals is to reframe political reporting to emphasize public-policy issues over traditional, political process coverage of campaign strategies and who's-ahead-and-who's-behind polls. "Public" news organizations appear to have generally achieved that goal: election-year issues tended to be emphasized over "process" topics. There were notable exceptions, however. Roselle, Maier and Potter, and Reynolds and Hicks found few to no public-journalism effects on the thematic aspects of election reporting by the U.S. television news departments they studied."

News-story sourcing, too, holds a special place in public journalism's philosophy, as "perhaps no axiom so distinguishes public journalism from traditional journalism as the promise to rely more on citizens and less on official sources for news commentary." But it has been a curiously difficult promise to keep, public journalism sourcing studies shows. "Public" newswork has not consistently elevated the numerical presence of ordinary citizens as quoted news sources in election reporting and routine coverage of community affairs. In most of the cases that have been studied, public journalism's presumably unique sensitivity to the unheard masses has not brought a full, immediately obvious, or practical change to long-standing newssourcing patterns. Traditional news-narrative conventions also may prevail even when "public" newswork does result in a numerically stronger news voice for ordinary citizens. Although more "average citizens" may appear and be quoted more often in the news, their narrative role may remain one of merely illustrating community problems; in effect, they remain the backdrop against which the "usual suspect" sources of experts and officials offer, in top-down fashion, substantive explanations of problem causes and solutions.

The remaining content-and-practices studies offer a mixed-bag assessment of public journalism's performance in the newsroom. In a national survey, for example, editors at "public" newspapers were more likely than their counterparts at traditional newspapers to say their publications report on solutions to community problems, convene community meetings, and reach out to readers by publishing reporters' email addresses and telephone numbers. Loomis concluded from his newsroom interviews that journalists can actually do public journalism without knowing it.

But for routine news, including a traditional emphasis on conflict, and for the visual, news-page design side of special-project reporting, "public" and non-"public" newspapers have been found to show few differences. Traditional storytelling devices have appeared in even the most "public" of project reporting. In one of the few studies of broadcast public journalism, Kurpius found that TV news departments fit a "public" model of newswork best when they hold democratically organized editorial meetings, yet their commitments to "public" newswork often are trumped by traditional business concerns.

## AUDIENCE EFFECTS

The ultimate goal of public journalism is to influence the civic attitudes and behaviours of news audiences. Changing people's attitudes toward the importance of civic involvement can be taken as a necessary precursor to changing their behaviours to bring about greater levels of involvement. Absent this ultimate "public" objective, there would be little point to the movement's efforts first, to engage journalists in a discussion about the perceived failings of traditional newswork, and second, to point them toward an alternative called "public journalism." But those two preludes to public journalism's goal of revitalizing communities' civic lives have met with spotty success generally. By implication, news audiences could be expected to respond attitudinally and behaviourally in ways that fall short of the movement's hoped-for civic effects.

Most of the sixteen audience-effects studies we reviewed looked at public-journalism reporting projects. Seven focused on election-campaign and community-issue projects by print and broadcast media partners, and five looked at single-newspaper projects. Two attempted to connect audience effects to variations in the intentions of newspapers to later do "public" election reporting.

## "CIVIC ATTITUDES" LEVEL OF ANALYSIS

With some exceptions, survey respondents who said they were aware of the public-journalism projects in their communities also tended to tell pollsters that the projects had a positive impact on their attitudes toward politics, civic life, and the involved news organizations. Public-journalism projects also have been credited with equipping "aware" respondents with greater knowledge of election-year issues and candidates' campaign strategies and tactics. Similar audience effects have been reported for newspapers staffed by journalists who expressed strong, prior intentions of later applying public-journalism newswork to the actual elections.

Partnerships between print and broadcast news organizations appear to increase the likelihood of attitudinal and knowledge effects. For example, public-journalism projects focused on a single community problem have been generally more effective at generating audience attention than those focused on several problems at once, according to Thorson et al. The researchers also credited increases in self-reported deliberation of community problems among respondents in Binghamton, New York, and Charlotte, North Carolina, to local "public" reporting projects that encouraged public participation in community problem solving activities. Conversely, they reported that projects in Madison, Wisconsin, and San Francisco that focused only on encouraging such deliberation did not lead to greater participation in problem-solving activities. However, few attitudinal and knowledge effects were found for the Charlotte Observer's 1992 "Your Vote" public-journalism project and the Bergen (New Jersey) Record's 1996 "Campaign Central" project.

"Civic Participation" Level of Analysis. There was no convincing pattern to the findings of audience-effects studies that looked for public journalism's influence on the civic-participation and voting behaviours, or at least the behavioural intents, of news audiences.

On the one hand, public-journalism reporting projects have been credited with increasing voter turnout, as well as survey respondents' interpersonal discussions about community problems and their participation in concerned civic groups. Friedland, Sotirovic, and Daily noted that survey respondents who said they were aware of the "We the People/ Wisconsin" project were more likely than respondents not aware of it to also say they had attended a community meeting, contacted a public official about a community problem, and voted in a recent election. Vercellotti's experiment with "issues" versus "horse race" political-news frames suggests that issue-oriented reporting is more likely to move audiences toward civic deliberation-a hoped-for effect of public journalism.

On the other hand, Vercellotti's work also suggests that news audiences may pay the most deliberative attention to the topic of a political-news story, regardless of its "issues" or "horserace" frame. The "We the People/Wisconsin" project had an inverse effect on civic engagement, according to Denton and Thorson's findings: the percentage of survey respondents who identified themselves as "likely voters" fell from 19% before the project to 11% immediately after it. Readers of the "public" Bergen Record were no more likely than readers of its non "public" competitors to talk about or vote in the 1996 election. Meyer and Potter reported that learning more about election-year issues from newspapers that showed high, beforehand intentions of doing public journalism election reporting did not necessarily lead large numbers of those readers to participate more often in civic affairs, voting included.

Among the remaining audience-effects studies, the public-journalism Wichita Eagle had a generally weak agenda-setting effect, compared to a local, non-"public" television station, according to Newby. Simmons, however, credited a strong agenda-setting effect to an unnamed Florida newspaper's public-journalism coverage of a proposed public-safety complex. And Zang found that most of the Bremerton Sun (Washington) readers she interviewed appreciated the newspaper's public-journalism projects on community problems.

## ARTIFACTS OF CONCEPTUALIZATION, MEASUREMENT, AND INTERPRETATION

Taken at face value, the forty-seven studies we reviewed collectively suggest that making journalism more public has made some notable differences, particularly in election reporting. We find reason to be skeptical, however, of the validity, reliability, and usefulness of several studies' findings. These works contain apparent conceptual or methodological shortcomings that are not unique to public-journalism research, but still risk unnecessarily fanning the flames of the already fiery public- versus traditional-journalism debate.

### CONCEPTUALIZING PUBLIC JOURNALISM

It was common among the evaluative studies either not to define the concept of "public journalism" or to define it in ways that did not show precisely how it differs from its putative adversary: traditional journalism. The result was that few of the studies were guided by clearly explicated conceptual or operational definitions of "public journalism." Indeed, more than a quarter of the works we reviewed conceded difficulties in defining the concept.

This is surprising and unfortunate, considering that some of public journalism's leading advocates have offered definitions that could have been used for inspiration. Many of the evaluative studies made a key assumption that the news organizations under investigation were practicing public journalism either because they participated in initiatives supported financially by such institutions as the Pew Centre for Civic Journalism, or because they themselves labeled their efforts as "public journalism."

Despite their sporadic efforts at theoretically guided definitions, many of the evaluative studies did appear to conceptualize "public journalism" generally as a journalistic movement whose primary goals are to increase civic commitment to and citizen participation in democratic processes. Still, the paucity of clearly and fully explicated definitions of "public journalism" could impose a number of limitations on attempts to evaluate the research that evaluates public journalism.

For one, the absence of such definitions would tend to frustrate efforts to determine if studies that inquired into journalists' affinity for public journalism actually measured the same underlying construct. It would do the same for efforts to determine if the "public" reporting projects under analysis shared particular distinguishing features. It also would tend to work against efforts to assess whether reported audience effects should be attributed to public-journalism content or noncontent factors.

To illustrate this critique, Bare scarcely explained the development of the belief-scale measures that served as the conceptual foundation of his work to identify characteristics that make a journalist a "public journalist." Jeffres et al. did not turn to the public-journalism literature in conceptualizing a press role they named "civic journalism/activist," nor did Weaver and Wilhoit in conceiving of a connection between public journalism and a "populist mobilizer" role that fit a handful of their journalist-respondents.

One also could argue the case that Meyer and Potter overreached their conceptual framework by applying their measure of twenty newspapers' beforehand intentions of doing public-journalism election reporting to tests for audience effects from the newspapers' later, overt newswork behaviours. They reported finding statistical relationships between the "intention" variable and positive audience effects, but found no discernable audience effects for the newspapers' actual reporting.

This seems counter-intuitive, given that Meyer and Potter offered no explicit evidence that the newspapers had publicized their reporters' before-the-election, public-journalism intents. Absent that publicity, one would more logically expect audiences to be influenced by journalists' overt newswork behaviours-the publicly observable, physical manifestations of their privately held intents. Loomis and Meyer58 took up this conundrum in a follow-up study and reported this solution: journalists' prior "public" reporting intents are connected to subsequent audience effects through the extent to which the annual corporate-report messages of newspaper-chain CEOs emphasized social responsibility.

## CONTENT ANALYSES

A key assumption of content analysis is that when coders assign content of interest to categories, they should be guided by "explicitly defined and accepted concept definitions. If the category definitions do not control [the] assignment of content, then human biases may be doing so... [and] findings are likely to be uninterpretable and unreplicable." Reliability is defined as the extent to which coders agree as they independently follow a study's coding protocols.

Coder reliability was not reported, however, in six of the studies that used content analysis. Another six underreported the extent to which their coders agreed, typically by providing an overall, simple-agreement coefficient that masks the reliability of individual variables by averaging all of them. Admittedly the constrained space of academic journals and books makes it difficult to fully detail how a study's variables were operationalized. But some accounting of this beyond merely listing category labels is important in judging a study's findings because variable definitions not only tell coders what content to assign where, they influence coder agreement as well.

Another issue in content analysis is who performs the coding. Three of the content studies were coded solely by their authors and one was coded by a lone research assistant. Reliability in these cases is of the weakest kind: intra-coder agreement, or "stability," a coder's agreement with himself or herself over time. Inter-coder reliability, or "reproducibility," is a better measure. It gauges the degree to which coding protocols yield similar results when applied by two or more coders and, ideally, none of them should be the researcher.

The idea is to demonstrate that the phenomenon being investigated exists independently-or outside the mind-of the researcher who designed the study. However, this was impossible to judge for eleven of the content analyses because they either made no mention of coders or did not make clear whether coding was done by the authors only, independent coders only, or the authors together with other coders. Three of the studies reported the authors and-others combination and although it is not the ideal scheme, it does lend itself to inter-coder reliability checks.

A chief goal of survey research is to generalize the responses of sample members back to the larger population that they are meant to represent. The accuracy of those estimates depends in part on how many sample members declined to respond and whether the nonresponders differed in fundamental ways from the population. The literature on survey methods notes that when people targeted as respondents have little to no specific interest in the research topic, they tend to not return mailed-out questionnaires or to decline telephone interviews.

"This means that mail [and other] surveys with low response rates almost invariably will be biased in significant ways that are related directly to the purposes of the research." Babbie advises that "a response rate of at least 50 per cent is adequate for analysis and reporting. A response of at least 60 per cent is good... [and] 70 per cent is very good [emphasis retained]."

All of the nonreporters were audience-effects studies. The rates for four of the journalist-attitude surveys fell below Babbie's standard for "adequate," which raises the probability of biased findings. One of the four-the APME et al. survey-reported a miscalculated "very good" rate of 70 per cent, but when corrected, the rate falls well below "adequate."

There was a marked tendency among the survey studies to dwell exclusively on the responses of sample members. But a sample is only a tool for making population estimates, the more relevant "bigger picture" that is uncovered by generalizing sample responses back to the larger population of interest. Only three of the survey studies reported the margin-of-sampling-error rates required for making such estimates.

Also in the survey studies, information about the questions posed to sample members was largely sparse or absent. Poorly drafted survey questions can interject bias into the data they return, so knowing something of how the queries were worded is useful in assessing survey findings. Survey questions should be short and unambiguous, free of biased or ill-defined terms and words, and not written in ways that would make them "leading" or "double-barreled." A question is considered "leading" when it tends to guide respondents toward a particular answer. It is considered "double-barreled" when it asks two or more questions, typically indicated by the conjunction "and."

By way of illustration, Arant and Meyer posed this double-barreled, agree-disagree statement: "My newspaper has an obligation not just to point out community problems and explain alternative solutions, but also to set up meetings and organization programs to solve the problems." It holds one "sub-question" about pointing out problems, a second about explaining solutions, a third about setting up meetings, and a fourth about organizing programs.

The trouble is that a respondent could agree (or disagree) with one or two or three of the four dimensions, and disagree (or agree) with the rest. An "agree" or "disagree" response would not represent absolute agreement or disagreement with the question's overall, intended premise. The APME et al. survey offers another example. In it, newspaper editors were asked, "Do you use the tools and techniques of so-called civic or public journalism?"

The key terms "tools" and "techniques" were not defined, and that makes the question ambiguous and responses to it difficult to interpret. Among other methodological shortcomings, the survey studies were largely silent on how or whether measurement instruments were pre-tested. Also, none of the journalist-attitude studies and only one of the audience-effects studies attempted some form of controlled experiment, although a number of the audience-effects works were explicitly or implicitly arrayed as naturalistic experiments.

## DATA INTERPRETATION

There was a tendency among many of the evaluative studies to generously interpret public-journalism performance data. This was particularly apparent in works that explored voter turnout as a key measure of the success of "public" election reporting. However, studies that claimed a causal connection between public journalism and voting failed to address adequately one of the two central assumptions of causality. Time-order admittedly was present: the public-journalism election projects under study occurred before Election Day.

It is a necessary but not sufficient condition for attributing causality. The second assumption is that one also must account for all other possible and knowable causal variables. On this, the audience studies that reported a public-journalism effect on voting did a generally poor job. Although it is probable that public-journalism election projects have had some (as yet undetermined) contributing effect on voter turnout, the complexity of voting behaviours makes it highly unlikely that they are solely or even mostly responsible for the observed increases in turnout.

To further illustrate this critique, Denton and Thorson credited the "We the People/Wisconsin" project with increasing respondents' self-reported interest in politics and knowledge of election-year issues important to state residents, even though both increases fell well within the margin of error they reported for their survey. Simmons did not account for contributing factors unrelated to public journalism when he concluded that a Florida newspaper's coverage of a controversial publicsafety office complex "ultimately set an agenda for public discussion about the... complex which had repercussions at the ballot box."

## DISCUSSION AND SUGGESTIONS FOR FUTURE RESEARCH

Overall, empirical research on public journalism's effects on journalists and news audiences has focused on a handful of news organizations and reporting projects. Much of what is currently known about public journalism comes from studies of its use by primarily the Wichita Eagle, Charlotte Observer and Wisconsin State Journal, and the "We the People/Wisconsin" project. And that is to say that little is known about public journalism's performance beyond these "jewel box" examples. Even less may be known when a healthy dose of skepticism is aimed at studies with apparent methodological shortcomings.

Future research must evolve to capture a wider array of newsorganization experiments with public journalism. Researchers must redouble their efforts to ensure methodological rigor in the conceptualization, measurement, and interpretation of public journalism's performance. To not do so would risk the often-voiced criticisms that public journalism is no more than "just good (traditional) journalism" or little more than a misguided attempt to replace valuable, longstanding journalistic practices.

Many of forty-seven evaluative studies we reviewed could be reasonably interpreted as supporting the notion that public and traditional journalism are not that dramatically different in how journalists conceive of and apply their philosophies and practices, and how that influences news audiences. Public journalism, when seen in this light, is one point on a continuum of journalistic practices that range from the disappointing to the ideal. It is another tool in the journalist's kit, not a self-contained kit in and of itself.

To be fair, however, public journalism has had some effect on journalists, news content, and audiences, even when one considers the apparent methodological shortcomings. But the effect also seems to have been a kind of half-half proposition.

Journalists appear to have a generally pluralistic attitudinal approach to newswork and this was reflected in coverage that displayed some of the presumably signature features of public and traditional journalism. Why and how this approach develops is an area richly deserving of future research. While it also has been shown that publicjournalism election reporting differs in some important respects from traditional reporting, there is more to be known about why a shift in emphasis from political-process topics to citizen-agenda issues has not brought more ordinary people into the news as information sources. Perhaps the unexpectedly high numbers of "usual suspect" elite sources found in public-journalism election reporting reflects an economic concern among for-profit news organizations with keeping informationgathering costs low.

It certainly costs less in terms of reporters' time and energy to turn to the more accessible and quotable candidates, politicians, and experts. Or it could be that despite the strength of their commitment to public journalism's ideals, "public" news organizations still define their electoral responsibility in traditional terms: as top-down rather than bottom-up agenda setting. They may still see their role as one of informing news audiences of the views of candidates instead of as one of bringing issues of concern to the governed to the attention of those who would govern.

More work is needed on the audience effects of public journalism. These efforts could be fruitfully guided by the literature on persuasion and voting behaviour. Also, one lesson from the media-effects literature is that it is difficult to pin down causal, media content-audience effects relationships, especially under naturalistic conditions. Controlled laboratory experiments could prove more useful for more convincingly identifying whatever causal factors may be behind any public-journalism influence on news audiences.

On a related point, future research should consider looking at the kinds of communities in which public journalism is practiced. For example, is public journalism practiced primarily by news organizations that serve affluent or deprived communities? Or that serve socially homogenous or heterogeneous communities? Or that serve communities where civic participation already is high or low? The answers to these and other queries could illuminate whatever causal link may exist between "public" reporting and civic participation. They also could shed light on the potential and desirability of using public journalism to help a community work toward consensus on how to address and overcome public-policy problems.

More work is needed, too, on understanding how the effects of public-journalism coverage are distributed within a given community. One could fruitfully ask whether public journalism helps reduce differences in political knowledge and participation among groups of high and low socio-economic status.

Or does it tend to stabilize, or perhaps even widen, any pre-existing differences? Researchers should consider as well the nature of community-problem solutions that public-journalism interventions seek explicitly or implicitly to move community residents toward.

Have solutions that are eventually enacted benefited everyone within a given community or have they tended to favour the interests of a community's most powerful segments? Have publicjournalism initiatives helped establish new community organizations or expand the missions of existing agencies? Have community agencies experienced measurable-and sustainable-increases in their membership or volunteer rolls as a direct or indirect result of "public" reporting?

The economics of public journalism's practice is another area deserving of future research. Leading public-journalism advocates have suggested that news organizations will find "public" newswork to be a profitable endeavor. We found no studies that attempted to systematically substantiate this claim. The literature is silent, too, on how news organizations plan and implement public-journalism initiatives. The success or failure of a project can depend on how it is designed and "sold" to rank-and-file journalists charged with enacting it. Public-journalism projects are similar to persuasive public-communication campaigns in terms of their ultimate objectives. But whether public journalists also are similarly as attentive in designing, executing, and following up on their efforts are questions deserving of scholarly attention.

In the end, it could be that public journalism's most unqualified success has been to keep "alive the soul-searching sparked by the poor coverage in the 1988 presidential campaign. It has helped revive [a] discussion about journalism's core values at a time when those values are under assault from the industry's profit motives." Its greatest impact may be more heuristic rather than practical. The idea of public journalism has prompted a much-needed discussion among scholars and practitioners about how to safeguard "journalism in the public interest" from an increasingly commercialized news-media system.

## Chapter 10

# A Quantitative Challenge

Editors and educators have long spoken despairingly of mathematical incompetence in the newsroom. Yet working with numbers is increasingly part of daily reporting. Today's journalists must analyse and interpret data-information-processing that demands math and computer skills. As Meyer noted, "They're raising the ante on what it takes to be a journalist... A journalist has to be a database manager, a data processor and a data analyst."

But the next generation of journalists, though well-versed with computers, may be no better with numbers. Applicants to the Columbia School of Journalism gave fewer correct answers on an arithmetic test than did a group of Japanese sixth graders. When asked, "What's with you and numbers?" their unanimous reply: "We chose journalism because we don't have to deal with numbers. We want to write."

While the profession's problems with math are well known, less understood is why many journalists have a hard time with numbers. This case study probes how journalists perceive the use of numbers in newspaper stories because little headway can be made in improving mathematical competencies in the newsroom unless the underlying reasons journalists shun numbers are understood.

Drawing from a series of focus groups with professional reporters, researchers, copy editors, and top managers, this study examines how journalists view the importance of math skills in covering the news, how capable they feel computing and interpreting numbers, and what they believe would be most helpful in improving their confidence and ability to work with numbers. The difficulty journalists have with numbers is well established. More than sixty years ago, Charnley found that daily newspapers repeatedly made numerical errors. Numerous replications of Charnley's study have confirmed his findings.

In recent years, reporter innumeracy has been blamed for inaccurate stories regarding political polls, banking, the homeless, African-Americans, the poor, child abuse, Social Security and Medicare, and drug abuse, among other issues. After reviewing more than 100 news stories on coverage of educational issues, investigators lamented the media's "appalling lack of understanding of statistics and social science research." Even the New York Times acknowledges it has problems getting its numbers straight.

But numbers are a fact of life for modern journalists. Noted Cohn in News & Numbers, "We journalists like to think we deal mainly in facts and ideas, but much of what we report is based on numbers. Politics comes down to votes. Budgets and dollars dominate government. The economy, business, employment, sports - all demand numbers.... Like it or not, we must wade in." Reporters are missing, for example, lifechanging demographic trends in America because of their ignorance of numbers.

A basic knowledge of math and statistics is essential for computer-assisted reporting. But to achieve mathematical literacy, journalists need to learn more than how to compute percentage change. Wrote Paulos in A Mathematician Reads the Newspaper, "It's time to let the secret out: Mathematics is not primarily a matter of plugging numbers into formulas and performing rote computations. It is a way of thinking and questioning that may be unfamiliar to us."

Despite research documenting the value of statistical analysis in reporting and the media's propensity to ignore or misuse numbers, the literature offers little insight on how journalists respond to numbers and why so many have trouble with them. The educational psychology literature, however, provides guidance on the related phenomena of math performance and anxiety, which have been much studied since publication of a controversial 1974 book in which two female researchers posited that men were inherently superior in mathematical ability to women.

Subsequent studies suggest a gender gap in math performance exists, with females reporting more math anxiety than males, though gender differences in math are not found across the board and, in fact, may be narrowing. Math anxiety, while a poor predictor of math ability, may be a good predictor of math performance, although the relationship between the two is frequently indirect.

The root cause of math anxiety, characterized as "a fear of mathematics or an intense, negative emotional reaction to anything remotely mathematical," arises from a variety of social and psychological phenomena. Factor analysis has identified six constructs underlying math anxiety: mathematics test anxiety, numerical anxiety, negative affect toward mathematics, worry, positive affect toward mathematics, and mathematics course anxiety. Numerical anxiety was the most removed from the others, demonstrating that "anxiety as a result of the manipulation of numbers is the sine qua non of mathematics anxiety."

Literature is lacking on the extent to which math anxiety is experienced by journalists, whether the increasing number of women in the newsroom may contribute to greater math anxiety in the newsroom, and what techniques are most effective for overcoming math anxiety and improving journalistic performance. Despite the importance of numerical accuracy, how journalists can be trained to avoid math errors and to increase math literacy also remains understudied.

Today's journalists must analyse and interpret data-information-processing that demands math and computer skills. As Meyer noted, "They're raising the ante on what it takes to be a journalist... A journalist has to be a database manager, a data processor and a data analyst." But the next generation of journalists, though well-versed with computers, may be no better with numbers. Applicants to the Columbia School of Journalism gave fewer correct answers on an arithmetic test than did a group of Japanese sixth graders.

When asked, "What's with you and numbers?" their unanimous reply: "We chose journalism because we don't have to deal with numbers. We want to write."

While the profession's problems with math are well known, less understood is why many journalists have a hard time with numbers. This case study probes how journalists perceive the use of numbers in newspaper stories because little headway can be made in improving mathematical competencies in the newsroom unless the underlying reasons journalists shun numbers are understood.

Drawing from a series of focus groups with professional reporters, researchers, copy editors, and top managers, this study examines how journalists view the importance of math skills in covering the news, how capable they feel computing and interpreting numbers, and what they believe would be most helpful in improving their confidence and ability to work with numbers.

The difficulty journalists have with numbers is well established. More than sixty years ago, Charnley found that daily newspapers repeatedly made numerical errors.6 Numerous replications of Charnley's study have confirmed his findings. In recent years, reporter innumeracy has been blamed for inaccurate stories regarding political polls, banking, the homeless, African-Americans, the poor, child abuse, Social Security and Medicare, and drug abuse, among other issues.

After reviewing more than 100 news stories on coverage of educational issues, investigators lamented the media's "appalling lack of understanding of statistics and social science research." Even the New York Times acknowledges it has problems getting its numbers straight.

But numbers are a fact of life for modern journalists. Noted Cohn in News & Numbers, "We journalists like to think we deal mainly in facts and ideas, but much of what we report is based on numbers. Politics comes down to votes. Budgets and dollars dominate government. The economy, business, employment, sports - all demand numbers....Open Coding. Four major categories and 14 subcategories emerged from the open coding analysis. Remarks noted in quote marks or italics are verbatim comments transcribed from the focus group transcripts. To protect confidentiality, names presented are pseudonyms. Numbers Are Pervasive. Subjects expressed widespread acceptance that numerical ability is essential for today's journalists. Numbers are important for covering everything from business to education, from the food section to sports. Numbers are one of the only ways to get a hold of what's going on in the community.

What we're finding is that numbers are the story. But subjects had not realized how pervasive numbers were in journalism.

Many were surprised that they had to learn math "on the job." The first thing that happens when you graduate from journalism school is that some editor is expecting you to have a basic grasp on how to figure percentage increase. A lot of people have to start learning from there. Learning math on the job is possible because the level of math required is not great. You can do good work and the skills you need are not any greater than what kids get in high school.

Possibly because the level of proficiency necessary was not seen as difficult, proficiency with words was valued above mathematical competency. A copy editor noted the newspaper would hire someone who did well on its copy editing test but not its math proficiency exam, but if applicants could not "correct the big flaws in the story, then we're not going to hire them, even if they're math whizzes." Mathematics, accordingly, is considered a value-added skill, not a baseline competency.

The subjects believed that numbers not only required computation but interpretation: figures should be explained in a way that readers can understand them. Mathematics requires precision, but analysis is as much an imprecise art as a science: "It's not only having the right number but putting the right words around it."

We rarely deal with hard numbers, absolutes like speed of light. We deal with floating percentages, mortgage rates—all dependent on different factors. If you change one little factor...you are describing a different set of conditions. A particularly vexing problem copy editors encountered was "apples and oranges comparisons," especially in stories with graphics. We routinely see discrepancies between graphics and stories.... The graphics will be in terms of percentages, but the story will talk in terms of levels. It's hard for readers to make that leap, and we don't help them at all.

Numbers Are Black and White. One way in which journalists believed numbers differed from words is that numbers were seen as starkly right or wrong-"there is no fudge." Readers could check the calculations, holding journalists to an unaccustomed standard of accountability. It's intimidating... handing over the numbers to be published. There's something about going out to the world that you want to make sure you have it right. There's a lot of double-checking and triple-checking.

The result is that numbers are considered "explosive, to be handled with care" because "if you miss one figure on a number, you've got a correction the next day." Everybody who has covered tobacco has at one time... made a mistake on the price.... And some grower would call up and say, "That's the stupidest mistake I've ever seen because it doesn't cost $89,000 a pound." Many subjects stressed the need for journalists to question their data rather than simply accept numbers at face value.

The most important thing to teach people is to remind them to look at what these numbers really represent, to force yourself to think of them that way and not just as digits floating in the air. That would save us making a lot of mistakes and create good stories.

While reporters generally are skeptical, they apparently have difficulty applying "common sense" to the numbers they report. The editor who relayed the story about tobacco prices noted that a common sense test should have caught the error.

You don't have to be a numbers expert to figure it out, to look at numbers and what they mean, to figure out whether they make sense to you or not.

Another common refrain was that when it comes to

numbers, reporters rely uncritically on the veracity of their sources. In some cases this reliance was seen as misguided faith.

One thing about numbers is that lots of times we think of our sources as infallible.

A few noted that sources seemed to control the information because they "owned" the numbers. But competing sources lead to conflicting information.

There are different sources for the same number found that often causes a problem.... One of the issues is figuring out your sources and who to believe.

Numbers provide credibility. Assignment editors believed the black and white nature of numbers provide "a certain credibility" to a story.

We don't want to bombard readers with facts and figures, but to some extent they really lend credence to a story.... It's important to have enough facts and figures to buttress a story.

Often, numbers in this sense would lead to enterprise stories.

Numbers stories are the ones that usually lead to something new and different and have actual credence. There are a lot of stories about mood, or somebody talking, "He said, They said." But with numbers you can actually take a bite out of something. They have more meaning. They're thoughtful.

Conversely, if reporters are not able to work with numbers in this way, they remain dependent on their sources for direction.

You're at the mercy of your sources to tell you what the story is unless you know how to think about the numbers.

If sources supply false information that remains unquestioned, the result can be a missed scoop. For example, journalists at a competing newspaper broke a story concerning illegally diverted federal funds because "they had done the math." More commonly, reporters miss significant news stories because they are not able to discuss the numbers involved.

Reporters may be interviewing somebody or reviewing

a document or a number that's important and they don't get it. They don't understand the significance of what they've just been told or what they've just read. It's not just how we report, but how we communicate with our sources.

One way to take control of the information, journalists noted, is to practice computer-assisted reporting, which is "all about creating new numbers." By manipulating source data, reporters can generate information nobody else has. The numbers are no longer open to easy challenge.

We often take bureaucrats' numbers and do something with them and we become the only source that has those particular new numbers. Who can say we're right or wrong?

Some subjects admitted to selective use of slumbers to lend credibility to what otherwise might be a shaky story.

We know that numbers are not infallible, but even when they're "right" they're not right. But we put them on a pedestal... and frankly, we use that to our advantage. We're not afraid of numbers... we use them to fudge our way around things.

Numbers as a Source of Anxiety. Focus groups at each levelreporting, copy editing, and upper management-included self-professed math phobes of both genders. These sufferers compare their math phobia to physical disability-it is like being "blind" or "paralyzed"-or to physical illness-a "virus" or "hives." As such, it is incapacitating: "Whenever I see numbers in the story I just kind of go into a little math tremor." A recovering math phobic admitted having flashbacks.

I still wake up at night sometimes if I have a story with numbers and do the math in my head before I can go back to sleep.

Noted a frustrated copy editor who was not math phobic, such incapacitation made some reporters reluctant to question their sources even when the numbers did not make sense.

It's a paralysis thing. They ask, "You want me to go where? Do I really have to go there? Let me try to find some reason why I don't have to go there."

For example, journalists at a competing newspaper broke

a story concerning illegally diverted federal funds because "they had done the math." More commonly, reporters miss significant news stories because they are not able to discuss the numbers involved.

Reporters may be interviewing somebody or reviewing a document or a number that's important and they don't get it. They don't understand the significance of what they've just been told or what they've just read. It's not just how we report, but how we communicate with our sources.

One way to take control of the information, journalists noted, is to practice computer-assisted reporting, which is "all about creating new numbers." By manipulating source data, reporters can generate information nobody else has. The numbers are no longer open to easy challenge.

We often take bureaucrats' numbers and do something with them and we become the only source that has those particular new numbers. Who can say we're right or wrong?

Some subjects admitted to selective use of slumbers to lend credibility to what otherwise might be a shaky story.

We know that numbers are not infallible, but even when they're "right" they're not right. But we put them on a pedestal... and frankly, we use that to our advantage. We're not afraid of numbers... we use them to fudge our way around things. Numbers as a Source of Anxiety. Focus groups at each levelreporting, copy editing, and upper management-included self-professed math phobes of both genders. These sufferers compare their math phobia to physical disability-it is like being "blind" or "paralyzed"-or to physical illness-a "virus" or "hives." As such, it is incapacitating: "Whenever I see numbers in the story I just kind of go into a little math tremor." A recovering math phobic admitted having flashbacks.

I still wake up at night sometimes if I have a story with numbers and do the math in my head before I can go back to sleep.

Noted a frustrated copy editor who was not math phobic, such incapacitation made some reporters reluctant to question their sources even when the numbers did not make sense.

It's a paralysis thing. They ask, "You want me to go where? Do I really have to go there? Let me try to find some reason why I don't have to go there."

wilM1 nxnÀÏn percentages, but the story will talk in terms of levels. It's hard for readers to make that leap, and we don't help them at all.

Numbers Are Black and White. One way in which journalists believed numbers differed from words is that numbers were seen as starkly right or wrong- "there is no fudge." Readers could check the calculations, holding journalists to an unaccustomed standard of accountability. It's intimidating... handing over the numbers to be published. There's something about going out to the world that you want to maxial Coding.

At this stage of the analysis, a dichotomy emerged that coherently defined the relationships across the categories outlined above: the division between math phobics and nonphobics. This dichotomy was pronounced: math phobia is similar to pregnancy in that you either are or are not.

Phobics approached numbers quite differently from nonphobics. Phobics spoke of numbers primarily in terms of generative situations, rarely in interpretive situations. Because generative situations are those that treat numbers as black and white entities, phobics envision numbers as either right or wrong. Journalists, who put the results of their calculations before the public, may experience an added element of performance anxiety.

It's really disconcerting. You get to the bottom line, a number. And there it is.

Consonant with the literature that numerical anxiety is the sine qua non of math anxiety, phobics could not see beyond this immutable aspect of numbers. The result is that "math is like a foreign language." For these individuals, step-by-step instruction with explicit rules, much like memorization of vocabulary and grammar, is required. I get confused because there is the twice as many thing and the double and the two times as much. And there's the percentage, which is different from percentage points, and all those little gray areas in there that have you completely flummoxed.... Make training as easy as possible: percentages, two times as many, more than, as much as, or all of that.

What is needed is "something like a style book for math." Phobics want a clear, rules-based approach to guide them in calculating numbers. I used to have this Dummy's Guide to Numbers could never keep straight when you subtract, when you add. So I had this key that said if you're trying to do this, then this is the formula; if you want to do that, then this is the formula. It was just great - and I lost it. [sigh] It was really very, very useful.

When nonphobics identified software programs to do just these types of calculations, phobics admitted they lacked the confidence to use even point-and-click technology. For phobics, technology added another level of complexity to numbers rather than helping them cope with anxiety.

Their lack of confidence makes it difficult to challenge sources, even when those sources are their own staff. [When questioning your reporters] it's just kind of a morass you're wading into. You just want to say, "Okay, that number's fine. I'm going to move along now." It's a temptation.

But math anxiety does not correlate with math ability. People may be capable of doing math but still experience high levels of anxiety. Higher error rates, then, will not necessarily be associated with those who experience math anxiety, although math anxiety can contribute to performance anxiety. Many subjects in this study who were phobic had performed adequately on a management-mandated math exam, although they said the test created "huge pressure" and caused employees to "break out in hives and sweat." What is at stake is not the ability to perform the job but the level of stress the job evokes.

Nonphobics viewed numbers as entities to be interpreted and applied to the everyday world (interpretive) as well as absolute results of calculations (generative). When faced with generative situations, these subjects believe a simple "common sense test" should be applied. I think the simple things are the lion's share of things we fall down in-and they seem like they're the easiest to fix. Just apply a common sense test-take a step back and read that sentence out loud to see if it makes any sense.

Such a concept is a paradox for those who are phobic: How can one apply "common sense" to something that is not intuitively clear? For nonphobics, it simply involves double checking for accuracy and logic, much as quotes would be double-checked for accuracy and meaning.

Nonphobics are inclined to play with numbers and use them to generate new story angles. They enjoy using numbers in interpretive situations. I happen to like numbers. I like them both for the joy of doing them and I like the analysis you can do based on the results.

For nonphobics, technology is empowering. They embrace interpretive situations and want more training in computer-assisted reporting techniques.

Math isn't that hard. It's either simple arithmetic, or if it's more complicated than that you can get a machine to do it for you.

Technology puts nonphobics in control of the questions that canbe asked as well as the answers that can be generated. One reporter crunched police data to show that crime clearance rates were lower than officially reported. When the reporter confronted police officials with the results, they were "clueless, they had no idea."

Lots of times we know much more about the story than the sources do. We've done the analysis and they haven't. They just aren't equipped to do it. They have the data, but they aren't equipped to do the analysis, so they can't double check our work.

Math-inclined journalists are more willing to turn to outside sourcesfrom the Internet to academics-to assist them in their work. Comfortable with interpretive situations, they seek not only accuracy but an understanding of what the numbers represent.

What emerges from this stage of analysis is that numbers function in many ways in the newsroom, but phobics can only perceive them as immutable. While nonphobics search for new story angles and new ways to obtain, process, and interpret data, phobics seek a few basic rules to keep them out of trouble. As a former math phobe noted,

For generations, reporters have been able to get away with their clumsiness with numbers by saying, "Well, I was good at English. " The more time I spend in journalism, the more I realise how blinded I was. It was like walking around with a hand covering one eye throughout my whole career because I was so afraid to deal with numbers.... If you can't speak math, you have no business being in journalism because that's much of the ball game.

Selective Coding. In the selective coding stage, the researchers identified a core explanatory concept as an overall theoretical formulation emerged. In this instance the key came from Bandura's social cognitive theory. Bandura posits the notion of self-efficacy, which he defines as "people's judgments of their capabilities to organize and execute courses of action required to attain designated types of performances." Bandura's premise is that beliefs determine behaviour; thus, how people behave is better predicted by their beliefs about their capabilities than by their actual capabilities. Self-efficacy is task specific. At any given time an individual's belief in his or her capabilities will determine whether or not to take on a task, the amount of effort that will be expended on the task, and how much persistence the individual will exhibit in the face of adversity.

Much of what was expressed by focus group participants fits this theoretical framework. Editors note that "a lot of reporters on staff just don't gravitate towards numbers stories because they get mind boggled," math-phobic journalists prefer to "move along" rather than deal with the perceived morass of numbers, and a fearful editor confesses she goes "into a little math tremor" until she musters the courage to seek help.

Low self-efficacy leads to stress, at which point the environment controls subjects rather than subjects controlling their environment, much in the manner in which math-phobic subjects talked about their phobia as a physical disability or illness. It is telling that the opening focus group question, a simple inquiry about how numbers are used at work, was generally met by a period of awkward silence - another indicator that mathematics is for many a subject outside their comfort zone.

As Bandura explains, low self-efficacy can give rise not only to anxiety but to despondency, a depressive condition in which people draw inward on their self-doubts. Conversely, high self-efficacy correlates with high motivation and a commitment to challenge. Nonphobic journalists want more statistical training to enable them to find stories they are missing and to better grapple with complex topics of concern to readers. High self-efficacy individuals are also more likely to seek support from others, as demonstrated by the willingness of nonphobic subjects to use outside experts.

According to Bandura, self-efficacy is a strong predictor of anxiety. Researchers have demonstrated the instrumental role that selfbeliefs of math ability play in math anxiety and subsequent math performance. Subjects' perceived math ability, not their actual ability, is key to determining whether they will fall on the phobic or nonphobic side of the analysis. Newsroom managers must learn to deal with the consequences of math anxiety because they are not in a position to proactively prevent its formation.

This qualitative examination offers a theoretical framework for understanding why innumeracy in the newsroom has been an enduring issue. Consistent with Bandura's social cognitive theory, research demonstrates that beliefs about math capability play a crucial role in students' choice of majors and careers. The subjects in this study were surprised to discover on the job that numbers form a basic part of the journalist's stock in trade. For people who are afraid of math, this realization jolted their assumption that they were equipped with the basic skills to excel in journalism; because of low self-efficacy, apparently many had chosen a career that they mistakenly thought would allow them to avoid mathematics.

A limitation of this study is that the results cannot be

generalized to the larger population. Quantitative studies are needed to confirm or deny the universality of the constructs that emerged from this research. But the emergent constructs are highly representative of the two divergent viewpoints-those who are math anxious and those who are not. As such, they present themselves as worthy of further examination and lead to the following suggestions for newsroom managers and journalism educators.

Bandura posits that actions become valued when the subject can see obvious reward, thus math becomes valued if it is explicitly shown to be an integral part of a career. Newsroom managers can provide early intervention during internships and in career development by emphasizing not just spelling sources' names correctly and writing a good lead or headline but also correctly calculating a percentage change and interpreting data from a spreadsheet.

However, rote mathematics will do little good unless reporters and editors also are shown how and when to apply the rules. Many said getting the "right answer" was not as problematic as figuring out how to use the data. Journalists need help with mathematical vocabulary and concepts so they know, for example, when to use the mean and when to use the median. As with words, fuzzy mathematical thinking leads to fuzzy description. Only by understanding the underlying mathematical concepts can reporters effectively explain statistics to their readers.

The dichotomy between math-phobic individuals and the nonphobic also underscores the need for a specialized training approach for those who possess greater math self-efficacy. For these individuals, workshops on basic math rules and their applications hold little appeal.

These subjects want to be exposed to new sources of data, to improve their technological skills, and to learn more about statistical analysis.

Advanced computer training is essential for this group - the data now available to journalists are too vast to cope with unaided. These subjects are receptive to workshops led by recognized experts - an approach that could intimidate the math phobic and shut down their learning. In short, the math-inclined need challenge, not reassurance.

Finally, a mechanism needs to be established to make math a more "top of the head issue," even for those already comfortable with numbers. By bringing these issues to the forefront, the common sense test is more likely to be applied. Newsroom managers need to establish a formal process by which numbers are routinely checked, not routinely passed over as someone else's responsibility. These numerical checks should not be just for accuracy but to ensure that the numbers make common sense and are expressed in terms that readers comprehend.

To help prevent innumeracy in the newsroom, journalism educators should take a stronger role in preparing a work force willing and able to work with mathematics. Much as journalism educators now require students to master the fundamentals of AP style, perhaps the time has come for journalism educators to make math a requisite skill for a degree in journalism. But this study underscores the need not only to emphasize math skills but to provide the support necessary so that journalism students who are acutely anxious with numbers can overcome their trepidation.

Under Bandura's programme of guided mastery, instructional material should be structured in easily mastered subskills from which principles are learned and applied, self-efficacy is promoted through a succession of exercises leading to independence, and motivation is nurtured by repeatedly showing that what is being learned has utility outside the classroom. The study raises several fundamental questions about the responsibility of journalism education for newsroom innumeracy.

For example, why isn't mathematics considered a requisite skill by most journalism education programs? Do educators contribute to the myth that math skills are not needed in journalism? Could it be that many journalism educators lack the confidence and skills to effectively work with numbers? These issues warrant further study.

Bandura shows that efficacy beliefs vary on several

dimensions: level (i.e., degree of difficulty), generality (i.e., degree of task specificity), and strength (i.e., degree of conviction). Recognizing that the confidence with which journalists approach math is multidimensional, we believe that further self-efficacy research would likely reveal constructs more broadly defined than the phobic-nonphobic dichotomy identified here.

Testing of newsroom math skills and confidence levels also is needed to investigate quantitatively the relationship between mathematics knowledge and mathematics self-efficacy among journalists. Research questions worthy of further study include: To what extent do journalists lack basic math skills needed for day-to-day reporting and editing? To what extent do journalists lack the efficacy beliefs needed to use their math skills effectively? What is the correlation of math skills and math confidence among journalists? How does confidence in mathematics among journalists compare to confidence in mathematics among other professionals? What training strategies would most effectively help journalists acquire not only requisite math skills but also the efficacy beliefs to use them well?

The implications of the growing feminization of the field needs further study. That women tend to experience more math anxiety is well documented. As more women come into newsrooms, it is possible that the door will be opening to increased math anxiety and attendant problems of mathematical inadequacy. Longitudinal studies are necessary to assess whether math anxiety levels correspond with the numbers of women in the newsroom. Managers in this study expressed hope that the newsroom culture would change from one of fearing math to one of embracing math as more computer-literate graduates joined their ranks. But this study suggests that computers are not an effective crutch for the math anxious. Further research is needed to explore the role of technology in making math accessible to the newsroom masses.

And foremost, a fundamental mindshift is needed in the newsroom. Journalism is no longer a refuge from mathematics, if it ever was. Numbers in the news should not be viewed as a "ticking time bomb," but as a journalist's ally, or at least a familiar acquaintance. But clearly, many journalists remain convinced that numbers are not-and should not be their calling. Researchers can make a worthy contribution by showing how to change these deeply embedded social norms.

## Chapter 11

# Journalistic Authority and the Coverage

The jailing of New York Times reporter Judith Miller in 2005 for refusal to testify before a grand jury led to outcries from journalists and calls for a federal shield law to protect journalists from being forced to reveal information about confidential sources. Miller, like journalists before her, maintained that forcing her to reveal her source's identity would hinder her ability to perform her job and was therefore a violation of the First Amendment. The courts disagreed and the spectacle created by an American journalist sitting in an American jail caused as much indignation and outrage (and detailed news coverage) as one would expect.

And, yet, an odd thing emerged in the news coverage. Along with all the legal details of the case, there appeared an insistent and ubiquitous reminder: Judith Miller had never written a story about the subject of the investigation. No one questions the truth of this fact (i.e., the grand jury was investigating the exposure of undercover CIA agent Valerie Flame's identity and Miller neither published her identity nor did she write any articles about the issue), but its presence is notable because it has no bearing on Miller's jailing.

Miller was jailed for refusing to comply with a subpoena. She was not jailed in spite of not having written a story, but with absolutely no regard for whether or not she wrote a story. Why, then, did this legally irrelevant fact permeate news coverage? More important, what can its presence tell us about the process by which journalists construct stories of the real? This chapter takes the ubiquitous presence of this legally irrelevant fact as an opportunity to observe the tension in professional journalism between the information ideal, which treats journalism as a mechanism for transmitting crucial facts to a democratically engaged public, and a story ideal, which emphasizes the work journalists do of Grafting compelling narratives out of facts they collect.

Journalism's avowed commitment is to the information ideal, which has at its centre the norm of disinterestedness. In embracing this ideal, journalists aim to avoid persuasion, manipulation, and rhetorical force through commitment to fact-centered, rational reporting.

At the same time, however, journalists are storytellers who organize facts they gather into meaningful, powerful narratives. The story ideal in journalism is patently at odds with the information ideal insofar as it privileges the ability of a given rendering of events to move and engage readers, drawing them into its worldview. The coverage of the jailing of Judith Miller illustrates that journalism's outward commitment to the information ideal veils its participation in the story ideal, and in this way disguises the story ideal's role as a source of moral authority for journalistic accounts of the real.

The collision between these two ideals is made visible through the presence of a legally irrelevant but morally charged fact in the coverage of Miller's jailing. Despite their manifest incompatibility, the information and story ideals work together to give legitimacy and authority to journalistic reports. Journalism embraces the information ideal and strives to transcribe reality directly, but it is simultaneously authorized and sanctioned by the moral force that is inseparable from the narrative form. News stories thus gain legitimacy as stories of the real on two levels.

On one level, they appear "real" in the sense of being a disinterested, disengaged, trustworthy transcription of events, offering as close an approximation as possible of direct access to what "really" happened. On another level, however, they appear real because they cohere with our shared sense of right and wrong, of a moral order properly maintained. Because news takes the form of narrative, its authority draws on both levels at the same time. It mingles the authority of disinterested objectivity (that is, of direct access to the real) with the authority of a shared moral order (that is, of a normative sense of rightness).

In the case of the coverage of Judith Miller, her not having written a story is important to the narrative (implicit in the news coverage and explicit on the opinion pages) that portrays Miller as a hapless victim of the courts, of the justice system, and, more concretely, of journalist Robert Novak.

The fact helps establish her role as the victim (and Novak's as the villain). Thus, though the fact is legally irrelevant (and forces the coverage into some moments of stark incoherence), it is morally central, and its pervasive presence in accounts of legal events makes visible the way story and information ideals work together to authorize journalism's stories of the real.

This study explores how tactics associated with objectivity create an authoritative basis for news stories, and then discusses how narrative, storytelling, and moral force confer a journalistic authority of their own.

It describes the legal context surrounding Miller's refusal to testify and uses textual analysis of Miller case coverage to show how the conflict between narrative and objectivity resolves itself in a way that allows the moral to act as a silent yet potent underpinning for the appearance of direct access to truth that objectivity claims to provide. This relationship between objective and moral authority reinforces the tendency of news to sanction and preserve the status quo, making journalists' convincing accounts of "the way it is" simultaneously accounts of "the way it should be," and the real, as presented on news pages, becomes synonymous with the right.

## THE AUTHORITY OF OBJECTIVITY

Authority is crucial to journalists, given that their job is to tell true stories about the world we live in. To do their jobs well, journalists rely on the ability to have their stories relied on, to have them considered "faithful rendering[s]... of what really happened." To be believed, journalists must employ techniques that make them appear credible. The work of journalists is, in many ways, that of "establishing, repairing and transforming the authoritative base for accounts of 'the way it is.'" Journalists deal in a genre that is legitimate only insofar as it is seen as true, and journalists thus dedicate much work to constructing their authority to tell stories of the true.

Journalism's most obvious and most potent source of authority has been its commitment to objectivity since at least the beginning of the last century. The ideal of objectivity aims to separate journalists from their stories, downplaying their role in generating the story and treating them instead as mediators who channel information from one group to another. This journalistic ideal was extolled by Lippmann as the best and perhaps only solution to what he saw as the primary problem faced by large democracies, the problem of information. Since members of large democracies need information beyond their "direct and certain knowledge," a scientific approach (that is, one that employs the method of objectivity) was needed to transmit that knowledge with a minimum of distortion.

To lay claim to the authority associated with science, journalists minimize their personal relationship to the story and emphasize the source. The tactics journalists use to create a sense of direct access have been called a "strategic ritual," a series of routine behaviours that mark the separation of fact from opinion and demonstrate journalists' distance from their stories. For example, journalists use a "plain style" of prose distinguished by its attempts to be, or to appear, free of style. By avoiding ornate or superfluous language, by being as efficient, compact, and direct as possible, the plain style seeks to make itself invisible and contribute to the sense that there is as little interference as possible between audience and source.

The plain style is able to draw authority from feigned naturalness only in the context of a commitment to the notion that language can be transparent, offering a direct view on what it describes. When language is seen as acting as a window on the thing it describes, the strategies of objectivity are able to give the impression of direct access to the world. Without that underlying epistemological position, the notion of the journalist as a conduit, a mediator, or a professional communicator is untenable, and it is impossible to derive authority from the apparent absence of the journalist.

But by resting on the assumption of language's ability to be transparent, objectivity can generate authority for a journalist's portrayal of events by creating the impression of the journalist's absence.

## THE AUTHORITY OF NARRATIVE

At the same time that they use objectivity to create a sense of transparency and derive authority from it, journalists also tell stories. Journalists adhere to the techniques mentioned above, but all the while, they are selecting facts to relate, describing relationships among them, and constructing a tale with a beginning, middle, and end. Thus, in constructing news, journalists also construct narratives, making coherent meaning out of what Arendt refers to as the "chaos of sheer happenings."

As narrative, however, news is unavoidably charged with moral meaning. White argues that a narrative always contains moral claims because it does more than record facts in the order of their original occurrence. Narrative introduces its own order, and in doing so, implicitly points to the possibility of alternative formulations, alternative orders. This recognition of other possible renderings of events implicitly contains with it a claim to its being the "right" version. Journalism's ability to authoritatively tell stories of the real is based on this claim, which is, at bottom, a moral one. As White puts it:

The events that are actually recorded in the narrative appear "real" precisely insofar as they belong to an order of moral existence, just as they derive their meaning from their placement in this order. It is because the events described conduce to the establishment of social order or fail to do so that they find a place in the narrative attesting to their reality.

Thus, to the extent that journalism is understood as narrative, its authority can be understood as deriving from the moral claims inherent in narrative. But this moral authority conflicts with the disinterested authority journalists derive from objectivity. As tellers of morally charged narratives, journalists are implicated in their stories in just the way they try to avoid by claiming the authority of objectivity. On the level of narrative, journalists don't gain authority by being an absence that doesn't interfere with direct access to the sources; they gain it through their own claims to the superiority of their narratives. Narrative authority rests on the very endorsement of a given moral order and personal involvement of the reporter that objectivity seeks to purge.

Ettema and Classer have shown how tension between objectivity and moral force in investigative journalism leads to the conservative nature of news. This tension is overt in investigative journalism because of that genre's open commitment to calling attention to wrongdoing while retaining a commitment to objectivity. Investigative journalists resolve the tension between the moral engagement of denouncing wrongdoing and the moral disengagement of objectivity by disguising their moral claims as empirical ones. This, Ettema and Classer argue, means that investigative journalism acts as a conservative force that "subverts] the critical discussion of values," rather than stimulating it.

The scope of Ettema and Glasser's work is limited to investigative journalism, where moral engagement is inherent in the traditions of muckraking and adversarialism. This study, however, shows that similar patterns can be observed in hard news. Even without a muckraking tradition, the narrative form gives hard news a moral dimension. Like investigative journalism, hard news attempts to use objectivity to eliminate moral engagement from its portrayals, but rather than making journalism amoral, objectivity only obscures hard news's claims about right and wrong, making them unavailable for open critical discussion. Mander has also addressed the role of moral force in news pages, arguing that in hard news the journalist's authority rests only in part on the perceived accuracy (or "objectivity") of the portrayal. Journalists also derive authority from a tacit contract with the reader, who agrees to believe the journalist's representation of events, but demands a moral evaluation of those events in return.

Mander therefore identifies the moral work that journalists do as part of the same contract that confers authority on them, but she stops short of the claim that moral work is itself a source of authority.

This study, however, concludes that the press plays a more invidious, and perhaps a more powerful, role in maintaining the status quo. Narrative does more than provide the reader with a sense of order; it also undergirds its portrayal of a social order with the power of the moral. The moral evaluation does not simply coincide with the objective presentation; it justifies and validates that presentation, so that the story itself comes to appear to be a direct reflection of truth that exudes a sense of rightness it could not otherwise claim.

The relationship that is being described here between objectivity and narrative is counter-intuitive, largely because it contradicts many of our assumptions about objectivity in journalism.

Objectivity is conventionally seen as an adversary of narrative, the tool that is used by journalists to expunge narrative and its moral implications from news coverage. But here we can see that objectivity and narrative actually work in concert: the former tells us what is true, actual, real, and the "way it is," while the latter tells us what is proper, appropriate, right, and "the way it should be." Thus, when the strategies of objectivity and the moral force of narrative come together in a single story, they tell us that what is true is what is proper, that what is actual is what is appropriate, that "the way it is" is also "the way it should be," and that what is real is also what is right.

## THE CASE FOR REFUSING TO TESTIFY

In refusing to testify before a grand jury about her confidential conversations with members of the Bush administration, Judith Miller argued (as have many other journalists throughout American history) that forcing journalists to reveal confidential information is a violation of the First Amendment's guarantee of freedom of the press. Two basic arguments are often made in favour of a testimonial privilege to protect them from subpoenas. The first is that journalists cannot do their jobs properly unless they are empowered to grant anonymity to sources, anonymity that won't be compromised by a subpoena.

The archetypical source invoked to support this claim is the whistleblower-the source who stands to lose a great deal by revealing information from which the public stands to gain a great deal. Such sources will never speak up, journalists argue, unless they can be sure journalists won't be subpoenaed and forced to reveal their identities. If such sources don't speak up, the public is the clear loser and the role of a free press in fostering an informed citizenry is clearly contravened.

A second argument is that subpoenas make it possible for law enforcement to co-opt the reporting journalists do. If law enforcement can wantonly demand whatever information it wants from journalists, all the reporting journalists do can be seen as potentially in the service of law enforcement. Subpoenaing journalists threatens to make them into "an arm of government" rather than an adversarial fourth estate.

This inherent tension between law enforcement and journalists did not manifest as a problem, however, until the late 1960s, when the Nixon administration responded to the burgeoning social activism of the day by subpoenaing journalists in a way that seemed at best unrestrained and at worst overtly hostile.

This change alarmed journalists, who in turn became less willing to cooperate with the government. The result was the 1972 Supreme Court ruling in Branzburg v. Hayes, in which the court found that while there is nothing to stop the passage of specific legislation to create testimonial privileges for journalists, no such privilege can be found in the First Amendment. Since 1972, many states have taken the Court up on its suggestion and passed laws that create a qualified testimonial privilege for journalists, but no equivalent federal law exists. Journalists, therefore, have neither constitutional nor statutory protection against being subpoenaed to testify in federal courts.

Thus, when Judith Miller found herself subpoenaed to testify before a federal grand jury about confidential conversations she had with high-level sources in the Bush administration, there was no law to protect her from being forced to testify. Though she (and Time magazine reporter Matthew Cooper, who was also subpoenaed) appealed to the Supreme Court to quash the subpoenas, the Court unanimously decided not to hear the case. Continuing her refusal to testify, Miller spent eighty-five days in jail. She was released when she eventually complied and testified before the grand jury.

For this study, the coverage of the Miller controversy from May 2004 to August 2005 was analysed. Though Miller was not found in contempt of court until October 2004, it was revealed in May that she and fellow journalist Matthew Cooper had been subpoenaed and could face jail for refusing to testify. This study thus encompasses the time from the original subpoena through Miller's incarceration on July 6, 2005. An entirely new pattern of coverage, driven by an entirely different narrative, emerged after Miller decided to testify and was released from jail, but that is outside the scope of this study. Two major dailies, the New York Times and the Washington Post, were analysed.

These papers were chosen for their elite status among U.S. daily newspapers, which suggests that they are likely to have a powerful impact on what stories are covered and how at papers across the country. The major newsweeklies, Time and Newsweek, were also examined, as were transcripts from the news programming on the television networks. The majority of the coverage of the case originated with the Times and the Post. It is worth mentioning that Judith Miller herself was a reporter at the Times and that Matthew Cooper was a reporter with Time magazine, so it is possible that personal relationships had their own impact on the coverage that came from these institutions. The networks did not cover the story in depth, but made reference to it at key dramatic moments, like when the Supreme Court denied certiorari to Miller and Cooper's case and when Miller was jailed.

## FINDINGS

### AN UNDISPUTED FACT

Throughout the coverage, references to Miller's not having written a story are ubiquitous, but their significance is most visible in those rarer instances in which reporters explicitly state that Miller is being jailed in spite of this fact. A key example comes from the New York Times' national desk on Oct. 8, 2004:

The reporter, Judith Miller, published no articles about the agent, Valerie Píame. Even so, the judge, Thomas F. Hogan, of United States District Court in Washington, ordered her jailed for as long as 18 months, noting that she had contemplated writing such an article and had conducted interviews for it.

Miller published no article, but the journalist tells us that she is being jailed "even so." The "even so" creates the sense of ironic injustice, suggesting that Miller's going to jail and her refraining from writing a story are in logical opposition to one another. But from a legal standpoint, writing a story is irrelevant to the charges against Miller, so her not having written one does nothing to exonerate her. Miller is being jailed for refusing to testify before a grand jury when subpoenaed to do so. Legally, she is not being jailed in spite of not having written a story; she is being jailed completely independently of the stories she did or did not write.

This relatively rare overt statement of the ironic injustice of Miller's jailing is surrounded by various other references to Miller's not writing a story that are unaccompanied by clear statements about the irony of the fact. For example, the following passage clearly treats the situation as ironic and contradictory, but it is unclear whether it is Miller's lawyer, Floyd Abrams, or the reporter who is pointing to the irony:

Speaking after the hearing, Mr. Abrams referred to the case involving Ms. Miller, who is facing a jail term even though she did not publish an article about Ms. Píame, as evidence of the "extraordinary reach" of the special prosecutor.

Again, Miller faces jail "even though" she didn't write a story. Here, the "even though" appears as a clause in Abrams' description of the case, but outside of quotation marks. It is, therefore, unclear whether the source or the reporter is characterizing Miller's situation as ironic, but the very ambiguity itself suggests that it doesn't matter. Attribution in this case is irrelevant because this ironic contradiction is the objective reality of the case.

In a number of other instances, the fact of not writing a story simply appears without any comment on the nature of its relevance. For example, in this Times story, the fact is set off as its own sentence: "A sixth reporter, Judith Miller of the New York Times, is in a Virginia jail for refusing to testify in the case. Ms. Miller never wrote about the matter," and in this Posi story, the sentence "Miller did reporting on the Flame story but never wrote about it" appears as its own paragraph with no explanatory text at all.

Miller's not writing a story becomes relevant only if the crime she faces jail for is understood to be writing the story that revealed Flame's identity in the first place, and not her refusal to testify. This is made very obvious by a moment from the network news coverage of the case. CBS news anchor Bob Schieffer reports, with obvious incredulity and outrage:

Unable to find out which of the government officials did this leaked Flame's identity to the press], the prosecutors are threatening to jail reporters unless they tell what they know, and that includes Judy Miller, who, I repeat, never wrote a story about it. What's next? Arresting people who decide not to steal a car."

Schieffer's analogy suggests that Miller might be jailed even though she refrained from committing the crime. This only makes sense when the crime that stealing the car stands in for is writing the story that identified Píame. Miller is innocent of that crime and that is what makes her jailing so shocking and unjust.

A similar confusion about what the crime is that Miller is being jailed for is evident in this headline for a Times story: "Little-Tested Law Is Used Against Journalists in Leak." The headline says a "little-tested" law is being used against the journalists, but that law is actually being used against Bush administration officials. The "little-tested" law is the Intelligence Identities Protection Act, which might have been broken by the administration official(s) who revealed Flame's identity to the press. This law was the basis for the grand jury investigation and is indeed "little tested" in that it has only been applied once since its adoption in 1982. It is not, however, the law being used against the journalists. Like the car analogy, this headline erases the contempt charge as the reason for jailing Miller and inserts a different charge in its place, one to which Miller's not writing a story might be relevant.

To fully understand the reason for the ubiquitous presence of this legally irrelevant fact and the accompanying confusion about the reason for Miller's jailing, it helps to note the contrast that the news coverage repeatedly draws between Miller's behaviour and that of columnist Robert Novak. Novak, after all, did write a story. In fact, he is the journalist who wrote the story that revealed the CIA affiliation of Valerie Plame. Highlighting the difference in their roles in Flame's exposure becomes an important task of the coverage: "In recent months, Mr. Fitzgerald has focused solely on Ms. Miller and Mr. Cooper. Mr. Cooper wrote about Ms. Flame only after the Novak column had identified her, and Ms. Miller, though she conducted interviews on the subject, has never written about it."

The contrast is clear: Novak revealed Flame's identity; Miller never wrote about it. It is made even clearer by the presence of Cooper. Cooper doesn't enjoy the pristine innocence of Miller who can be extolled for never writing any story at all. Cooper's innocence has to be established somewhat more carefully; he did write a story, but only after Novak did. This finer distinction between Novak and Cooper makes clear that the real crime isn't just writing about the matter, but revealing Flame's identity. Miller's innocence (and the injustice of her jailing) lies in the fact that she didn't commit this crime.

The "innocence" in question, of course, isn't legal innocence, but innocence in the context of the narrative about the case that is being constructed by the journalists covering it. On the news pages we can see only the shadow of this story and of the implication that Novak is guilty and Miller innocent. On the editorial pages, however, standards of objectivity and professionalism don't preclude overt moral claims, and there we find undisguised accusations and condemnations as well as impassioned defenses. Exploring this coverage will help us understand more fully the way right and wrong are figured in the narrative surrounding the case and thus the moral implications of the facts that appear in the news pages.

## THE MAKING OF A VICTIM AND VILLAIN

On the opinion pages, the opposition between Miller the good journalist and Novak the bad one is explicitly and repeatedly stated. Two main offenses mark Novak as a villain: writing the column that exposed Piarne in the first place, and failing to publicly disclose both whether he had been subpoenaed by the court and whether he had testified. The first grievance is voiced in an opinion piece in the Washington Post that argues that Cooper shouldn't be imprisoned because "Cooper didn't Out' Valerie Plame as a CIA operative-that was columnist Robert Novak."

Outing Plame is the offense, the reason for imprisonment, and Cooper's innocence it contrasted against Novak's guilt. Similarly, another Post editorial suggests that outing Plame was the real crime:

Special Prosecutor Fitzgerald is charged with investigating whether the leak of Ms. Flame's identity by one or more administration officials to columnist Robert D. Novak two years ago constituted a criminal act. Yet so far the only person to actually face jail time in his prolonged investigation is a reporter who never wrote a story about Ms. Plame, let alone revealed her CIA affiliation.

The leak was to Novak, we are reminded, and Miller's innocence is marked on two levels: She didn't commit the big crime of revealing Flame's CIA affiliation, and she didn't even commit the small one of writing about the story at all. Again, this passage suggests that Miller's facing jail would be more appropriate if she had been the one to write the story that blew Flame's cover (or, somewhat inexplicably, if she'd written any story about Plame at all), but it wasn't her, it was Novak, so he should be the one in trouble.

Writing the column that exposed Flame was an offense both because it put Miller in a position to face jail in the first place, and because it was seen as journalistically ignoble. Leaking Flame's identity to the press was seen as an attempt by the Bush administration to undermine one of its critics. Flame's husband, Joseph Wilson, had criticized the administration's claim that Saddam Hussein had attempted to buy uranium from Niger. Far from participating in the vaunted journalistic tradition of comforting the afflicted and afflicting the comfortable, Novak's role appeared to be that of Bush administration shill, passing on information that was whispered to him, not in the public's interest, but in the interest of smearing an enemy of the administration. This ignoble deed had now led to a situation in which a journalist (a journalist who wasn't Novak) was going to be incarcerated. Novak's ignoble deed started everything, so that deed became the crime and Miller's incarceration was unjust because she was innocent of that crime.

The second offense that marks Novak as a villain was violating an unofficial journalistic code by keeping quiet about his status with respect to the investigation. He refused to say whether or not he had been subpoenaed, whether or not he had testified. A typical quote comes from the Los Angeles Times editorial page:

What Novak has done or failed to do as a journalist remains shielded in mystery because Novak refuses to talk. Traditionally, journalists have publicly explained their status and their position in such controversies-as have various other reporters in the Plame affair. Knowing where Novak stands in this case would be important because the other journalists involved-especially Judith Miller of the New York Times-need to know his position so they can form a unified front against government threats.38

This passage overtly positions Novak as a journalistic villain. His refusal to reveal his status is an overt violation of journalistic codes (what is done "traditionally" that allows them to fight the government effectively). Judith Miller is positioned as the victim of Novak's transgression-she stands in for all journalists who are prevented from banding together by his choice to keep quiet about his status with the courts.

Novak is thus seen as victimizing Miller through both his acts of villainy. She is the victim of his outing Flame in the first place because she is the one facing jail, and she is the victim of his choice to keep his own counsel with respect to his testimony because she doesn't know how best to strategically respond to government threats.

Thus, the lines get clearly drawn on the editorial pages. On one side we have Miller, the good journalist. In her virtue, she doesn't do the administration's dirty work by publishing information to discredit its critics, and she refuses to compromise her journalistic integrity by revealing the name of her source on the stand. She also publicly discloses her status-the fact that she has been subpoenaed and that she is resisting the subpoena. On the other side is Novak, standing for all threats to true virtue. In his villainy, he is on the side of the government: he will helpfully publish dirty secrets about Valerie Plame and he will keep quiet about his role in the investigation.

The unambiguous nature of these roles is crucial to their ability to generate a compelling moral story. Right and wrong are firmly established; order and disorder are clearly understood; the only question that remains is how the former will be able to triumph over the latter.

In the context of this juxtaposition of victim and villain, the moral weight of the repeated fact that Miller didn't write a story becomes perfectly clear. Not writing a story contributes to Miller's innocence not in a legal sense, but in the moral order established on the editorial pages. The fact contributes to the establishment of an unambiguous opposition between good and bad, right and wrong, guilt and innocence. In this case, writing the story that exposed Valerie Plame's identity was bad, wrong, guilty, so Miller's not writing one helps establish her as good, right, and innocent.

This understanding of the way guilt and innocence are constructed on the editorial pages helps explain both the reason the fact of not writing a story permeates the news coverage and the coverage's moments of confusion over the reason for Miller's jailing. The fact is there not to transmit information, but to establish Miller's moral rightness. The confusion over the reason for Miller's jailing is necessary to maintain the clear distinction between the victim and the villain in the tale. This understanding also clarifies other moments of slippage in the news coverage, moments that otherwise appear incoherent.

For example, in the following passage from an article that appeared on the news pages of the Washington Post, Miller's actions are contrasted with Novak's. However, the two actions don't actually stand in contrast to one another, except insofar as Miller's mark her innocence and Novak's mark his guilt: "Stone and other legal experts say they assume that Novak has testified under some sort of waiver or compromise. Miller, by contrast, never wrote a story about the Plame matter."

On the surface, it is illogical for the second statement in this passage to follow from the first. Since the first statement suggests Novak probably testified, the logical contrast to it would be a statement pointing out Miller's continued refusal to testify. But as it stands, the first statement is about Novak's choice to testify, the second is about Miller's not having written a story. These two things are only in contrast in the context of the moral universe that is established on the editorial pages. According to that framework, Novak's guilt is marked by his refusal to tell whether or not he has testified, and Miller's innocence is marked by her not having written a story. The contrast isn't actually between testifying and writing stories, but between a morally debased journalist's actions and those of a morally upright one.

By looking to the narrative that was generated in the opinion pages, characterized by a firm and unambiguous distinction between the victim and the villain of the tale, we can explain what seemed to be inexplicable facts appearing on the news pages. Without the moral force of this narrative, many facts presented in the news coverage of the jailing of Judith Miller don't make sense. If we understand journalism only in terms of the information model, if we confine our understanding of journalism to the rational transfer of information, it is impossible to account for the continued reiteration of the fact that Miller wrote no story. It is only by going beyond the information model to investigate how journalism, even hard news, functions as a story that we can make sense of the coverage of Miller's jailing. The coverage was animated both by the information ideal's desire to adhere to the fact-based strategies of objectivity and by the story ideal's unavoidable commitment to a given moral order.

But the lesson to be drawn from this case study is not simply that news is both story and information at the same time. Rather, this case provides an opportunity to observe how these two ideals offer different kinds of authority to journalists. In the information ideal, journalists use the strategies of objectivity to claim the authority of transparency, the authority of direct access to a single truth. In the story ideal, journalists use narrative to create moral authority, the authority of the "rightness" of one rendering of events over another, the rightness of one world order over another.

In this example, we see how the authority of narrative and the authority of objectivity don't just peacefully and separately coexist. Rather, they are complementary; the former lends its force to buttress the latter. In reminding us that Miller wrote no story, the coverage is, on one level, merely transmitting an undisputed fact. But as we have seen, it's a fact that is heavily freighted with moral meaning; it tells a story about good and bad, right and wrong, a victim and a villain. By adding its moral authority to the disinterested authority of objectivity, this fact brings to an objective news story the sense of describing a moral order that is normatively right.

In this way, news that appears to make truth claims that are devoid of moral force, resting its legitimacy on the strategies of objectivity alone, is actually drawing on the moral force of narrative. This moral force allows what is presented as objectively true to also appear natural, eternal, and indisputable. While such news appears to be offering unmediated access to the real, what it really offers is a version of the real that is made incontrovertible by its conflation with the right.

## Chapter 12

# Journalists Values and Roles

While Weaver and Wilhoit and others have identified the various roles that journalists perceive themselves as performing, social psychology research suggests that individual value systems may determine how journalists perceive different roles. Moreover, it provides a basis from which to explore why journalists embrace particular roles over others. Personal values and demographic factors contribute to a web of context through which journalists view their roles and make decisions about which functions they feel are central.

The values that we hold, or the philosophical principles on which we base our reasons for doing things-claims to truth, social justice, fairness-constitute the engine that drives many discussions about the behaviour of media practitioners. Individual values, conceptually more fundamental than the roles we see for ourselves in society, inform as well as lend context to the functions journalists undertake. This study seeks to examine how incorporating value-theory research might expand our understanding of journalistic role conceptions established by the studies of Weaver and Wilhoit, Voakes, and others.

There is little question over whether ethical frameworks are used in journalistic decision making. The most substantive discussions revolve around the factors that influence that process or the philosophical underpinnings of a democratic free press. Others have sought to explore the journalistic applications of particular philosophical approaches. This study explores the suggestion that the conventional applications of philosophical approaches alone do not adequately explain journalistic behaviour and the roles embraced by journalists on a daily basis.

## VALUE THEORY RESEARCH

Research into values has an extensive history in sociology and social psychology and has culminated in a body of theory that suggests individuals conduct their social lives according to a "value system"-"a hierarchical arrangement of values, a rank-ordering of values along a continuum of importance." Research also has produced sophisticated assessment instruments used in value analysis, most notably the Rokeach Value Survey that has been widely used since the early 1970s.

The Rokeach Value Survey, which assesses the respondent's rankordering of eighteen values in two categories, has been independently validated and used extensively to compare value systems of individuals as well as diverse cultures. Rokeach's definition of value has informed much contemporary value analysis: "More formally, to say that a person 'has a value' is to say that he has an enduring belief that a particular mode of conduct or that a particular end-state of existence is personally and socially preferable to alternative modes of conduct or end-states of existence." Values, research suggests, are relatively stable over time for members within a given group. Ranked values obtained by individuals and groups also have been directly linked to behaviour.

Using the Rokeach Value Survey, researchers have examined the influence of values on television viewing behaviour,9 the value systems of city planners and managers, and how values guide the ideological outlooks of social workers. The value survey also has been used to examine how specific instrumental values and internalized messages work together when individuals self-assess their behaviour.

The value-theory research of sociologists has not been widely utilized by media theorists, who have largely focused their work on cognitive psychology and on normative frameworks drawn from philosophical approaches. Black and colleagues examined how the content of an ethics course alters the value systems of journalism students. Viall proposed applying a modified Rokeach survey to explore journalistic values, but only in a notably constricted approach.

Other researchers using the Rokeach Value Survey have noted that the value list does not adequately represent "basic human rights" such as dignity, privacy, and protection from harm. This study adds six values to the list of eighteen instrumental values included in the Rokeach Value Survey. Values added to the instrument for this study should help to close that "basic human rights" gap.

## CONCEPTIONS OF JOURNALISTIC ROLES

Much media research has implicitly depended on assumptions about journalistic values, but has stopped short of analyzing how a value theory might be at work. The landmark studies by Johnstone and colleagues, Culbertson, and Weaver and Wilhoit examine the professional roles-what could be referred to as the generally held teleology, or end purpose, of journalism. In their 1992 study, for example, Weaver and Wilhoit categorized survey responses as reflecting how journalists assessed their professional roles based on "interpretive," "disseminator," or "adversarial" values. This study focuses on the dynamic of interaction between those professional roles and the motives behind them. Journalists were asked to rate the importance of various media roles-for example, to "investigate government claims," to "avoid stories with unverified content," to "let people express views"-as well as to rank a set of values according to their perceived importance to journalistic work.

In an earlier study that visited the issue of professional roles, Janowitz found that, over time, people working in journalism changed their perceptions of the role of journalism in society from one of strict neutrality to one that attempts to explain the news by putting it in a broader context. Echoing Lippmann, Janowitz wrote that earlier models had journalists adhering to a role that emphasizes objectivity to provide verifiable information to the public. "The model was reinforced in part by the increased prestige of the academic social researcher, and it assumed that, through the application of intellectually based techniques, objective and valid results could be obtained." In time, the model evolved from one of detachment to one of involvement, giving prominence to the role of the interpretive or advocate journalist.

The philosophical values on which these journalistic roles are based are conceptually more fundamental than the roles themselves; the three previously mentioned survey items related to the work of Weaver and Wilhoit-to "investigate government claims," to "avoid stories with unverified content," to "let people express views"-can be considered to refer to the principles of truth, justice, and equality. Consequently, it is not unreasonable to expect that perceived roles and underlying principles correlate with one another-not only in the sense that journalists endorse various media roles and corresponding values, but that values, even potentially conflicting ones, are held simultaneously. Such pluralism was a key finding in Weaver and Wilhoit's 1992 survey of journalists: "[M]ost journalists strongly endorsed a combination of two, and sometimes three, core roles. At least superficially, then, most journalists saw themselves as serving seemingly contradictory functions" [authors' emphasis]. Preliminary findings of the 2002 survey update by Weaver, Beam, and colleagues suggest similar pluralistic role conceptions.

Measuring individuals' value systems and examining how certain values are given more weight than others offers direct insights into the motivations of behaviour-including the decision-making process. This study is motivated by the following research questions:

*RQ1:* What are the value systems of journalists?

*RQ2:* What is the relationship between the values that journalists rank highly and the roles that they embrace?

*RQ3:* What are the relationships between the roles that journalists embrace, the values that they rank highly and demographic factors such as age, length of time in their position, length of time in the profession, and length of time spent in a community? Because the link between personal values and professional roles is such an intuitive one, bodies of research on both topics have remained distinct, and the relationship between the two has not been explored in a systematic way.

The literature and reflections of individual journalists are filled with anecdotal references suggesting the two are related. Shoemaker and Reese, while arguing that the individual journalist has less of an influence on news content than do organizations or social systems, nonetheless note that an individual journalist's characteristics can shape what that reporter thinks is important and that reporter's definition of news. Journalists regularly note how their personal values and outlooks are brought to bear in their professional lives.

Journalists' perceptions about what is news are influenced as much by their personal experiences as by their training and newsroom socialization. In this sense, news content can be highly individualized. "Reporters bring their own expertise to bear-their environment, their heredity, their biases. If you have all males on the campaign, there won't be any questions about abortion rights. If you have no people of colour, you may not get a question about reaction to the beating of Mr. Byrd in Jasper," said Ann Scales, an African-American reporter for the Boston Globe who covered the Gore campaign during the 2002 presidential election.

While Scales points out how who she is affects how she does her job, Louise Knott Ahern, the education reporter at the Riverside, California, Press-Enterprise, suggests that core personal values are intrinsically tied to her professional behaviour. "...[I]f you're not going to be an ethical person in your life, you're not going to be an ethical journalist. Do you cheat on your taxes repeatedly? Do you find kids smoking pot, and say, 'Way to go, Johnny'? You know? You're not going to be an ethical journalist. If you're not that way in life, you're not going to be that way in your reporting." The approach that a reporter takes to a story and the series of decisions she makes regarding what facts are newsworthy and what facts can be ignored-her "bias," some would say-are "the inevitable consequence of the combinations of one's experience and inbred nature."

While much research has been conducted independently on value theory and on the roles that journalists see for themselves in society, few efforts have been made to explore the link between the two. However, both bodies of research represent different ways of examining the internal forces that drive reporters and editors. Social psychology research suggests that media practitioners operate by constantly reassessing the primacy and relevancy of each within a set of fixed, so-called instrumental values as they are applied to diverse questions. We also can, based on the assumptions about journalistic values that fill the literature of media ethics theory, hypothesize the following:

*H1:* Newspaper journalists who rank the values "Courageous," "Independent," and "Just" highly will endorse an adversarial function of the press.

Based on research that establishes a relationship between values and behaviour, the value systems of journalists help shape how they perceive their function in society. The nature of the adversarial role as defined by Weaver and Wilhoit represents strong support for the watch-dog responsibility of journalism and a "skeptical" outlook, both of which suggest the values of "Courageous" and "Just." Weaver and Wilhoit also concluded that so-called adversarialist journalists placed great value on job autonomy-which, of course, corresponds with the value of "Independence."

*H2:* Newspaper journalists who rank the values "Minimizing harm," "Fair," and "Self-controlled" highly will endorse a disseminator function of the press.

Defining the disseminator role, Weaver and Wilhoit characterized journalists who embraced it as "audience-oriented" and "cautious," which corresponds with the values of "Minimizing harm" and "Self-controlled." The authors also described disseminators as "considerably less accepting of controversial reporting practices, such as posing as someone else or using unauthorized documents," which also suggests the value of "Fair."

*H3:* Newspaper journalists who rank the values "Civic-minded," "Imaginative," and "Capable" highly will endorse an interpretive function of the press.

While Weaver and Wilhoit are less precise in their description of the interpretive role, they suggest that journalists embracing this role express strong support for the concept of the press as a public service, which corresponds with the value "Civic-minded." The interpretive role also presumes a more active approach to the news that calls for a greater use of individual creativity. This suggests that the values of "Imaginative" and "Capable" rank highly for journalists embracing the interpretive role.

This project is based on a nationwide random-sample mail survey, stratified by state, of 600 newspaper journalists conducted in early 2002. The individual journalists constitute two groups: newspaper reporters and newspaper editors, with one of each drawn from each newspaper in a process of stratified random selection. The number of newspapers needed from each state for proportional representation was calculated, with a target total of 300. To prevent the large number of small daily newspapers from being overrepresented, major metro dailies with circulations of 150,000 or more were weighted by assigning each of them two consecutive numbers instead of one, thereby doubling their chances for selection.

A single editor (team editor, metro editor, city editor, managing editor, etc.) and a single reporter were selected using a table of random numbers applied to each group on each newspaper's staff list. These staff lists are commonly available on newspaper Web sites. Phone calls were made to verify the presence of each selected journalist when necessary. The initial mailing was in mid-January 2002, the second mailing was during the third week of January, and a third wave was during the first week of February.

Respondents were presented with a sheet of movable adhesive tabs, each listing one of the 24 values. They were asked to rank them in importance by placing each tab next to one of the printed numbers between 1 and 24. The overall value hierarchy was derived by obtaining the average ranking for each value. The brief descriptors that Rokeach originally used to present each value were retained. To assess respondent positions regarding journalistic roles, reporters and editors were asked to respond to 14 statements on a 5-point Likert scale, with 5 = extremely important, 3 = neither important nor unimportant, and 1 = extremely unimportant.

The survey elicited 355 usable responses from journalists at 239 newspapers, representing a response rate of 59%. Respondents ranged from neophyte reporters just on the job at small rural papers for a few months to veteran executive and managing editors at some of the country's largest metro dailies. With one exception, the demographic makeup of this study's respondents does not deviate dramatically from what Voakes found in 1997 and Weaver and Wilhoit found in 1994. Women made up 48.7% of respondents in this study, compared with 37% for Voakes and 34% for Weaver and Wilhoit. Whites made up 94% of the respondents, while Blacks constituted 3.2% and Hispanics 1.4%.

## A PROFILE OF JOURNALISTIC VALUES

The profile of journalists' instrumental values that emerges from the survey places a strong emphasis on a mix of competency-based and morality-oriented concepts, much of which would be expected to describe the professional outlook of journalists. Three respondents did not rank the values but completed other sections of the survey, giving the value rankings a total of 352 valid responses. An analysis of this journalistic value hierarchy has been reported elsewhere; this study, however, focuses on the value rankings as they are related to journalistic role conceptions.

"Honest" was ranked the most important value by far by most journalists; more than one-third of all journalists ranked it first, and another sixty-two journalists ranked it second. More journalists ranked "Honest" in either one of those positions than all other positions combined. "Honest" was followed by "Fair." Roughly half of all journalists placed this value in one of the top three spots. Those two morally oriented values were followed by two values that Rokeach related to the concept of competency: "Responsible" and "Capable." Nearly one-half of the journalists ranked "Responsible" at positions two through five.

When testing his original list of instrumental values on different populations, Rokeach said the average intercorrelation among the rankings for all the instrumental values was -.06, which suggested that each of the values could be considered discrete, valid measures for different concepts. While several of the original values do significantly correlate with each other due to an intrinsic parallelism of the concepts involved (i.e., "Responsible" and "Self-controlled"), the intercorrelations for the rankings of the original values by journalists in this project mirror intercorrelations that Rokeach found in his general-population studies.

To Rokeach's 18 values, 6 others were added for this study to reflect the most predominant values commonly found in the media ethics literature: "Fair," "Just," "Aboveboard," "Empathetic," "Minimizing harm," and "Civic-minded." The 6 journalistic-oriented values added by this project also show negligible intercorrelations, with averages ranging from -.03 to -.059, suggesting that each of the added values is in fact measuring additional concepts and not simply other dimensions of values already listed. Among the 18 instrumental values, the highest negative intercorrelation Rokeach found was -.38.

Roles Embraced by Journalists. Responses to 14 journalistic "function" statements generally correspond to what Weaver and Wilhoit found in their survey ten years ago, with some notable differences that may be due to changes in cultural and professional emphases over that time period. The response rate for this final section of the instrument was slightly lower, at 53% (N = 328).

Most of the role-conception items were from Weaver and Wilhoit and can be grouped into the authors' factors of the predominant "interpretive," "disseminator," and "adversarial" functions. Journalists gave "Get information to the public quickly" the highest overall average. They gave "be less critical of officials during national crisis" the lowest, at 2.3, closely followed by "set the political agenda" at 2.6.

This study's three hypotheses predicted that journalists who rank particular values as highly salient also would embrace certain journalistic role conceptions over others. Specifically, Hl predicted that journalists ranking "Courageous," "Independent," and "Just" highly would endorse an adversarial role; H2 predicted that those ranking "Minimizing harm," "Fair," and "Self-controlled" high would endorse a disseminator function; and H3 predicted that those ranking "Civic-minded," "Imaginative," and "Capable" high would endorse an interpretive role.

The predicted relationships did not produce significant Spearman's rho correlations, so data analysis did not show support for Hl and H2. Spearman's correlations also did not appear to provide immediate support for H3. While the survey included several statements used by Weaver and Wilhoit as indicators of the degree to which journalists embraced the adversarial, disseminator, and interpretive functions of the press, only the two statements associated with the adversarial role ("Be skeptical of public officials" and "Be skeptical of corporations") produced a Cronbach's alpha (.95) strong enough to constitute an index.

A linear regression model showed some support for H3 when accounting for the demographic variables. H3 hypothesized that journalists who ranked the values "Civic-minded," "Imaginative," and "Capable" highly also would be more likely to embrace the interpretive function of the press. In the regression model, the individual values served as the predictor variables and the role-conception statements served as the dependent variables. For one of the interpretive-function statements, "Influencing public opinion," the value "Civic-minded" proved to be a significant predictor of some of the variance, with a modest yet significant change in the r-square (.025).

Years spent in journalism also were a good predictor in explaining some of the variance in the extent to which journalists embraced the statement, "Influencing public opinion." The longer journalists were in the profession, the more likely they were to support that statement. The models also showed that the same demographic variables of age and years in journalism produced significant r-square changes for two of the four statements associated with the interpretive function: "Providing analysis and interpretation of complex problems" (.022), and "Discussing national policy while it is still being developed" (.015).

The journalism ethics literature is rich with speculation on the values of journalists, both what people believe they are and what they ought to be; the results of this survey provide a quantitative profile of journalists' actual value systems, which offers a more solid ground on which to theorize about how journalists should conduct themselves. The profile simultaneously points to areas where the theory of media ethics and the practice of newspaper journalism converge as well as to wide gulfs between the hierarchy of values that journalists have and the approach that ethicists say journalists ought to take to their jobs.

Several patterns emerge between the values and journalists' assessments of various roles and functions. The two statements that constitute the adversarial role ("Being constantly skeptical of actions taken by public officials" and "Being constantly skeptical of actions by businesses and corporations") are both positively correlated with "Above-board" and "Broadminded," and negatively correlated with "Polite." Again, this indicates the immense importance placed on the need for credibility (though not necessarily civility) among those journalists who take the watchdog role as their primary function.

A third statement that could be considered a measure of the adversarial-oriented role, "Being less critical of public officials during a national crisis," was negatively correlated with "Fair," "Imaginative," and "Independent," and positively correlated with "Responsible." The more that journalists indicated that government should be supported in times of national crisis, the less highly they ranked the values of "Fair" and "Independent." While the correlations are relatively weak, they are significant, indicating some relationship. At the same time, journalists who ranked "Responsible"-as well as "Obedient"-highly appeared to indicate that being less critical during crises was part of what it means to be a responsible journalist. Only one of the two statements ("Getting information to the public quickly") associated with the disseminator role was significantly correlated with any of the values.

Journalists appear to hold a deep ambivalence toward the so-called interpretive function of the press. While the values such as "Broadminded" and "Courageous" are positively correlated with several of the statements ("Providing analysis and interpretation of complex problems" and "Investigating claims and statements made by the government"), "Responsible" is negatively correlated with the first statement, suggesting that journalists remain uncomfortable with being perceived in any way as activists.

In addition to these three journalistic role conceptions, the 1992 survey data by Weaver and Wilhoit as well as the 2002 survey data by Weaver, Beam, and colleagues suggested the emergence of a fourth role-that of "populist mobilizer," which "developed and channeled" the public's interest in intellectual and cultural issues after grabbing audience attention.

Several statements served to assess support for this role, including "Setting the public agenda," "Developing intellectual and cultural interests of the public," and "Giving ordinary people a chance to express their views on public affairs." Weaver and Wilhoit concluded that the support among journalists for these statements was "tantalizing evidence that the spirit of the 'public journalism' movement may have established a foothold."

Correlations between the mobilizer statements and the value rankings in this project seem to provide qualified confirmation of this. The value "Civic-minded" is positively correlated with the statement, "Developing intellectual and cultural interests of the public." However, even here journalists appear to shy away from any behaviour that might smack of advocacy: The value "Fair" was negatively correlated with another mobilizer statement, "Setting the public agenda," and none of the values was correlated with a third statement, "Giving ordinary people a chance to express their views on public affairs."

While results yielded little support for the study's specific hypotheses, the data clearly suggest some connection between journalists' value hierarchies and the roles that they embrace. The results also suggest that these two overlapping realms require further research. The survey instrument used here could be applied to broadcast and Internet-based journalists as well, providing potentially valuable comparative profiles. Similar comparisons can be explored regarding journalistic role conceptions among different groups of journalists as well as differences in how these roles are perceived by journalists and the general public.

Several suggestive relationships between journalistic values and roles emerge from this study. But given the research that has explored at length the forces of newsroom socialization the relationships are surprisingly weak ones. While previous research has suggested that social control in the newsroom is a strong shaper both of the values that guide their work and how journalists perceive their function in society, this study suggests that newsroom socialization does not exert a strong influence on general values, or vice versa, given the weak correlations between role priorities and the value rankings. Rather than consider values-whether general or specifically journalistic-as products of a singular newsroom socialization dynamic, research may need to differentiate the various "environments" in which particular values and role conceptions are formed. Values, beliefs, and behaviour interact, as Voakes suggests, in "a dynamic swirl of social factors."

It seems likely that journalistic role priorities are influenced more by the newsroom environment and professional socialization, whereas more general values are shaped by family, religious, and cultural environments. Also, while the value profile of newspaper journalists that emerges is valuable and suggests many different applications, this study also illustrates the difficulty in assigning such broad, generalized values to specific behaviours.

Several associations that emerge in this study are worth considering. The value profile established in this study elaborates upon-and in some cases contradicts-what journalists have reported regarding self-perceptions of their professional roles. Weaver and Wilhoit concluded in their 1992 study that 51% of journalists reported that the disseminator role was "very important," 63% reported that the interpretive role was "very important," and 18% placed a similarly high priority on the adversarial role.

However, just as interesting is the finding that the data showed more correlations among the top six values and the two statements associated with the adversarial role-being skeptical of government and being skeptical of business-than with any other set of role conception statements. And in all, the adversarial role statements were correlated to ten of the values ranked by journalists. While these correlations are somewhat weak by objective standards, they are among the stronger correlations in the data, and they are statistically significant. They also may reflect the recent findings by Weaver, Beam, and colleagues that more journalists placed importance on the watchdog function of the press in 2002 than in 1992.

The emphasis on the adversarial role also is underscored by the frequency with which five values in particular - "Broadminded," "Fair," "Courageous," "Imaginative," and "Independent" - correlate with various role statements that suggest a watchdog function. Two of those values rank among the top six. In fact, among the entire list of twenty-four values, the adversarial role is linked to more values than any other role, based on correlations between these values and the two role statements that indicate support for the watchdog function. In total, the adversarial role is linked to five values, while the disseminator role is linked to only three ("Capable," "Fair," and "Responsible").

The interpretive role, which Weaver and Wilhoit found

to be most widely endorsed by journalists, is linked to only two values ("Broadminded" and "Courageous"), and both of those are values where the adversarial role also shows strength. In other words, journalists may disavow the public notion of an over-aggressive journalist, yet they consider such a watch-dog function as critical to what constitutes being a credible journalist. However, like the research by Weaver and Wilhoit, this study finds those sometimes contradictory roles that journalists endorse-and the underlying values that are their foundations-can be held simultaneously.

The role conceptions research and this value profile both speak to the internal forces that drive journalists. This study reveals some intriguing links between the two approaches. What remains unclear is how the two interact, and to what extent journalists' values and role perceptions influence how they go about the daily job of reporting and presenting the news.

Clarifying these relationships in future research will require revisiting some theoretical constructs used in this study to represent values and roles. It is obvious, for instance, that the "Civic-minded" value triggered possibly negative associations with public journalism in the minds of some journalists, rather than the idea thatjournalists have a role in the cultivation and maintenance of community. Additionally, the theoretical linkages between some of the findings that were not initially hypothesized should be put to test in future studies. More importantly, however, this study points up the need for more research that brings to bear value theory and social psychology on the profession of journalism and the journalists themselves.

## Chapter 13

# Operationalizing and Analyzing Exposure

Measurement or manipulation of exposure is the foundation of research examining effects of mediated information such as news, music videos, Internet sites, and advertising. It is equally fundamental to studies of intentional influences on that environment such as behaviour change communication campaigns. Our ability to test theory and to establish media or campaign effects is a function of our ability to successfully manipulate or measure exposure to mediated communication, and to analyse effects of that exposure.

Exposure, in principle, is a straightforward concept. McGuire's information processing model, for example, distinguishes exposure as the prerequisite for subsequent attention, comprehension, and retention. Accordingly, we may define exposure as the extent to which audience members have encountered specific messages or classes of messages/media content. However, operationalizing such a definition is a messy business. This definition says exposure refers to a person's merely encountering the messages, whether or not they are noticed enough to be remembered.

After all, noticing the relevant messages in the communication environment is almost certainly confounded with variables that may predict attention to the content of that message, such as prior knowledge or involvement with the topic. It is also quite possible that exposure may leave an affective if not a cognitive impression of some kind, even if the messages have not been attended to well enough to be remembered. However, if messages are not processed thoroughly enough to be recalled, how can exposure be self-reported? As a result, operations for exposure either take the conservative position of estimating exposure from the possibility of exposure, absorbing the error associated with not actually encountering the messages of interest, or use various techniques to obtain self-reports of exposure, and then use various strategies to control the effects of selective attention due to prior knowledge or involvement which would otherwise undermine causal claims.

Each available approach involves significant trade-offs and uncertainties. Some of these strategies have recently been evolved or incorporated into studies of exposure, making a critical review of methods used to study exposure effects timely.

## USING SELF-REPORT MEASURES OF EXPOSURE

The most straightforward way to assess people's exposure to mediated communication is to ask them. Given the thousands of messages and other mediated content to which an individual is exposed in a month, the accuracy of such recall is often problematic.

Since exposure to messages and media is, outside of the research lab, volitional and self-selected given prior knowledge, involvement, and other variables typically associated also with outcomes of interest, the direction of causality is also problematic. The task of the media effects researcher using self-report measures is to minimize these problems insofar as possible. The issues with respect to such operations are well-recognized and will therefore be only briefly reviewed here.

## GLOBAL SELF-REPORT

One may simply ask respondents how often they watch the news, play "first-person shooter" video games, or listen to conservative talk-show radio programming. Perhaps the best-known, though widely criticized, example of such analysis is found in early cultivation research in which amount of television viewing was correlated with fears concerning crime and violence. Problems include the lack of specificity regarding the actual content of media exposure represented by global self-report, which would result in underestimates of effect sizes and lack of control for third-variables and reverse causality. One strategy to address effect size problems is to increase specificity of exposure measures.

Asking about frequency of watching specific crime dramas and reality cop shows is more precise than asking about overall TV viewing if one is interested in effects of violent TV content.

Specificity of media exposure measures should include separate measurement of media types (such as television, radio, and newspapers) as well as of media content. Another approach to obtaining detailed information about specific media use is media diaries. Respondents are asked to record all of their use of specified media over some time frame. Problems include motivating respondents to provide complete and accurate record keeping, and the time-consuming task of coding and entering data from such diaries.

A primary weakness in the use of global self-report measures is the inevitable uncertainty concerning the exact nature of the relevant content of the media to which respondents report exposure. This uncertainty can largely be removed when content analyses of those media are conducted in conjunction with the survey of exposure self-reports. Such content analyses permit quantification of specific elements of media content, such as valence of coverage, sources used, and ethnicity of people portrayed. This should facilitate more precise theoretical specifications of mechanisms as well as increasing predictive power. The claim that one has characterized the content of a medium is only convincing, however, insofar as one has successfully defined a corresponding population of messages and has randomly sampled or taken a census of those messages.

## RECALL AND RECOGNITION

More precise than global exposure self-reports, but also

more resource-intensive, are exposure self-reports that involve the recognition or recall of specific messages. In recognition measures, messages (or sometimes verbal descriptions of specific messages) are presented to the respondent.

In recall measurement, the respondent is asked to describe content of messages that he or she has seen, which then must be analysed by coders to assess the accuracy and completeness of recall.

To use these methods, one must have a relatively small population of messages from which to sample test messages (for recognition measures) or against which to compare open-ended recall measures.

Such approaches, then, are typically more appropriate for the evaluation of specific media-based campaigns than for studies of the existing media environment, unless one is interested in the impact of specific programs, articles, or other messages. In general, recognition measures appear to be preferred over recall for several reasons.

Coding of free or cued recall is time-consuming, difficult, and error-prone. More important, people who process messages with relatively little attention are likely not to remember them in the context of a free recall task, but are more likely to recognize them. Therefore, recognition measures are probably less confounded with variables related to attention such as prior interest in the topic than are recall measures, and therefore are closer to the conceptual definition of exposure.

One of the principal problems of recognition measures, however, is the tendency of people to report recognizing messages that they in fact have never seen. The primary reason is probably respondent uncertainty: people are exposed to a great many messages on most topics, and it is easy to mistake a message presented in a recognition task with other rather similar messages that one may have seen. Other possible reasons include social desirability-the belief by a respondent that he or she "should" have seen the message-or simply response set when other messages in a test group are in fact recognizable.

A simple strategy for handling this problem is through use of foils or ringers. These are messages that could plausibly have been of the type being tested, but were never shown and are different enough from messages actually shown that legitimate confusion is unlikely.

Recognition of foils can be used as a statistical control for response set and social desirable response bias; analysis of foils in a treatment/control design also suggests that simply using a "might have seen" response category, and coding it as "never seen," can reduce error due to false recognition. Analysis of foils/ringers and "maybe" responses are useful for reducing the impact of false recognition, social desirability, and response set, but they do not address underlying problems concerning direction of causation, third variable explanations, and selective exposure.

## THE DOSE-RESPONSE PROBLEM AND USE OF COVARIATES

As Hornik points out, the relationship of amount of exposure to media effects is a key applied question, on which the expenditure of many millions may depend. Establishing a "dose-response" relationship between exposure and outcomes also goes a long way towards validating the effect of a class of messages.

Unfortunately, in field contexts amount of exposure is self-selected, not manipulated. Exposure is typically a mediating, rather than a truly exogenous, variable: It may be substantially influenced by both baseline scores on an outcome variable and by many possible third variables (also known as endogeneity). Baseline scores can only be effectively controlled in longitudinal research.

Use of statistical controls or covariates can manage third variable problems-to the extent that they are well-measured, that all relevant third-variables are identified and incorporated into the model, and that no variables are mistakenly included as covariates when in fact they are mediators of effects. This ideal scenario can only be approximated, and there is always a substantial degree of uncertainty concerning the appropriateness of one's choices of control variables. Moreover, large numbers of covariates make for cumbersome models that use up degrees of freedom and statistical power (overparameterization), and can only accurately account for variables with a linear relationship to the outcome variable.

One statistical method recently applied to exposure studies in the evaluation of the National Youth Media Anti-Drug Campaign is the use of propensity scoring. This was done because this government-sponsored campaign was national in scope and begun before the evaluation began. Absent control groups, control over exposure levels, or a baseline, evaluators were dependent on assessing dose-response effects while trying to control for all the many variables that might predict variation in exposure to campaign advertising. Propensity scoring involves building a statistical model predicting the likelihood of a given level of exposure from a variety of exogenous variables that are likely to be related to exposure.

A single vector can be calculated from this model and applied to adjusting the outcome of interest for this propensity to be exposed. This strategy has a number of desirable statistical qualities. Analyses are not encumbered with a long series of control variables-even if hundreds of covariates are incorporated in the model used to create the propensity score, only one propensity weighting must be used in adjusting a given analysis. Moreover, propensity scores do not assume a linear relation to the outcome as covariates do, and can be balanced over levels of the outcome variable.

Propensity scoring, then, addresses the degrees of freedom and linearity problems with covariate analyses, but remains as dependent as traditional covariate analyses on identifying all key third variables and measuring them with a minimum of error. Moreover, researchers using propensity scoring may be especially prone to inadvertently using mediators as covariates, because there is no price paid in statistical power or model complexity by adding in additional variables to the propensity score model.

A critical assumption when covariates are used is that they are all exogenous-that is, none of them in fact serve as mediators of exposure effects. For example, in political communication, one might want to use political discussion as a covariate, under the assumption that it might predict exposure to political coverage in the media as one seeks out information to use in such discussions. However, if effects of political coverage are mediated by political discussions (which might, for example, encourage incorporation of new information learned from the media into knowledge structures), then its use as a covariate or as part of propensity scoring might help eliminate media effects that in fact are present.

## MANAGING PROBLEMS OF CAUSALITY USING LONGITUDINAL ANALYSES OF EXPOSURE

### CAUSALITY AND ENDOGENEITY

The problem of reverse or reciprocal causality (or the endogeneity of exposure) is, as noted above, a fundamental challenge in most media effects questions. Research in selectivity suggests people are likely to seek out, process attentively, and remember information that interests or is relevant to them.

These selectivity m echanisms, then, are likely to increase self-report of exposure to a given type or class of messages. For example, consumer research shows that people who have an interest in a type of product are more likely to report having seen such advertising, more aggressive youth are more likely to seek out violent media content, and more politically involved people process mediated information with more attention.

One cannot ascertain in cross-sectional data whether exposure items are measuring exposure, or salience of the type of information conveyed to people predisposed to seek out and recall such information. For example, in political communication, cross-sectional studies that link exposure to political knowledge may inflate the strength of such relationships. People who have an interest in and are knowledgeable about politics are probably more likely to seek out and recall mediated information, as well as having such mediated information increase their knowledge.

Conversely, youth exposed to an anti-drug advertising campaign may be more likely to notice and recall such messages if they are experimenting with or using drugs, which would militate against finding favorable impacts of exposure in cross-sectional data.

In fact, one might state as a general principle that cross-sectional analyses that assume unidirectionality exaggerate the relationship between exposure and outcomes when the messages are consistent with the outcome, and underestimate it when the messages-as in many health prevention contexts-are intended to decrease a behavioural or attitudinal outcome of interest that may in turn be predictive of attention to the message.

The true relationships cannot be estimated with confidence. Structural equation models or instrumental variables may be used with cross-sectional data to estimate reciprocal paths. Causal models of cross-sectional data can provide useful initial evidence regarding the relative strength of reciprocal relationships, but can hardly be regarded as providing definitive evidence.

## LONGITUDINAL ANALYSES, SELECTIVE EXPOSURE, AND CAUSALITY

One approach to reducing these problems is to use longitudinal data analysis. Studying longitudinal effects of exposure on change in political knowledge or marijuana use, controlling for prior levels of knowledge or use, is more convincing with respect to causal influence than are cross-sectional analyses, as one can control the time-ordering of effects and the influence of prior scores on the outcome measures; in other words, one is testing the effects of exposure on change in the outcome variable.

The simple use of lagged prediction, however, may not go far enough; the contribution of selective exposure may be to some extent controlled (insofar as it is captured by the influence of baseline scores on the outcome variable), but it is still not understood unless it is explicitly modeled. Use of longitudinal data permits comparisons, for example, of nested structural models positing selective exposure effects versus selective exposure plus media effects paths.

In such models, model fit for a stability model plus the lagged selective exposure effect can be assessed. Fit can then be reassessed with the lagged media effect path added, and a chi-square difference test computed to ascertain whether adding the media effect path or paths to the selective exposure paths resulted in a statistically significant improvement in model fit.

Cross-lagged panel regressions, however, have been criticized as being statistically inferior to growth curve models. Growth curve models focus on analyzing individual respondents' developmental trajectories in a longitudinal data set, and identify coefficients for averaged trajectories that can serve as variables in a regression or structural equation model. Multi-level growth curve models can also separate out effects of "trait" and "state" components of predictor variables, which can be important in analyzing effects of media exposure.

For example, the author and colleagues used multi-level growth curve models to test the "downward spiral" hypothesis that while aggressiveness in adolescents tends to increase use of violent media content (selective exposure), this exposure would reinforce that aggressiveness (media effects).

Use of the multi-level model made it possible to look in particular at effects of variation in aggressiveness over time and not simply at aggressiveness as a trait, which is less likely to be subject to media influence. By modeling both selectivity and media effects, using either growth curve or more familiar cross-lagged models, one can move beyond simplistic discussions of competing causal directions and specify ways selectivity and effects of exposure to media content may reinforce each other or cancel effects out.

Instrumental Variable Approaches. Still another approach

to improving causal inference in pre-post and other longitudinal designs is to utilize instrumental variables, a technique widely used in econometric analyses.

Instrumental variables in the present context are variables that are associated with exposure but not with the outcome of interest. A classic hypothetical example would be an international development effort in which some members of the population are blocked from receiving a radio broadcast because of a mountain blocking radio reception.

Area of residence-if not confounded with income, social status occupation, and so on in ways that might also be related to outcomes of interest-can then serve as an instrumental variable estimating relationships between exposure and outcome, and exposure-outcome relationships can be estimated using two-stage least squares methods, irrespective of possible reciprocal relationships between exposure and outcome.

The problem is that it is often difficult or impossible to identify variables strongly predictive of exposure that are conceptually and empirically independent of the outcome of interest. As a result, exposure studies using instrumental variables to control endogeneity are at best a rarity.

## THE PROBLEM OF LAGGED EXPOSURE EFFECTS

There are significant challenges to analyzing exposure using lagged longitudinal analyses, besides logistical issues such as cost, confidentiality, and respondent mortality. Effects of message exposure may be short-lived. If so, longitudinal lags (typically one-half year or more) may be too long to detect lagged effects of message exposure, especially for a message processed incidentally and with little attention, such as with advertising.

A more sensitive way to capture the effects of message exposure, especially regarding short-lived effects as in the case of advertising, is to use time-series analyses. Such analyses, however, are most effective when exposure measures are not dependent on self-report, and therefore are discussed later.

## EXPOSURE AND ATTENTION: CONCEPTUAL AND ANALYTIC ISSUES

McGuire's information-processing model of persuasion highlights exposure and attention as the two prerequisite conditions for message influence. Some media effects research treats these variables as additive, controlling for exposure before analyzing the effects of attention. Other research argues that effects of exposure should be weighted by attention,

The latter argument is attractive at first glance. Certainly, it is likely that the degree to which exposure affects an individual is a function of the amount of attention that individual pays to the message. However, this is also methodologically problematic. Attention is inherently confounded with the prior knowledge, interest, and attitudes that give rise to attention.

Such prior variables might independently be related to the outcome of interest independent of exposure. Weighting exposure by attention might produce effects that are primarily due to attention's antecedents, not exposure. Moreover, there are serious statistical questions raised by using multiplicative terms without using the additive terms in the same model. If such an approach is to be explored, use of the main effect terms as well as the weighted term is to be recommended.

## ESTIMATING EXPOSURE FROM THE POSSIBILITY OF EXPOSURE

An alternative to exposure self-report measurement is to identify or manipulate the possibility of exposure to a set of messages in a given population. The classic way to do this is through experimental manipulation in a laboratory setting or in the field. Experimental manipulation, however, is not the only way to study possible exposure. One may use instead reach and frequency, using the traditional media planning terminology.

Studies of advertising can take advantage of data concerning amount, type,, and placement of advertising available (at non-trivial cost) from Nielsen and other market research firms. If one is working in cooperation with advertisers, as in the evaluation of a counter-advertising campaign, one can use media buy records to identify levels of possible exposure. Conceptual and methodological problems with respect to using each of these methods to operationalize exposure are discussed below.

## EXPERIMENTAL MANIPULATIONS OF EXPOSURE

Of course, the only certain way to demonstrate causal relationships between exposure to media content and subsequent effects is through experimental designs. There are good reasons, though, that such studies do not fully dominate the media effects field. The following briefly reviews the problems and opportunities associated with experimental manipulations of exposure.

## LABORATORY EXPERIMENT

Experimentation is well understood by social scientists, but it may be useful to note issues that have particular impact in research on effects of exposure to mediated messages. For example, the complexities of selective exposure, information clutter and competition, the casualness with which much information is processed in real-world settings, the social contexts in which messages are received and discussed, and the cumulative effects of exposure to many hundreds or thousands of messages over a period of years cannot typically be reproduced in the laboratory. Experiments build theory and help elucidate processes, but these theories and models must be tested in the social environment as well.

The choice and presentation of message stimuli to which research participants are exposed in particular pose difficult problems. There has also been considerable debate over how possible it is to cleanly manipulate message variables, and the appropriate ways to analyse message differences in an experiment.

Several researchers have argued that the key distinction is between true manipulation of a message (e.g., varying the source attribution) and operationalizing a message variable by presenting participants with various exemplars of different types of messages, such as humorous versus fear-inducing advertisements.

There is some consensus that in the latter case at least random effect models are appropriate, as the message variable has been operationalized through selection of examples rather than through a crossed experimental manipulation. Use of random sampling to create a pool of experimental stimuli to be used in an experiment more closely approximates the real media environment, and results in a more ecologically valid operationalization of exposure than would otherwise be the case.

Manipulation of exposure can be made a little less artificial by providing people messages outside of a laboratory environment. For example, some market research firms maintain panels of people who have agreed to serve as research respondents. Respondents can be sent experimental stimuli, thus providing a high degree of control over exposure outside of a lab setting. Similar methods may be possible using respondents recruited through the Internet and then randomly assigned to experimental conditions.

## FIELD EXPERIMENTS AND QUASI-EXPERIMENTS

The gold standard for any study of media or campaign effects is the group randomized trial, in which entire communities are randomly assigned to media treatment and control conditions. The strength of inference such studies make possible is impressive. Communication effects are studied in "real world" community settings, with all the complexities of audience selective exposure and attention, multi-step flow, and community process intact. Communities are in many respects a natural unit of analysis for exposure to mediated communication, as broadcast areas for radio and television, and circulation areas for newspapers, largely correspond with physical communities.

Media markets typically become the necessary unit of randomization in field experiments in which broadcast media or newspapers are involved. As noted earlier, this approach assumes that research participants have been adequately exposed to the message simply because they reside in a media treatment community. Such an assumption makes for a conservative test, given the degree to which exposure depends on access to specific forms of media and selective attention to the messages provided.

The primary difficulty, though, is that the gold standard requires lots of gold. The expense of community intervention trials, such as those using media markets as the unit of randomization, has increased tremendously with the recent expectation that community trials be analysed using clustered or nested analyses in which the primary unit of analysis is the community.

This represents a very serious challenge for researchers. Communication interventions typically have small effect sizes. Such effects are non-trivial given the ability of such campaigns to reach much or most of a population. However, an expectation that such studies should be analysed at the community level of analysis reduces power to detect effects considerably. The costs of community-level media intervention studies precludes in most cases obtaining an adequate number of communities to assure reasonable power. For example, the author and colleagues are currently analyzing results from a field study of 16 communities to test the effects of using media in communities and schools to reduce teen substance use.

Effects on virtually all attitudinal and behavioural outcomes are significant or highly significant when analysed at the individual level (with an N over 3,000); some outcomes of interest, though, no longer remain significant analysed at the community level (N = 16), though fortunately major intention and behaviour treatment effects remain statistically significant even at the community level. Effect sizes even for outcomes that go to non-significant, though, are relatively robust relative to typical campaign interventions.

Group randomized trials, then, have a substantial risk of resulting in Type II error that might mitigate against socially important findings. Sophisticated journals will accept analyses of studies where treatments are applied at the community or institutional level (e.g., schools) that do not conduct a full hierarchical analysis of the data, but normally expect that these analyses are statistically adjusted for community-level or other clustering effects using procedures such as generalized estimating equations.

## CROSS-OVER DESIGNS

Another model-the cross-over quasi-experimental design-has the potential to permit field experimentation in which media markets are used to manipulate exposure, but at a much lower cost than community-randomized designs. Cross-over designs, in which a control group is given the intervention treatment after post-test is completed on the original treatment group in the expectation that an effective treatment should replicate effects on the control group, are commonplace in biomedical research. Indeed, such designs are standard when withholding the treatment entirely raises ethical problems. Such cross-over designs are, unfortunately, a rarity in media effects research. One example is a recent study of anti-marijuana advertising that compared two similar communities in Kentucky and Tennessee, one community exposed to the advertising, one the control.

This would hardly have been considered a publishable design, but for the use of the cross-over procedure. Successful replication of treatment effects in the control community eliminates many alternative explanations for treatment effects, such as uncontrolled variability between communities or history effects. It is conceivable that history effects might have generated experimental effects first in the experimental community and then in the erstwhile control community, while simultaneously lowering effects subsequent to exposure in the original experimental community-but the probability of such a pattern seems small indeed. As noted below, the explanatory power of this cross-over design was also enhanced by the use of time-series data collection.

Cross-over designs using only a few communities exposed and unexposed to a media treatment do not rise to the same unambiguous evidentiary standard as the community-randomized designs described above. However, they provide an attractive alternative to community-randomized designs to explore important research questions that would otherwise be impossible to study rigorously in the field given resource constraints, or when ethical or political considerations require that communities receive equivalent treatment exposure.

## TRACKING STUDIES AND OTHER TIME-SERIES ANALYSES

Another technique in the cross-over study of anti-marijuana advertising was the use of rolling cross-sectional data collection and interrupted time-series data analysis to assess exposure effects. Rolling cross-sections involve collection of data at regular, closely spaced time points, such as every week or every month, typically over at least 30 or more points in time. Interrupted time-series can be used to statistically test for the effect of an intervention in changing the slope of the outcome behaviour as plotted against time. Such analyses can also potentially be used to estimate the "half-life" of message effects and, if carried out long enough, can identify confounds such as seasonality effects that might otherwise lead to misinterpretation of longitudinal findings.

Face validity of intervention findings are much enhanced when time-series analyses show that desired effects closely follow increasing distribution of and exposure to the messages of interest, and that these effects decay predictably when message exposure is withdrawn.

Rolling cross-sectional data collections and the resulting time-series data sets are known in the advertising industry as tracking studies. Tracking studies take advantage of a unique aspect of paid advertising campaigns: precise knowledge, on a week-to-week basis, of advertising placements and the consequent reach and frequency, or possible exposure, of the communication effort. Typically, tracking studies have modest objectives, testing for ad and brand recall and recognition to ascertain whether expenditures are achieving expected levels of awareness.

However, such studies can also be used to assess impacts on self-reports of attitudes and behaviours. Causality in such analytic models is relatively unambiguous, as exposure can be measured exogenously, using Gross Rating Points (GRPs) or other measures of exposure inputs, and not through exposure self-report. It is also possible to use self-report measures of exposure in time-series analyses; however, assertions about causal direction are much weaker when self-report measures of exposure are used than when reach and frequency measures operationalize exposure. The assumption that messages placed were actually seen is an uncertain one, but should lead to conservative estimates of effects free from selectivity and other confounds.

Another approach to the use of time-series analyses to investigate exposure effects has been pioneered by David Fan. Fan and others using similar techniques assume exposure, and link rolling cross-sectional outcome data with rolling cross-sectional content analyses. The latter poses significant logistic challenges, which have been addressed through computerized content analytic strategies using key terms to identify stories on a topic and the valence of the story. AP wire stories represent the media environment. Time-series analytic techniques are applied to test the association of fluctuations in amount and valence of media coverage with fluctuations in relevant public opinion polling that is carried out in an on-going way.

Such an approach has limitations. The AP wire is an imperfect indicator of all U.S. media coverage. There is no measurement of individual-level exposure to such news as a mediator of coverage effects on attitudes or behaviour-again, this method focuses on possible versus actual or self-reported exposure. It is possible that third variables may drive both coverage and behaviour (though this possibility can be tested through examination of evidence for a slight lag in exposure effects on outcomes).

Many of these limitations, however, should increase conservativeness of findings. The more serious limitation is that these techniques can only be employed for exposure to media for which on-line sources over time are readily available, and for outcomes that are tracked regularly through on-going surveys. When such studies are an option, however, they permit exceptionally robust inference concerning real-world effects of media exposure on national populations.

The array of designs and analytic techniques available to study effects of media exposure permits convincing inferences when results triangulate across methods. This is illustrated in particularly concise and dramatic fashion in a recent meta-analysis of media violence studies, in which studies are separated by method, variation in effect size by method indicated, and the overall convergence of effects shown.

Media effects theories are theories of process, of cause and effect. Longitudinal designs that permit modeling of process over time or field experimental designs that permit unambiguous causal tests are where maturing theories must find their supportive evidence. Longitudinal designs also permit-indeed, they demand-explicit theorizing regarding the role both of selective exposure and media effect. In the realm of media campaigns, rolling cross-sections and time-series analyses offer researchers the opportunity to evaluate campaign impact with a precision that has previously been unattainable, and cross-over designs may increase the viability of quasi-experimental studies.

Simple cross-sectional surveys and small-scale experiments provide excellent opportunities to ascertain if theoretical propositions and hypothesized mechanisms are viable and worthy of further exploration. They are insufficient to test whether these mechanisms operate as hypothesized in the larger social world. Expanded use of more sophisticated designs and methods is necessary if the media effects and campaigns research area is to continue to advance.

# Chapter 14

# Search of a Model

Some commercial television news operations around the United States are moving toward a public journalism model of coverage. Public journalism is a model in which media organizations structure coverage in ways that encourages the democratic process and create connections to diverse communities. "It begins with the understanding that journalists have a fundamental responsibility for strengthening civic culture." It is about making public life go well? The concept of community is used as it is in social network analysis where community means the interconnected relationships among people who share a common goal, neighborhood, and/or relationship. Communities overlap and individuals may be members of multiple communities. For instance, a person can be an active member in a neighborhood, coach little league baseball, and work as a professor.

All of these roles make that person a member of different communities. Thus, diversity of communities can be thought of in racial and ethnic terms, geographically, professionally, and socially. Here communities are developed in the way Fisher studied the network connections among individuals in his book on community structure. Fischer's view of communities is important to public journalism because it facilitates journalists within this structure in thinking about the almost endless ways to represent diverse communities in the news.

## LOCAL TELEVISION NEWS

Underlying the broad goals of public journalism is the

desire to improve the marketplace of ideas through dialogue among citizens; government; and media, in this case television news. In Iyengar terms, it is moving the coverage of a community from the episodic toward the thematic. This involves changing the professional practices of journalists. Bernstein and Lacy studied the contributions of local television news to the marketplace of ideas and found a fairly high amount of government coverage, much of it imported from outside the coverage area.'

Kaniss found that spot news tended to push government and issues out of coverage patterns. Bernstein and Lacy also found smaller television markets tended to provide less contextual information compared to larger markets, though it is not clear what the level of contextual information was for large market stations.

Kaniss said journalists know where to find stories to meet professional values. Tuchman developed the news net metaphor for news coverage to describe how journalists meet professional norms through their routines. She noted that the size and quality of the net determines the size and quality of the stories captured by that net. Gans said ideology is generally excluded from news coverage. However, Fishman points to ideology as an idealized road map for journalists in their work. In many ways, what public journalism attempts to do is improve the quality of this idealized road map.

Money also enters the equation for coverage. McManus found the greater the station's available resources, the more active the journalistic discovery. He noted that even stations with great resources primarily rely on passive means of reporting. But money is not the only concern. Journalists also tend to have different concerns about content than citizens. Crane found television journalists focus more on story format than on quality of content, Berkowitz also found news judgments based on technology concerns, like having good video, in addition to resource concerns. Many of the tenets of public journalism hinge on helping journalists improve active discovery outside of the newsroom and have citizens as the judges of quality work.

One element missing from the television news literature is a discussion of citizens or community within the newsgathering process. Audience is not a replacement for this, since citizens don't have to be viewers of a particular station or even of television news. The basic understanding of audience ignores the individual's role in multiple communities and the value of community connections.

Community connections serve two important purposes for journalists. They allow story ideas to be generated through citizens at the community level (often referred to as bubbling-up from the community) and they help journalism organizations present information more accurately by more accurately reflecting the reality of the community represented in the news story.

These efforts vary across stations by level of commitment, allocation of resources, station market position, and the conditions under which the station conducts public journalism. Even within divergent levels of public journalism adoption, there are important similarities.

Public journalism, as practiced by television stations, is spread along a broad continuum. It is not possible in this study to explain all of the forms it takes. The best way to gain an understanding of public journalism in a television form is to observe newsrooms and interview the managers and journalists about the way they practice it and their vision for its development. This takes advantage of grounded theory techniques as described by Strauss and Corbin.ts Specifically, it allows emergent categories to inform theory building throughout the research process.

This research compares three station types to better understand the origins and consequences of television news organizations implementing public journalism and how this implementation alters journalistic norms and routines. To a certain degree, comparisons of each type are also being made to non-public stations.

Organizationally, the stations have a commitment to the communities they serve. The stations promote themselves as community leaders with a local focus. Organizations attempting public journalism tend to be among the stations in the ratings race for top position. This may be a function of the resources solid ratings can provide for a station. Thus, the availability of resources is another commonality.

Station market position may also determine the form of public journalism coverage a station adopts. Market position is the focus the station takes in developing its products, in this case news, and promoting those products. Market position may be a key element in understanding the form of public journalism a station is willing to develop. This seems plausible since it takes into account the institutional history at the station. It also acknowledges that dramatic changes in how the station presents its chosen image to the audience is unlikely, since images are generally developed more gradually and purposefully.

Four basic market positions were evident in this research. A public affairs position is one where the station focuses on government processes and civic issues. Community service stations create an image of being helpful and friendly in the community, often sponsoring charity events and giving news coverage to these events and groups. Crime and disaster stations promote their ability to capture hard news quickly and without a lot of extraneous material. Often crime and disaster stories are imported from other areas outside the station's viewing area to fill the newscast with sufficient death and destruction. Stories also tend to be shorter and faster paced, often earning these stations the title "flash and trash" in the industry.

A fourth market position is emerging, though is not fully developed. It is a public journalism market position. These stations focus on enterprise reporting and knowledge of the communities in the coverage area. Stations moving toward the public journalism position pull elements from the issues focus of the public affairs image and the community connections from the community service image. Both of these adopted elements are modified to fit public journalism ideals.

Television markets also may help determine the type of market positions the audience finds acceptable. Certainly, some markets, like Minneapolis, Minnesota, have a stronger civic character that might cause news organizations to more seriously consider a public journalism market position. Other markets may be more parochial, lacking that strong civic culture and thus making it more difficult for a public journalism market position to take hold.

## EXPECTED TYPES OF TELEVISION PUBLIC JOURNALISM

Early in the research process, I observed television newsrooms and conducted preliminary interviews. This exploratory research led to the development of three expected types of public journalism television organizations. The types are integrated station, special projects station, and publicity station. These types categorize the different station approaches to implementing public journalism. These are mutually exclusive types. A station cannot be in more than one category, but a station can conceivably be in a state of transition. These types are not necessarily exhaustive categories, because new types may emerge as visionary news managers further develop public journalism. However, it is significant that these stations chose to move toward a public journalism form of coverage. The value of this research is the development of a model for analyzing how work is accomplished.

The organization and practice of public journalism coverage is important because each model provides a view into the structure of the station, particularly the way newsrooms are organized. Organizational structure and public journalism are not automatically linked, because non-public journalism stations can be organized to gather high quality news, and poor quality stations can do public journalism.

The integrated station incorporates public journalism coverage into its normal daily routines. A current trend in broadcast journalism is for managers to say public journalism is being incorporated into daily coverage. However, this is difficult to accomplish and few stations have any proof of successfully accomplishing that goal. Though elements of public journalism are developed at the individual level, the organizational structure is what makes this development possible.

Organizationally, public journalism is incorporated into daily news in different ways. Sometimes it might be part of a special report or series; on other days it might involve taking a public journalism tack on coverage of a planned news event. Taking advantage of enterprise ideas at daily editorial meetings is the most common method for incorporation of public journalism into the daily mix of news.

The special project station handles public journalism on a project-by project basis. This category is a wide-ranging continuum. Some stations do a single project and abandon public journalism, while others make long-term commitments to the principles of public journalism. Like the integrated station, there is a commitment to public journalism. However, the level of commitment among project-focused stations varies. During the project there is a well-defined role for public journalism in the news operation.

Organizationally, special project stations have a more structured management style. Station managers often dictate the direction of the project work, creating a more formal organizational structure than was found at the integrated stations. At project stations, the work is done on the periphery or even outside the newsroom and is rarely included in any daily work, except for promotional pieces on the day of an event. The focus is trained on a single topic area, which limits the opportunities for crossing over into daily news coverage. The projects are generally conducted over longer periods of time, often several months or even an entire year. Managers are responsible for developing and implementing the project, and there is generally a limited number of news staff involved in the project.

Community outreach is strong, much like at the integrated station; however, many project stations limit the majority of outreach to the project topic. Issues and values discussions are often relegated to the project meetings, limiting the debates to a smaller group within the station. Project stations also tend to have strong station manager support, but fewer middle managers are involved in the process, thus limiting the communication among news staff. This organizational structure limits the opportunity for spillover of public journalism into daily news coverage.

Publicity stations tend to be organizationally structured with a strong centralized management style. Decisions are made at the upper management levels with limited input from workers. The focus in editorial meetings is on logistics of coverage rather than content issues, which were likely to have been decided in earlier management meetings. Meeting involvement is limited to journalists and often only news managers. Community outreach may be significant through the station's community affairs office, but is limited in the newsroom. These stations may conduct some town hall meetings. However, the structure of these meetings was promotionally based and lacked strong attempts to better understand community viewpoints.

Publicity stations focus time and resources on promoting connections to communities. Little effort is placed on actually creating opportunities for journalists to spend time in various communities or creation of meaningful connections. Resources are allocated in such a way that the coverage decisions are made and then, almost as an afterthought, the community labels are put on the elements to promote a non-existent connection.

These are the stations that give public journalism a bad name. They use a few of the tenets of public journalism to attract an audience, often pandering to the audience to accomplish higher ratings. While none of the stations examined in this were publicity stations, one station did appear to be moving toward this category. Publicity stations are not likely to continue as publicity focused public journalism stations for long. Either they will choose to allocate resources to solidify their public journalism work or, more likely, will move on to another quick fix to avoid a loss of viewers and ratings.

## STATION SELECTION

Stations selected for this project cover large, medium, and small markets; included both old-timers and relative newcomers to public journalism work; and cut across a variety of issues from elections to crime to economic problems. This variety is important in thinking about the ways in which public journalism is created and applied by television stations. Most important in the selection of these stations was that they are exemplars of public journalism.

This project is the extension of evaluative work done for the Pew Centre for Civic Journalism. Five of the stations, WISC (CBS affiliate in Madison, Wisconsin), KRON (NBC affiliate in San Francisco, California), WSOC and WBTV (ABC and CBS affiliates respectively in Charlotte, North Carolina), WBNG (CBS affiliate in Binghamton, New York) were selected by the Pew Centre for analysis as varied examples of successful public journalism efforts. I was the researcher who conducted the television data gathering for the Pew project. KVUE and KARE were added for this study because the original sample lacked examples of integrated forms of public journalism.

WISC was included in the sample because it is one of the oldest public journalism projects in the nation. KRON was chosen because it had just completed a successful election project and was beginning to consider extending its effort beyond elections to a project on transportation. That eventually did occur. WSOC was picked because it had completed a strong project with the Charlotte Observer, but was not interested in continuing their efforts at that time. WBTV had just begun to work with the Observer on a new public journalism project on elections, which is why it was included. WBNG might be one of the more interesting stations in this study. While the stations selected include small, medium, and large market sizes, WBNG faced one of the largest challenges in the smallest market doing public journalism successfully at that time. This station was chosen partially because of the parochial nature of the communities it covered.

## FIELD WORK STRUCTURE

This research uses comparative methods to study the patterns across cases. The comparative method has a long tradition in sociological analyses where the number of cases is small but the explanatory value of each case is high. This method stresses the logic of cases instead of the ability to generalize from the data.

The comparative method is particularly good for studying emergent phenomenon, like public journalism. Ragin described the comparative method in his seminal book on the subject as the study of how conditions work together in one setting compared and contrasted to how they fit in a different setting. This method is accepted in the broader social sciences. Though extremely valuable, it has yet to find wide adoption within communications research.

## ETHNOGRAPHIC DATA

The ethnographic fieldwork extended the data in the following ways. First, it provided a sense of the larger organizational structure of the newsroom, specifically on where power lies within the newsroom. Second, it allowed a view into the daily inner workings of the newsroom, a view of processes of completing work on deadline. Third, it provided the opportunity to watch the inter-relationship of employees as they conducted their work. The ethnographic data often helped identify particular employees as important interview subjects or helped develop additional questions for particular interviews. It also provided the basis for understanding the content of the interviews, as well as a general perspective of the overall news operation.

A total of ninety-three interviews were conducted over the course of ten months. Interviews averaged thirty minutes each. All interviews used the same interview protocol and the same approach to data collection. However, the protocol was tailored to address the specific focus of each station. Only one station, WSOC, refused to provide a list of news workers or to allow observation of the newsroom. Some observations were conducted while waiting for journalists and managers I was scheduled to interview who were late for their appointments. These journalists and managers gave examples and information that supported my limited observations of the newsroom in their comments.

The interviews were structured as the "nonscheduled standardized interview" or the "focused interview." The questions were open-ended and offered the ability to leave the interview schedule to explore interesting veins of discussion during the interview. The interviews were recorded and professionally transcribed. The transcribed interviews were analysed using QSR*Nudist 4.0 qualitative analysis software.

## WORKING HYPOTHESES

Four basic working hypotheses were developed for this project. Each addresses a specific area within the larger research question of how implementation of public journalism affects the journalistic and organizational structures within the television station. It is important to remember that in this form of comparative work, hypotheses are developed as expectations of findings rather than quantitatively testable elements. Thus, it is best to think of these working hypotheses as units that focus the research and the areas of analysis.

*H1:* The station's market position prior to attempting public journalism will affect the form of public journalism selected at the station. Stations with a community service or public affairs market position are expected to engage in higher levels of commitment to public journalism.

*H2:* The organizational structure at the station will dictate the level of acceptance of public journalism at the station. Stations with more decentralized newsrooms are expected to more readily adapt to public journalism forms of coverage.

*H3:* Managers who can lead through providing a vision of what they are developing for the future will implement public journalism forms of news coverage without disruption of traditional journalistic norms and routines.

*H4:* Over time, the level of station commitment, both in prioritizing coverage efforts and allocating resources to public journalism, will determine the type and format of public journalism undertaken by the station. Note that commitment and execution of public journalism operate to a certain level of independence. Thus, it is possible to have a high level of commitment to a basic format of public journalism. It is also possible for a station to have a limited commitment to a complex public journalism project. However, neither of these scenarios is expected to last long, since the lack of balance of resources to complexity of endeavor is likely to kill the effort.

## STATIONS STUDIED

Site visits and resulting interview and ethnographic data supported two of the three main types. The only type not found was the publicity station and that is likely due to the selection criteria focus on the most successful stations conducting various forms of public journalism. However, one station and possibly another may be moving toward this third type. The following, section describes the types of stations and the public journalism they do based on the data.

## SPECIAL PROJECT STATIONS

By far the largest group in this study was the project station. Six stations fit in this category. The greatest range of public journalism is also within this category. Some project stations had a long-term commitment to public journalism, while others were simply testing the waters. The greatest transition of stations in this study was found in the group that showed a limited-term commitment to public journalism. There is no clear predictor as to the direction a station might go after the initial test project. Some stations stopped doing public journalism after the initial project, while at other stations managers decided to make a longer-term commitment.

Three stations, Charlotte's WSOC-TV and WBTV-TV, and WCCO-TV in Minneapolis, were categorized as a limited-term project stations for this research. Both Charlotte stations partnered with the Charlotte Observer newspaper for different projects, at slightly different times. WSOC-TV called the project "Carolina Crime Solutions," while the newspaper used the title, "Taking Back Our Neighborhoods."

The newspaper carried the larger share of the burden, but recognized the greater reach a partnership offered into the communities involved in the project. WSOC's news director made it clear that they would consider other projects, but that this was a self-contained effort. The majority of the news staff was not involved in the project. This station has since moved away from public journalism and might be moving toward a publicity station, if anything at all.

WBTV worked on election coverage with the Charlotte Observer. The station's involvement was largely limited to the acting news director and the station's political reporter. Other stations from across the state were also part of this project, but were not included in this research study. Primarily the acting news director, who was committed to the public journalism goals, orchestrated WBTV's effort. It was apparent during the research visit that the commitment would wane if the acting news director were not involved. She has since left the station.

WCCO-TV has a historically strong commitment to conducting town hall meetings with citizens, which is one of the tenets of public journalism work. The data collected from those sessions by the station show some elements of publicity-focused stations, in addition to the civic-minded work. During the course of this fieldwork, WCCO abandoned the "Feedback 4" community meeting sessions and moved toward strictly image-building efforts in the newscasts, with one exception.

The station continued to compete in long-form journalism, which the station promoted as the "Dimension" report. This news product continued to develop elements to public journalism in the coverage routines, though the community connections built during previous town hall meetings appeared to be diminished.

Three longer-term project stations included WISC-TV in Madison, Wisconsin, KRON-TV in San Francisco, California, and WBNG-TV in Binghamton, New York. While this research was being conducted, these stations were continuing their commitments to public journalism projects.

WISC is one of the grandfathers of television public journalism. Its "We the People, Wisconsin" project is a partnership with the Wisconsin State Journal newspaper, WHA public radio and public television, and Wood Communications, a public relations firm. WISC is committed to conducting quarterly public journalism projects with this large partnership well into the future. The station is also involved in a second project called "Schools of Hope."

KRON differed slightly from WISC. Like WISC, the first project the station did was election focused and involved a partnership with the Salt Francisco Chronicle and KQED public radio and public television. At the time, KRON was not sure whether it would continue doing public journalism work, so it began as a short-term project station. During the course of the fieldwork on this project, KRON decided to take on a new public journalism project on transportation issues. Now the station's incoming news director says the station plans to continue this type of work, making it a good fit in the long-term project category. The station's most recent project, "About Race," not only won the time period when it aired, but is also receiving national attention and awards.

WBNG is in the smallest market studied for this research, but the station is a heavyweight in the market, garnering larger ratings than its competitors combined. The station has wonderful resources and facilities and has played a significant role in its partnership with The Press & Sun Bulletin in the project "Facing Our Future." This multi-year project is part of the station's identity according to the general manager. Like the other longterm project stations, the project remains encapsulated as special projects with little or no crossover into the daily news coverage routines.

## INTEGRATED STATIONS

KVUE-TV in Austin, Texas, and KARE-TV in Minneapolis, both owned by Gannett, fit the integrated station category. Neither of these stations see public journalism as a moniker for their newscasts, yet both stations have strong community affairs departments that work closely with the news department in developing citizen sources in a wide range of communities. It is also interesting to note that the news directors at both stations are supportive of the ideals of public journalism and believe their stations are conducting that type of community-connected work. Still the majority of news workers does not know much about public journalism and do not believe their station does that sort of work. This belief changes when public journalism is described to them as citizen-based, community-focused coverage.

KVUE-TV was chosen for this research study because of the policy news managers developed to assess the meaningfulness of crime stories before allotting time in the newscast for those stories. The crime guidelines, though limited to a specific category of stories, fit the context, depth, and enterprise elements of coverage that are indicative of public journalism work. When asked if the guidelines had spilled over into other coverage, news workers responded that crime coverage is now held to the same, tougher standards of the other categories of coverage.

KARE-TV was chosen for this study because of the public journalism types of stories it broadcasts, particularly in its long-format news stories segment called "Extras." This is in direct competition with WCCO's "Dimension" reports. It is interesting to note that unlike WCCO, the type of coverage created in the Extra's unit does spillover into the daily coverage. This may be due in part to the fact that KARE reporters and photographers are allowed, and even encouraged, to develop stories to work on in the Extras unit. Though there is an Extra's unit staff, general assignment staff can and do move in and out of the Extra's unit when stories warrant extra airtime and preparation time.

Organizationally, these integrated stations have decentralized management structures with most decisions made by teams. Editorial meetings are open to anyone who cares to participate; however, the final decisions remain with the journalists. These meetings are often the place where issues and values discussions occur in the newsroom. Integrated stations place a greater value on these principled debates than other stations.

There is a clear reward system for enterprise reporting, which reinforces the value managers say they place on enterprise story ideas. There is also a concerted, stationwide effort to reach into the community, particularly areas not normally covered by the news department. This would include neighborhoods that receive little or no coverage, minority groups and organizations, and issues that journalists have yet to discover in their coverage area (but are known within the community). This broadens the scope and reach of the station's newsgathering efforts.

Both stations tend toward consensus building techniques in daily decision-making. The result is overall coverage that is citizen and community focused. At these stations, public journalism norms and routines are part of the continual process of creating the news product and the managers at these stations are actively engaged in further developing these norms and routines within the station.

## Journalistic Norms and Routines within Types

Journalistic norms and routines are well documented, as noted earlier. The normative structures include objectivity, professionalism, typifications of news, and source selection. The journalistic routines include editorial meetings, the allotment of resources (both air time and newsgathering resources), the daily expectations placed on news workers (submission of enterprise story ideas or beat checks), and the daily news management expectations that develop the newscast structure. Some stations have less traditional routines, such as regular company awards meetings or scheduled internal teaching and critique sessions. These routines channel the way news work is done.

Challenges to norms or routines are often the rallying point for journaltists who are resisting change. It is important to note that the resistance to the change toward public journalism varied by station type. The stations moving toward a publicity mode were looking for a short-term ratings fix and tended to have poor internal communication between staff and managers. Project stations saw more resistance to change toward public journalism based on normative challenges. Part of this resistance resulted from a lack of communication with the news staff not involved in the project.

This communication void created two sets of news workers, with one group left out of the process. This was followed by a perception of disproportionate resource allocation. However, as individuals were brought into the project, their challenges diminished or even disappeared based on their new understanding of public journalism. Integrated station managers met with the least resistance in moving toward public journalism. Solid internal communication, involvement of every news worker in the process, solid encouragement, and rewards helped minimize resistance.

## The Role of News Meetings

News meetings are an important part of most local news operations. Generally, news departments hold two major news meetings each day.

The morning meeting is the largest in terms of attendance, potential stories on the station's "day sheet," and the amount of resources to be allocated for coverage. The afternoon meeting generally addresses assignments for the night crew and any developments on stories since the morning meeting.

Integrated Stations. Traditionally, newsrooms start editorial meetings with a "day sheet," a list of all the news items the assignment desk is aware of for that day. These are usually planned or scheduled news events and news conferences, items called into the station's news tip line, stories to follow up from the morning newspaper, or stories from the station's own follow-up file.

Integrated station news meetings tended to be open, enterprise-focused and decision-making by consensus. As a result the meetings were also the longest of the stations studied and tended to have a decentralized system of discussing issues instead of logistics.

One key component of news meetings at integrated stations was their inclusiveness. Anyone who wanted to attend was welcomed and even encouraged. Unlike the traditional separation of news from the rest of the station, the integrated stations' news meetings included people from sales, promotions, community affairs, interns, and anyone else who wanted to sit in on the meeting. At KVUE and to a lesser degree at KARE, news workers are expected to attend.

Integrated station meetings tend to begin with the enterprise ideas first. One news manager says, "In the morning meeting, the staff knows that they like to be heard from and so that's a good time to said, 'Hey, I heard this thing yesterday, and we can do something on this because it's a good forum for that.'" News workers say they expect the daily discussion of stories at this meeting, not logistics so much as issues.

The news selection process is also different. The integrated stations based decision making on democratic group consensus. Ideas are bantered about until someone says they want it or the group discards the story. KARE's news director says, "The hardest thing in our morning meeting is we all want to talk about the issues. You know, everybody has an opinion. And everyone gets really charged. And that's why our morning meetings sometimes go so long, is because everybody wants to talk." This system is important because it covers a larger range of ideas and communities in the coverage area simply by having a wider range of individuals included in the meeting. News workers say managers encourage participation and because of that encouragement the news staff is not intimidated about speaking their mind. In fact managers tend to have less say in these meetings than their counterparts at other stations studied.

Special Project Stations. The meetings at long-term project stations tended to focus more on research results and the logistics of coverage than on issues discussions. Managers' input carried a lot more weight in the morning meeting at these stations. Also, the preparation for morning meetings is not as thorough as at the integrated stations. Not everyone contributes to the meeting. After one meeting, a WISC reporter said, "Some people don't much seem to be interested in anything and it seems that a lot of people come into meetings with hardly anything, which to me seems strange."

These stations tended to mention research results as a reason for choosing certain stories for coverage. A news manager at a long-term project station said, "...even though we're driven by research, we decide things by democracy."

Long-term project stations had a greater reliance on the assignment desk for both story assignments and for managing coverage logistics. Integrated stations also used the assignment desk for logistics, but the assignment desk played a much smaller role in story development.

Short-term project station news managers tended to have pre-editorial meetings. The editorial meeting was strongly influenced by the news managers. In many ways the coverage was set before the editorial meeting even began. The morning meetings had low attendance, except at WSOC where the news director instituted mandatory attendance a few weeks before the research visit. Managers at all three stations said they welcomed reporter input, but little was forthcoming. Since the story coverage decisions were already finalized, these meetings tended to be almost entirely logistics focused. These stations had the strongest assignment desks of the stations studied, with little outside input.

WCCO was the only station visited twice during the research period. The first visit was at the beginning of this research and the last was near the end of the project. The time between visits was a little more than a year. During this time, the station underwent significant change, moving away from public journalism. At the first visit, this station held editorial meetings that mirrored, or were even more issue focused, than the integrated stations in this research. By the time of the second visit, the editorial meeting was completely dominated by a new executive producer, a position the station had previously left unfilled. Most notably missing from this newsroom after the change were the in-depth issues discussions.

**Marketing of Television News**

Today marketing is a key component of television news. What used to be considered a four-letter word in newsrooms is now gaining acceptance as the way the system works. Marketing is now an accepted element in television news production. Stories are often planned out in advance to allow time for the promotions department to create promotions and attract an audience.

Each station has a moniker it uses to present its image to the public on a regular basis. A change in that moniker often signals a change in the focus in the news department. During this study, only one station went through an image change. WCCO changed from "Your News Station" to "The Home Town Team." The difference in the two images is significant. "Your News Station" fit the traditional station-of-record role the station arguably still maintains. "Home Town Team" is a softer image, presenting a stronger sense of connection to the community.

At integrated stations, community service is a key component in the station market image. Integrated stations go to great lengths to connect with citizens and community leaders. This is important because it shows a depth of commitment toward including a wide range of perspectives in the creation of the news product. A strong emphasis is also placed on listening to citizens' criticisms, ideas, and opinions as a way to improve news.

Special project stations tend to use community forums as a form of marketing and positioning. These stations have a commitment to bringing community leaders from all levels into the station to talk about issues and coverage. WISC's news director says the key is listening to what citizens have to say.

**Enterprise Reporting**

Enterprise reporting is one of the keys to conducting

public journalism in daily news. It is also the point of crossover from project-focused coverage to daily coverage using public journalism techniques. Integrated stations, by definition, are already doing public journalism on a regular basis. The norms and routines at these stations are deeply rooted in the enterprise reporting tradition. News workers are expected to contribute enterprise story ideas on a regular basis, if not daily.

The enterprise stories are highly regarded and are rewarded at these stations. Employees are encouraged to consider coverage of neighborhoods and communities not normally captured on the news radar. The norms and routines of coverage at these stations focus on the solicitation of story ideas from all parts of the community and all departments of the station (including sales) and on the discussion and deliberation of these ideas in an open and continuing forum.

The hope for greater use of public journalism practices in daily coverage is found in the long-term project stations. Though none of the long-term project stations showed much change in daily coverage routines as the result of the public journalism projects, this may change. News directors at both WISC and KRON indicated an interest in achieving greater implementation of public journalism ideals in the daily news product.

Managers at the special project stations said they valued enterprise reporting, but the submission levels were lower than at the integrated stations. A common theme among reporters at these stations was the lack of weight their ideas carried in the meetings. Some news workers have said they don't submit ideas because their ideas do not get used. To some degree this may be a resource issue, though it would be wrong to say that a lack of resources is the main cause.

News workers appear to feel free to voice their opinions, even when those opinions are unpopular. This indicates a level of autonomy within the newsroom that is important for the development of even a low level of enterprise story ideas. Still the reporters seem to rely on the assignment editor for stories.

At short-term project stations the routines of enterprise reporting appeared to be limited or missing. This was particularly noticeable in the editorial meetings, where managers control most of the discussion.

One other place in which enterprise reporting is firmly situated is long— format news. The two Minneapolis stations in this study present long-form news stories in their late newscast. KARE's "Extra" and WCCO's "Dimension" both buck the trend toward shorter stories with less depth. These stories can range upward of five minutes, depending on the night. Both stations have separate units within their newsrooms responsible for producing the long-form stories that use a more enterprise-focused structure.

KARE regularly allows general assignment reporters and photographers to rotate into the Extra's Unit when they present a good enterprise story idea and simply need longer preparation time or greater airtime to complete the work. WCCO was less likely to allow such a rotation. Thus at the integrated station, there was an additional incentive for developing enterprise reporting.

## Conclusions

Some community-conscious television stations around the country are making concerted efforts to develop a television version of public journalism. It is already apparent that there are some conditions under which public journalism is more likely to flourish in television. The key elements are the station's market position, organizational structure, the norms and routines of journalistic work, and the depth of commitment to public journalism. This development in television news is taking several forms.

Integrated stations tended to develop out of the community service market position. Managers at integrated stations tended to see public journalism as an extension of the station's collective understanding of the communities served. They have issues-focused editorial meetings and place a high value on enterprise reporting with a connection to a variety of communities. This does not mean all of the coverage at these stations is civic— based, but that there is a growing effort and a system of support for creation of community-based enterprise reporting.

The commitment to the ideals of public journalism is strong because it is an engrained part of the station structure. It appears that stations using the community service market position see public journalism as a way to extend that brand and to add a harder edge to their newsgathering. Many of the connections to the community are already present at the station, but those connections are maintained outside of the newsroom. It is a simple process to expand the community connections beyond the community service office and into the newsroom.

Special project stations tended to have developed out of the now disappearing public affairs market position. Traditionally, these stations have focused heavily on politics, government, and big business in a beat reporting structure. For these stations the move toward public journalism signals a move away from traditional beats and toward more community sources in their reporting.

The problem is that very little crossover occurs between the project and daily reporting. Some of this structure is created by the designation of certain employees as the public journalism staff.

This creates a barrier between the project and daily news coverage. However, stations with a long-term commitment to public journalism projects still encased public journalism within a special projects unit on the periphery of the newsroom.

The short-term project stations tended to come out of a crime-focused market position. Though these stations do solid public journalism work within the project, the work tends to be even more isolated from the newsroom. Often a single person coordinates the entire effort.

For public journalism to thrive and succeed in television, it must become part of the daily news process. This is not to say that the integrated station type is an ideal in its current form. There is a lot to be learned from the project focus, including depth of coverage and greater focus on specific civic issues of importance to the community. Market position plays an important role in the development of public journalism.

Community service stations and public affairs stations tend to be the organizations working to capture the developing public journalism market position.

The station's roots appear to determine the format of public journalism chosen, with public affairs stations tending toward project status and community service stations choosing a more integrated form. These choices affect the structures of journalistic practice within the news organization.

Integrated stations tend toward more issues discussions within the editorial meetings and place a higher value on enterprise reporting.

The focus on enterprise story development and the placement of value, and in some cases rewards, on meetings with a true dialogue among equals helps improve the level of issue discussions at the editorial meetings. This also encourages more informal discussions of key issues within the newsroom.

Project stations mix logistics and issues discussions within the editorial meetings. These stations appear to value enterprise reporting, but do not have high expectations or a rewards system for developing enterprise pieces. Shorter-term project stations tended to use editorial meetings for logistics discussions, with almost no value placed on enterprise reporting.

Ultimately, all of these elements point to a level of commitment to public journalism, a commitment that requires time to develop and cover enterprise stories, a value placed on connecting to communities and citizens to hear their voices, resources to allow more coverage time and/or greater airtime to tell a story that is issues oriented and meaningful, a story in which the members of the community see themselves and their views accurately reflected.

No station has developed a perfect model. However, it is apparent that far-sighted news managers hold the key to changing routines within the organization to address challenges to journalistic norms. The data collected at these stations suggest journalistic routines are more important than journalistic norms in determining coverage patterns. Most of the criticisms of public journalism by journalists in this study were based on challenges to routines rather than norms. This means managers, not individual news workers are the key to the success or failure of the public journalism effort.

## Chapter 15

# Media Reporting and Perceived Credibility

This chapter examines the reporting of online polls and their perceived credibility. In the last several decades, the public opinion poll has been acknowledged as a necessary tool for probing the complexity of people's beliefs and attitudes on certain issues. Poll data serve as the quantification of those beliefs and attitudes, which tends to make them appear more real and provides us with "a sense of definiteness."

A substantial body of research suggests that the use of surveys in journalism provides more reliable information than other methods about the state of public opinion. Mendelsohn and Crespi, for example, argue that the reporting of poll results by the news media satisfies" the public's curiosity about the world in which it lives." Similarly, Paletz et al. notes that, "Polls are newsworthy: they are topical, related directly to issues in the news, are up-to-the-moment."? Especially during elections, many researchers have found that poll results become special news items that enhance people's curiosity to know who will win the election.

People today are more likely than in earlier times to quote the latest poll when they discuss a pertinent issue, probably because the news media include polls in many of their stories. The growing popularity of opinion polls can be documented by the sheer number of polls that have been reported by major news organizations in the past years. For example, two prestigious national newspapers and three television networks' evening news programs-the New York Times, Washington Post, ABC World News, CBS Evening News, and NBC Nightly Newsreported more than 11,000 opinion poll results during the three years of 1996 to 1998.

Along with the proliferation of traditional polls, an increasing effort during the past few years has been made to take the pulse of the public through the Internet. As the number of Internet users has increased dramatically, both public opinion pollsters and news organizations have come to recognize the advantages of online polls and turned to them. However, there has been much criticism that the respondents of online polls are nonrepresentative and demographically quite different from the general population. Despite these problems, some analysts of public opinion (pollsters and journalists) assume that most people do not differentiate sufficiently between representative opinion polls normally found in newspapers and television news and nonrepresentative online polls.

As one business journalist put it, "The technology is way out in front of opinion at this time, and may only serve to create the illusion of decisiveness when the public is still largely uncertain." If this is the case, perceptions of public opinion in society could be distorted by those who rely extensively on or participate in online polls. In this respect, the questions of how online public opinion polls are reported in the news media and how they are perceived by people are both theoretically and practically important, and deserve to be closely examined.

## RELATED STUDIES

## THE CONTROVERSY OVER ONLINE POLLS AND MEDIA REPORTING

In the past several years, the number of news stories reporting online polls has rapidly increased. The topics of online polls range from politics and economics to entertainment and sports.9 Some advocates of these polls emphasize their relative advantages over traditional polls.

Researchers from Harris Interactive (formerly, Harris Black International Ltd.) have argued that "Internet polling is less expensive and faster and offers higher response rates than telephone surveys/" They also claim that their Internet polling correctly predicted seventy-one of seventy-three election races in the 2000 U.S. presidential election. Similarly, Adam Schoenfeld, vice president for Jupiter Communications, has claimed that "the size of the response was an impressive demonstration of how an online computer service can almost instantly measure public opinion on an issue."

The biggest concern of opponents of online polls is that a large sample size alone is an insufficient criterion to generalize the findings to the population. Thus, despite the fact that online polls often have thousands of respondents, these numbers are meaningless because the respondents (usually) have not been selected from a complete sampling frame or through a reliable sampling procedure.

In fact, most online surveys found on the Internet today allow respondents to simply log in their opinions and then instantly see how other people have responded to the same questions. While these "quick" polls are certainly entertaining, they lack any validity because of the respondents' self-selection into the poll sample. As a result, the demographics of Internet users sampled in online polls are not the same as the general population. Many surveys have reported that Internet users are more likely to be white, better educated, and more affluent than the average American. Therefore, it is highly questionable that most online polls provide an accurate representation of people's opinions in general.

It should be noted that some efforts have been made to alleviate the problems of self-selection and skewed demographics of online poll respondents. Harris Interactive's online interviewing, for example, relies on a database of more than seven million panel members "who have opted in to receive invitations to take part in online surveys." Interviews are conducted using a self-administered, online questionnaire, via proprietary, web-assisted interviewing software. Since this sampling method also does not result in a representative sample (for example, only people with computers can complete the survey), Harris Interactive weights completed interviews with several demographic variables (e.g., sex, age, education, race, and ethnicity) and a composite "variable representing the propensity of an individual respondent to be online" to generalize survey results to the national population. Despite this rather sophisticated sampling and weighting procedure, serious doubts remain about the representativeness of these samples.

Despite these doubts about how representative online polls currently are, recent studies have documented a growing use of Internet polls by the news media. Wu and Weaver, for example, found that the number of online poll stories had notably increased between 1992 and 1995. More recently, based on their content analysis of online poll reports between 1996 to 1998, Kim and Weaver found that the reports of online polls were much more likely to focus on nonpolitical subjects such as sports and entertainment than were the news reports of traditional random-sample surveys.

They also found that online polls were more likely to be conducted by media organizations, whereas traditional polls were more likely to be based on surveys conducted by nonmedia organizations. In addition, in terms of methodological information, online poll stories were less likely to conform to AAPOR standards than traditional poll stories. Given that we encounter more and more online polls in the news media today, it seems important to assess the reporting of online polls by the traditional news media.

## POLLS AND CREDIBILITY

The correlation between message attributes (e.g., sources and stylistic variables) and perceived media credibility has been analysed in a number of studies. Although their findings have been mixed, many different dimensions of source attributes have been found to impact audience beliefs about message credibility. One of the first studies concerning message credibility, particularly of news sources, was by Greenberg and Miller. Their findings suggested that message acceptance had to do with source credibility, and the effects of low credibility could be obviated by delaying source identification until after the message was provided. Based on the assumption that different methods in news reporting provide different message credibility, Moiser and Ahlgren examined whether newspaper readers evaluated "precision journalism" news stories as more credible and reliable than traditional news articles. Emphasizing several dimensions of credibility-including clarity, accuracy, trustworthiness, and believability-they found that news stories including precision journalism techniques, such as survey research and opinion polls, were evaluated as no more credible than news articles using traditional reporting methods.

Regarding credibility of online information, some research has explored the effects of Internet-related sources on people's perceived credibility. Johnson and Kaye, for example, examined how reliance on online information versus traditional media influenced online source credibility of politically interested online users. Their survey found that heavy online users evaluated political news online as more credible than political information presented in the traditional news media. In other words, perceived credibility of online news might be related to how often people use the Internet.

In an experimental study concerning readers' perception of print and online news stories, Sundar found "striking similarities between the factor structures underlying receivers' perceptions of print news and online news." He concluded that subjects use the same four criteria in their perception of print and online news stories-credibility, liking, quality, and representativeness. In other words, subjects' evaluations of the news stories were not influenced by whether the stories were presented online or in print.

On the other hand, there is evidence that the use of quoted sources can increase the perceived credibility and quality of online news stories. In an experiment with forty-eight subjects, Sundar found that news stories with quotations were rated significantly higher in credibility and quality than identical stories without quotations. Since online news readers do seem to note the presence of quotes in online news stories, it is likely that they process and evaluate online news stories as actively and deliberately as stories printed in a newspaper.

More recently, Flanagin and Metzger conducted a survey to assess people's perceptions of the credibility of various categories of Internet information compared to similar information provided by other traditional news media. They found that respondents considered Internet information to be as credible as that obtained from television, radio, and magazines, but not as credible as newspaper information. Their findings suggest that credibility varies across media channels.

The perceived credibility of public opinion reports has been analysed in two studies. Paletz and his colleagues attempted to answer the question of how public opinion polls were presented by the news media and to what extent polls were depicted as reliable and credible.

Based on their examination of poll reports in the New York Times and two television networks (NBC and CBS), Paletz et al. argued that the credibility of polls was related to the identification of poll conductors.

The authors found that poll stories that mentioned prestigious polling organizations such as Gallup and Harris were perceived as more reliable and credible. Later, by manipulating experimentally source credentials and affiliations, Salwen found that the use of probability sampling methods increased subjects' evaluations of poll trustworthiness, expertise, and objectivity.

In sum, previous findings concerning poll reporting and perceived credibility of online information suggest that people's perceptions about message credibility could vary by the type of opinion polls they encounter: traditional telephone or nontraditional online. Based on the findings mentioned above, however, the perceived credibility of polls may be independent from whether they are presented online or in the traditional news media. Given that more and more individuals are able to access online information and to navigate the Internet, this study explores how people perceive online public opinion polls and whether there is a different level of credibility between online and traditional roll reports.

## RESEARCH QUESTIONS AND HYPOTHESES

This study aims at expanding research about the effects of online poll reporting by examining people's perceptions of online polls in general and by assessing the perceived message credibility associated with traditional polls and online polls. Given the advantages of methodological triangulation, this study is based on a content analysis of media reports of online polls, a telephone survey focusing on people's perceptions of polls, and an experiment designed to test differences in perceptions of traditional and online polls. Our first research question is:

*RQ1:* What is the content and form of online poll reports in the news media, especially in terms of subjects and conductors?

Another goal of this study is to analyse whether people perceive traditional and online opinion polls differently. Because many people might not differentiate sufficiently between the two different types, some might perceive online polls (especially those with very large samples) as more accurate or reliable than traditional polls that use smaller random samples. If this is the case, perceptions of public opinion in society could be distorted for those who rely heavily on online polls. The survey reported here investigates people's perceptions of online polls in general, compared to traditional random-sample polls. Thus, the following research questions are proposed:

*RQ2:* What are people's attitudes toward public opinion polls, particularly online polls, in general? Do they perceive any differences in the trustworthiness and credibility of traditional and online polls?

*RQ3:* What are the major predictors of the perceived credibility of public opinion polls? Is exposure or attention to traditional or online polls related to general beliefs about the accuracy and trustworthiness of polls in general?

The purpose of our experiment was to see if the

relationship between content attributes and their perceived credibility found in previous studies varies with type of opinion poll results in a news story. In other words, from the literature review, we suspected a certain effect of content attributes, particularly source and type of poll, on message credibility. Therefore, based on the findings of previous studies and our reasoning, it is hypothesized that:

*H1:* The credibility of a news story reporting the results of a traditional random-sample poll conducted by a prestigious polling service will be greater than the credibility of a news story reporting the results of an online poll conducted by the same service.

Since reputable media organizations usually acknowledge in their poll reports that online polls are not representative of the overall population, attentive media users should be aware of the basic differences between traditional and online polls. We therefore hypothesize that:

*H2:* The differences in perceived credibility of the two story versions reporting traditional and online poll findings will be greater among the subjects who recognized the type of opinion poll during their reading than the subjects who didn't.

## CONTENT ANALYSIS OF ONLINE POLL NEWS STORIES

To answer the question of how online polls are presented by the news media, we content-analysed news media coverage of them during 1996 to 1998. According to our search, the first online poll story appeared in 1992. With key words such as "online poll" and "internet poll," our search of the Lexis-Nexis data base yielded 680 online poll reports. Collected poll reports were carefully screened to ensure that they meet the inclusion criteria that the story either was exclusively devoted to the reporting of online polls or used their findings as an integrated part of the news content. Excluded were news items that did not include online poll data or used the term "online poll" as a part of the text without focusing on online poll results. Specifically, we collected the data repeatedly under all six news file categories of the Lexis-Nexis data base-newspapers (PAPERS), major newspapers (MAJPAP), news magazines (MAGS), newsletters (NW-LTRS), transcripts (SCRIPT), and wire services (WIRES).

To examine the way online public opinion polls were reported in news stories, 310 online poll stories were systematically selected from a total of 621 articles published after 1996. Each story was coded for year of publication; conductor of poll (media organizations, commercial polling services, research/professional institutes, etc.); focus of poll (politics, sports, life styles, entertainment, etc.); and type of medium (newspaper, television, wire services, etc.).

About 10% of the total sample (30 stories) were analysed by two coders to test intercoder reliability. Kripendorff's Alpha was.90 for poll conductor and 94 for subjects. The overall coefficient for all measures was 92, indicating an acceptable level of coding reliability.

## SURVEY ABOUT PUBLIC OPINION POLLS

The survey data for this study come from a telephone poll conducted in March and April 1999 among a representative sample of 767 respondents living in Northern Virginia and Maryland. The telephone interviews, which lasted about ten to twelve minutes, were conducted by trained undergraduate students who participated in a research methods class taught at George Washington University. The sample, provided by Genesys, was drawn from all telephone banks in the two target areas with one or more published listings. All numbers were dialed a minimum of seven times, and one respondent was selected randomly within each household. The response rate was 51%.

The survey focused on measuring peoples' attitudes toward public opinion polls in general, their awareness of differences between traditional random-sample and online polls, and their individual exposure to both types of polls. Several questions, partly adapted from Kohut and Roper, were designed to assess people's attitudes toward public opinion polls.

One question tapped respondents' trust in polls by asking them, on a three-point scale, "how often you think you can trust poll results to represent what people think about important issues" (1 = only some of the time right; 3 = almost always right). Credibility of public opinion polls was assessed by asking respondents "whether you think that a random sample of 1,500 or 2,000 people can accurately reflect the views of the nation's population" (0 = no; 1 = yes). Perceptions of the social influence and public impact of polls were measured by asking "how much you think that poll results affect or change things" (1 = almost no influence; 4 = too much influence) and "whether you think that most polls work for or against the best interest of the general public" (0 = work against; 1 = work for).

In order to assess whether people differentiate between the representativeness of traditional random-sample and online polls, respondents were asked "whether you think that either polls you see in the newspaper or on TV or online polls you see on the Internet or on AOL provide more accurate reflections about the views of the nation's population" (1 = news media poll; 2 = online poll; 3 = same accuracy).

Exposure and attention to public opinion polls were measured by asking respondents to state "how often you read poll results when you see them in the newspaper" (I = never; 4 = always) and "how much attention you generally pay to polls when you read the newspaper or watch the evening news" (1 = no attention; 4 = a lot of attention). Similarly, exposure and attention to online polls were assessed by asking "how often you participate in online polls when you see them on the Internet or on AOL" (1 = never; 4 = always), and "how much attention you generally pay to poll results when you see them on the Internet or on AOL" (1 = no attention; 4 = a lot of attention).

Because exposure to news in the mass media and online is likely to influence the perception of public opinion polls, respondents were asked how many minutes a day they typically spend reading a daily national newspaper, watching the national network evening news, and listening to radio news. In addition, they were asked a set of standard questions to assess their gender, age, education, race, party affiliation, and income.

Experiment on Message Credibility. The experimental component of our study seeks to discover whether college students, as a highly educated group with a presumably better understanding of public opinion polls, perceive traditional and online polls differently in news stories. One hundred and forty-four students from introductory communication courses participated in our experiment. The subjects were mostly undergraduate students attending Indiana University. Subjects in classrooms visited by the authors voluntarily participated in the study.

The questionnaire was introduced as part of a study dealing with people's perceptions of news coverage on a current political issue. A majority of the subjects were female (71%), journalism majors (70%), and lower-division students (80%). The subjects were randomly assigned to two groups. Each group was exposed to one of two versions of a news story concerning a public opinion poll about President Clinton's impeachment. There were no significant differences between the two experimental groups in terms of demographics, media use, and experience with traditional and online polls, suggesting that the randomization of treatment worked well.

The news story used was slightly modified so that one version presented online poll results, while the other presented traditional opinion poll results. The news story based on the random-sample poll referred to a "Times/CBS telephone poll" with a sample of 653 respondents, as originally published in the New York Times, while the news story using the results of the online poll cited a "Times/CBS online poll" with a much more typical online poll sample of 10,653 participants.

After reading the news article, subjects were asked to complete a series of questions mainly designed to assess the subjects' perceptions of the poll results in the story. Some questions concerning media use and demographics of the subjects were also included. In order to investigate the polls' effect on message credibility between the traditional poll story versus the online poll story, this study measured the subjects' evaluation of poll credibility in the news story40 and believability of the story.

A poll credibility index was computed by summing each person's scores on the three credibility composite measures: trustworthiness of poll results, honesty of pollsters, and truthfulness of respondents. Cronbach's Alpha (a) for the reliability analysis of the "poll credibility index" was.67. The total number of subjects who answered all three items was 117. All three composite measures and believability of story were measured with a four-point scale.

## THE REPORTING OF ONLINE POLLS IN NEWS MEDIA

It's clear that the number of news stories about online poll results grew dramatically beginning in 1995 after a rather slow start from 1992 to 1995. Along with this growth in numbers, there was a slight increase in the proportion of news stories exclusively reporting on online poll results and a slight decrease in those integrating online poll results with other findings. Online polls reported in newspapers were also mostly carried out by media organizations (72.1%), but there were some from other sources as well, such as commercial firms (9.3%; e.g., Gallup or Harris), research institutes and educational organizations (7.7%; e.g., universities).

TV networks carried more politics (33.3%) and entertainment (28.3%) online poll reports, whereas newspapers' online poll reports were more likely to focus on sports (39.2%). Online polls carried by magazines, wire services, and newsletters focused on lifestyles (31.6%) and economics (19.3%). Overall, the reports of online polls were much more likely to focus on sports, politics, entertainment, and lifestyles than on economics, technology, health, or education.

The news story used was slightly modified so that one version presented online poll results, while the other presented traditional opinion poll results. The news story based on the random-sample poll referred to a "Times/CBS telephone poll" with a sample of 653 respondents, as originally published in the New York Times, while the news story using the results of the online poll cited a "Times/CBS online poll" with a much more typical online poll sample of 10,653 participants.

After reading the news article, subjects were asked to complete a series of questions mainly designed to assess the subjects' perceptions of the poll results in the story. Some questions concerning media use and demographics of the subjects were also included. In order to investigate the polls' effect on message credibility between the traditional poll story versus the online poll story, this study measured the subjects' evaluation of poll credibility in the news story40 and believability of the story.

A poll credibility index was computed by summing each person's scores on the three credibility composite measures: trustworthiness of poll results, honesty of pollsters, and truthfulness of respondents. Cronbach's Alpha (a) for the reliability analysis of the "poll credibility index" was.67. The total number of subjects who answered all three items was 117. All three composite measures and believability of story were measured with a four-point scale.

## THE REPORTING OF ONLINE POLLS IN NEWS MEDIA

It's clear that the number of news stories about online poll results grew dramatically beginning in 1995 after a rather slow start from 1992 to 1995. Along with this growth in numbers, there was a slight increase in the proportion of news stories exclusively reporting on online poll results and a slight decrease in those integrating online poll results with other findings. Online polls reported in newspapers were also mostly carried out by media organizations (72.1%), but there were some from other sources as well, such as commercial firms (9.3%; e.g., Gallup or Harris), research institutes and educational organizations (7.7%; e.g., universities).

TV networks carried more politics (33.3%) and entertainment (28.3%) online poll reports, whereas newspapers' online poll reports were more likely to focus on sports (39.2%). Online polls carried by magazines, wire services, and newsletters focused on lifestyles (31.6%) and economics (19.3%). Overall, the reports of online polls were much more likely to focus on sports, politics, entertainment, and lifestyles than on economics, technology, health, or education.

Exposure and attention to public opinion polls were measured by asking respondents to state "how often you read poll results when you see them in the newspaper" (I = never; 4 = always) and "how much attention you generally pay to polls when you read the newspaper or watch the evening news" (1 = no attention; 4 = a lot of attention). Similarly, exposure and attention to online polls were assessed by asking "how often you participate in online polls when you see them on the Internet or on AOL" (1 = never; 4 = always), and "how much attention you generally pay to poll results when you see them on the Internet or on AOL" (1 = no attention; 4 = a lot of attention).

Because exposure to news in the mass media and online is likely to influence the perception of public opinion polls, respondents were asked how many minutes a day they typically spend reading a daily national newspaper, watching the national network evening news, and listening to radio news. In addition, they were asked a set of standard questions to assess their gender, age, education, race, party affiliation, and income.

Experiment on Message Credibility. The experimental component of our study seeks to discover whether college students, as a highly educated group with a presumably better understanding of public opinion polls, perceive traditional and online polls differently in news stories.

One hundred and forty-four students from introductory communication courses participated in our experiment. The subjects were mostly undergraduate students attending Indiana University. Subjects in classrooms visited by the authors voluntarily participated in the study. The questionnaire was introduced as part of a study dealing with people's perceptions of news coverage on a current political issue.

A majority of the subjects were female (71%), journalism majors (70%), and lower-division students (80%). The subjects were randomly assigned to two groups. Each group was exposed to one of two versions of a news story concerning a public opinion poll about President Clinton's impeachment. There were no significant differences between the two experimental groups in terms of demographics, media use, and experience with traditional and online polls, suggesting that the randomization of treatment worked well.

The newsIn short, contrary to what was expected, neither the two story versions using different types of polls nor readers' recognition of the type of poll in the news story was associated with their perceived message credibility. Overall, although the two hypotheses for this study were not statistically supported (at the.05 level), our findings suggest that people's perceptions of message credibility were slightly influenced by the type of opinion poll in the story.

This study has explored U.S. news media reporting of online polls and public perceptions of online polls as compared with more traditional random-sample polls. Given that more and more people access the Internet and use its information, this study adds to recent attempts in our field to explore people's perceptions of Internet information, especially the perceived credibility of online public opinion polls.

The findings from the content analysis reported here show that there has been a sharp increase in the number of online polls reported in traditional news media from 1995 to 1998, at the same time that there has been a slight decline in integrating the findings of these polls with other evidence of public opinion. This is a troubling trend for anyone concerned with accurate and representative reporting of public opinion, given the fact of the unrepresentative samples responding to online polls and the lack of control over who responds.

Moreover, the slight increase in the exclusive reporting of online poll results in the traditional news media is not an encouraging trend for pollsters or for journalists who care about providing accurate information about public opinion. This is especially true for television news, which carries a much larger proportion of media-sponsored online polls than other news media. In addition, a comparison of the specific subjects of traditional and online poll reports suggests that online poll reports were much more likely to focus on sports and entertainment, rather than more serious issues, than were news stories based on traditional randomsample surveys.

Some confounding findings were observed from the survey and experimental studies. While it is encouraging to find that about 60% of respondents in the survey consider opinion polls found in traditional news media such as newspaper and TV more accurate than those found on the Internet, our experimental analysis reveals that perceptions of message credibility among college students who participated in the study were not statistically different between the two story versions concerning traditional random-sample and online polls. However, three of the four measures of credibility were rated slightly higher by those who received the traditional poll story version, supporting the survey finding of more perceived accuracy of polls carried by traditional media.

This finding may signal another troubling trend. As more and more online poll results are reported in traditional news media, it may become more difficult for people to discriminate between the two.

Taken together, these findings suggest that the traditional news media should be careful about what kind of poll results they report, and how they report them if they want to preserve their own credibility as well as that of carefully conducted public opinion polls.

Finally, the regional survey data and the homogeneity of subjects (college students) in the experiment limit the generalizability of the findings. Future research based on more representative data than ours is needed to examine the credibility of traditional and online polls and the news reports that are based on them.

## INFLUENCING THE PICTURES IN OUR HEADS

The agenda-setting influence of the news media is not limited to this initial step of focusing public attention on a particular topic. The media also influence the next step in the communication process; our understanding and perspective on the topics in the news. If you think about the agenda in abstract terms, the potential for a broader view of media influence on public opinion becomes very clear.

In the abstract, the items that define the agenda are *objects*. For all the agendas we have discussed, the objects are public issues, but they could be other items or topics such as the agenda of political candidates during the presidential primaries. The objects are the things on which the attention of the media and, subsequently the public, are focused.

In turn, each of these objects has numerous *attributes*, those characteristics and traits that describe the object. For each object there also is an agenda of attributes because when the media and the public think and talk about an object, some attributes are emphasized, others are given less attention, and many receive no attention at all. This agenda of attributes is another aspect of the agenda-setting role of the news media.

To borrow Lippmann's phrase, "the pictures in our heads, " the agenda of issues or other objects presented by the news media influence what the pictures in our heads are about. The agenda of attributes presented for each of these issues, public figures or other objects literally influences the pictures themselves that we hold in mind.

Images held by the public of political candidates and other public figures are the most obvious examples of attribute agenda setting by the news media. During the 1976 presidential primaries, the descriptions by Democrat voters in upstate New York of their party's contenders for the nomination already showed considerable correspondence (+.64) in early February with the media's presentation of these men. By late March, the match had increased to +.83. Voters not only learned the media's agenda of attributes; with additional exposure to the news, they learned it even better.

In the national contest that year between incumbent President Jerry Ford and challenger Jimmy Carter, the median correlation across the entire election year between the Chicago *Tribune's* agenda of attributes and the pictures of these two men in the minds of Chicago-area voters was +.70. In local politics, voters' images of two candidates for mayor of Victoria, Texas, in the 1990s also significantly matched the descriptions in their local newspaper (+.60). There are many other examples.

There also are examples of attribute agenda setting for public issues. The aspects of issues selected for attention by the media influence the public's perception of these issues. For a broad and recurring issue such as the economy, one set of attributes consists of the perceived causes and proposed solutions for the specific economic difficulties of the moment.

Among the general public in Minneapolis, the correspondence between the *Minneapolis Tribune's*, agenda for these aspects of the economy and the public's picture of the economy was a strong +.81. Another set of attributes consists of the various arguments pro and con regarding the proposed solutions to these economic problems.

In Minneapolis, the degree of correspondence there between the media and public agendas of attributes was less but still a substantial +.68. Discussion of the economy in the news had major influence on how the public were thinking about this issue.

In a very different setting, a local environmental issue in the MidWest, there was a similarly strong level of correspondence (+.71) between the pictures in people's minds and local newspaper coverage on six aspects of a project to develop a large man-made lake in central Indiana.

Which aspects of an issue are covered in the news—and the relative emphasis on these various aspects of an issue—makes a considerable difference in how people view that issue. From the pattern of the total news coverage, the public learns what journalists consider the important issues are and who the prominent public figures of the day are. From the details of this coverage— the agenda of attributes presented by the news media—the public forms its images and perspective about these issues and public figures.

Influencing the focus of public attention is a powerful role, but, arguably, influencing the agenda of attributes for an issue or political figure is the epitome of political power. Determining the way that an issue is framed—setting the ground rules for deliberation, if you will—can significantly influence the ultimate outcome. In the first year of George W. Bush's presidency, the specter of soaring electrical bills and sporadic power outages in California, coupled with rising gasoline and natural gas prices across the nation, easily propelled the energy issue onto the national agenda.

But beyond these dramatic effects on public attention, how was the energy issue to be framed? For the Bush administration, the priority framing was the need to produce more oil, natural gas and coal to meet the nation's energy needs. Framing the energy issue in terms of conservation was downplayed in Washington, D. C. but not by other voices across the country. How to frame this issue became something of an issue in its own right.

There are obvious implications here for the traditional journalistic norms of accuracy, balance and fairness. The traditional conflict narrative—the "he said, she said" school of journalism—juxtaposing the administration's position with the conservationist's position is grossly inadequate for reporting this situation. For a complex issue such as energy, there are many, many aspects to be considered, which is to say that there potentially is a vast agenda of attributes to be reported.

The task for journalism is to go beyond stenographic coverage of the most vocal framers of an issue—even beyond in-depth investigation of their claims and assumptions. True enterprise reporting means identifying as many of the aspects of an issue as possible and putting them on the agenda for consideration. But those are only the first steps in the natural history of an issue, the beginning of raising consciousness about it. The continuing news story is the lengthy process of public deliberation about this agenda, a process of working through that can eventually lead to thoughtful public policy decisions about the best course of action.

The initial point made here is that the news media have a central agenda-setting role in that process—identifying the major issues of the day and presenting the full agenda of attributes for those issues. There is nothing in this task that calls on journalists and the news media to abandon their neutrality or ideas about fairness and balance. It simply is a more systematic and responsible version of what the media presently do in a more willy-nilly way.

## THE PUBLIC AND THE MEDIA

Although the influence of the media agenda can be substantial, information and cues about object and attribute salience provided by the news media are far from the only determinants of the public agenda. People still, at some point, decide for themselves what really matters to them; there is a difference between the importance attached to events by the media (and therefore initially by people) and the relevance of those events to people.

The substantial influence of the news media has in no way overturned or nullified the basic assumption of democracy that the people at large have sufficient wisdom to determine the course of their nation, their state, and their local communities. In particular, the people are quite able to determine the basic relevance —to themselves and to the larger public arena—of the topics and attributes advanced by the news media. The media set the agenda only when their news stories are perceived as relevant by citizens.

In many instances, the desire by journalists to tell a good story overrides thoughtful judgments about what the public really needs to know and blinds journalists to the public's depth of interest. The intensive news coverage on the Clinton-Lewinsky scandal spectacularly failed to set the public agenda and sway public opinion about President Clinton's ability and right to serve.

Despite gargantuan play and persistent digging for the tiniest detail, "All Monica, all the time" wound up demonstrating only that the media voice has limitations. Overwhelmingly, the public rejected the relevance of that scandal as the basis of their opinion about the president's success or failure at governance. Surveys consistently showed that while people condemned Clinton the man, they continued to accept Clinton the president.

Clinton-Lewinsky was hardly the first time that journalists have misjudged the public's appetite and interest. Large portions of journalists' professional judgments about what should be on the news agenda are routinely ignored by the public, a pattern of behaviour vividly reflected in the declining readership for daily newspapers.

On a typical day in 1980, about two-thirds of the adult population read a daily newspaper. By the end of the century, this figure had slipped down to 57%. There is a similar decline in television news viewing, both for network television and local television.

This decline in the size of the audiences of the news media as well as the presence—or, sometimes, absence—of specific agenda-setting effects by the news media can be explained by a basic psychological trait, the innate need within each individual to understand the environment around them. Whenever we as individuals find ourselves in a new situation, there is an uncomfortable psychological feeling until we explore and mentally grasp at least the outlines of that setting.

Recall your first semester in college when, most likely, you were in a geographically and intellectually unfamiliar environment, or your initial feeling on moving to a new community or visiting a foreign city. This innate need for orientation also exists in the civic arena. Voters in Austin, Texas, were asked to vote for or against the construction of a lightrail system by the local transit authority. In this situation, there was a very high need for orientation, at least among those citizens who intended to vote in the referendum.

Few Austin residents really understood what light rail was or how the benefits and costs of light rail—which was to be paid for by an existing sales tax—compared to other options such as more expressways for automobiles. The Austin *American-Statesman* attempted to satisfy this need for orientation with extensive coverage and discussion on numerous aspects of the city's transportation problems.

Because it is a psychological trait, the degree of need for orientation varies greatly from one individual to another. For most individuals in Austin, there was a high need for orientation regarding light rail. They were concerned about the city's traffic problems but had little understanding of what light rail might contribute to the solution of this problem.

For other individuals, there was little or no need for orientation at all. They just weren't interested and didn't intend to vote in the referendum. Recurring situations in which need for orientation is typically high are party primary elections and local nonpartisan elections for judges, situations in which voters often have little or no information about the candidates.

And every 4 years there is the high-water mark of national civic involvement and need for orientation as people briefly tune in to politics and make their decision about how to cast their vote for president. In all these situations, and many more, people experience a need for orientation, a need for some kind of mental map and understanding of where they are.

Need for orientation is defined by two components: relevance and uncertainty. Relevance is the initial defining condition that determines the level of need for orientation for each individual. If a topic is perceived as irrelevant—or very low in relevance—then the need for orientation is low. Individuals in this situation pay little or no attention to news media reports on this topic and, at most, demonstrate weak agenda-setting effects.

For individuals among whom the relevance of a topic is high, their degree of uncertainty about the topic determines the level of need for orientation. If this uncertainty is low, that is, they feel that they basically understand the topic, then the need for orientation is moderate.

These individuals for whom a situation has high relevance and low uncertainty will monitor the media for new developments and perhaps occasionally dip into a bit of additional background information. But they are not likely to be avid consumers of news reports about the topic. Agenda-setting effects among this group are moderate.

Finally, among individuals for whom both the relevance and their uncertainty about a situation is high, need for orientation is high. These individuals typically are avid consumers of news reports about the topic, and strong agenda-setting effects typically are found among these individuals.

To demonstrate the usefulness of need for orientation in explaining the public's behaviour, let's look at that high-water mark of American politics, the presidential election, and see how attention to the news media and their agenda-setting effects vary according to individuals' levels of need for orientation.

Both frequent use of the news media to follow the election and the agenda-setting effects of the news media on the perceived importance of the issues steadily increase with the level of need for orientation among members of the public. When the news media do provide information that citizens find relevant and useful in coming to a decision about how to cast their ballots, there is a substantial audience—and there is substantial media influence on the priorities that citizens assign to the issues of the day. In this situation, the public and the news media are partners in public life and a common search for understanding.

The vast range of differences among individuals in their need for orientation about public affairs identifies three major publics for news: Information-seekers, monitors and onlookers. There is, of course, also a nonpublic, that 10 per cent or so of the adult population who seldom follow news in any fashion: newspapers, television or online. Our focus here is on the three publics that are involved to varying degrees in public life and the use of news media.

Information seekers, who most closely resemble the

idealized citizens of democratic theory, are persons to whom elections and a wide variety of public affairs are highly relevant. Typically, they make an effort to acquire a considerable quantity of information about public affairs because they have a high need for orientation. Some individuals are situation-specific information seekers because there is an immediate decision to be made—those high-need-for-orientation people in the election example presented or many of the voters who went to the polls in Austin, Texas, to say "Yes" or "No" about light rail.

Other information seekers have an abiding, long-term interest in some aspect of public affairs. In *"The American People and Foreign Policy,"* Gabriel Almond called this group the "attentive public." These are persons with high interest in an issue, considerable knowledge about the issue, and a pattern of regular acquisition of new or additional information about the issue. Similar attentive publics have been identified for a variety of other topics.

There also is evidence of a general attentive public, that is, information seekers who routinely cast their net widely in the daily news report. Among the members of this public, there is a systematic and cumulative progression through three or four categories of information in the daily newspaper.

From the broad array of national and international news typically found on the front page and in the first section of the newspaper, this general attentive public moves on to reading local governmental news, then to other political news. If we define this general attentive public as those persons who regularly read all three of these types of news, it is about one in four or five members of the community.

If we add reading the editorial and op-ed pages to our definition of the general attentive public—in other words, increase the requirement to regularly reading four types of news—then this public is about one in six or seven members of the community. Most individuals who immerse themselves this deeply in the daily newspaper also make extensive use of television news.

Another public consists of monitors, those individuals

who monitor or scan the ongoing stream of news for information specifically relevant to them and their lives. These individuals generally are satisfied with knowledge *of* the issues of the day rather than detailed knowledge *about* the issues of the day.

Monitors become an attentive public only when an issue with rather immediate consequences for them moves onto the community or national agenda, something they see as a threat or an opportunity. Schudson observed that this public based on a strategy of monitoring now has displaced the information-seeking public as the majority public.

Although there is a long-running debate about whether the information seeking public ever was the majority, there is considerable contemporary evidence that monitors, persons with only a moderate need for orientation about public affairs, now are the modal public.

For example, there is the pattern of declining levels of newspaper reading and television news viewing already noted in this chapter. For newspapers, this decline is largely the result of frequent readers, those who regularly read a daily newspaper on four or five weekdays, becoming occasional readers, those who read a daily newspaper only a few times each week.

Large numbers of persons formerly with a high need for orientation now have only a moderate need for orientation. When the entertainer Eddie Fisher, by divorcing Debbie Reynolds and marrying Elizabeth Taylor, revealed himself as someone likely to test the attentiveness of the public with a string of wives, *New York Times* columnist Russell Baker says he realized for the first time that "there might be a lot of things that were not worth keeping up with.

This, " he explains, " "was a moment of liberation. " ... Will ignorance of the exact cause of death, of the subcommittee's vote, or of the names of Eddie Fisher's wives come to be seen as a sign of a disciplined resistance to the blandishments of the current noise?

Additional evidence that many persons are satisfied with no more than a moderate need for orientation is found in analyses of how people reach their voting decisions. A simple calculus based on a few orienting cues is sufficient for many: how a candidate stands on one or two issues that an individual finds particularly relevant or the images of the candidates based on a handful of attributes.

"*Low-information rationality*, or 'gut' rationality, best describes the kind of practical reasoning about government and politics in which people actually engage, " concluded Samuel Popkin in *"The Reasoning Voter."*

A third public, onlookers, is those persons for whom civic life has little personal relevance. These are the individuals with a low need for orientation, persons for whom the daily newspaper and television news may be more of a pleasant distraction and source of entertainment than a source of orientation to civic life.

Many of these persons are registered to vote, but they do not appear at the polls with any regularity. The fact that onlookers do make some use of the news media and do appear at the polls from time to time is cause for a degree of optimism. Onlookers are potentially reachable—and will become participants in public life—if the news agenda strikes a resonant chord.

Finding those resonant chords for all three of these publics means that journalists must be more than creators of interesting and compelling stories based on the traditional news values of journalism. Journalists must be communicators who are concerned about the effects—and especially, the lack of civic effects—of their messages on the public.

More specifically, journalists and news organizations need to work at tailoring their messages to reach all three publics. One strategy used by many newspapers is to use summary boxes and graphics to highlight the key aspects of major news events, then present all the details in lengthy, more traditional stories.

The boxes and graphics service the monitors and might even entice the onlookers. Detailed stories serve the information seekers. Online news sites can reach these disparate publics with attractive home pages and summaries complemented with hyperlinks that can take the audience deeper and deeper into the aspects of the topic about which they want more knowledge.

## WATCHDOG ROLE OF JOURNALISM

The goals of the revered watchdog role of journalism typically include rooting out the malfeasance, conflicts of interest and corruption in public life. The news media are the public's surrogate looking over the shoulder of public officials, institutions and businesses. This tradition of investigative reporting is a steeple of excellence in the profession of journalism. But this watchdog role often is too confined to the actions of individuals in some narrow setting.

Frequently, the focus is on indictable crimes. An expanded notion of this watchdog role will be more successful in gaining the attention of all three publics for the news. When the city of Philadelphia built a new convention centre, the city's news media were diligent in digging out instances of corruption in who benefitted from the disbursement of public funds. But the larger watchdog role of questioning whether the city really needed this facility or whether these funds might be better invested in other public works was never on the media agenda.

In the summer of 2001, the Austin, Texas, *American-Statesman*— along with the city of Austin and the U. S. Attorney—was in diligent pursuit of what happened to the $1.45 million in public funding and another $3.70 million in private funding for Vision Village, a 4-year-old project that has yet to produce any of its promised 156 low-cost housing units.

Pursuit of this story is an important watchdog function. But the larger watchdog role for all the local news media in Austin is the question of how to provide affordable housing for both the chronically depressed portions of the city and, increasingly, for middle-income citizens priced out of the market by the city's economic boom. It is likely that the Vision Village situation ultimately will be resolved by the civil and criminal courts.

The judicial process will not resolve Austin's housing situation. But the Austin news media can put this situation on the public agenda and keep it there through the long period of working through to some resolution. It took Austin more than 15 years to settle the matter of building a new airport. Building individual housing is much more complex. In short, the watchdog role of the news media cannot be limited to an investigative series of reports—even if it wins a prize—or a running story on one aspect of a larger community situation.

The news media frequently are agenda setters. But what is the civic relevance and utility of the items placed on the agenda? Jay Rosen commented in *"What Are Journalists For?"* that "the point of having journalists around is not to produce attention, but to make our attention more productive.

"News media need to be creative watchdogs and agenda setters scanning the horizon for the gaps in current public life. Part of this larger watchdog role is functioning as social radar, not just a chronicler of what government and other institutions are doing right now, whether good or bad. This means discovering the concerns of citizens and defining what the public needs to know in very expansive terms.

After extensive discussions involving a substantial cross section of community leaders as well as key members of the newspaper's own staff, the San Antonio, Texas, *Light* began 1992 with a full editorial page spread in the Sunday newspaper proposing that the community focus on eight specific issues affecting the city's children. Although most newspapers try to stimulate public opinion with their editorial page, few systematically formulate such a highly focused editorial agenda and then follow through with extensive running news coverage.

The effects were dramatic. Funding by the city of San Antonio for 10 children's programs increased by nearly $6 million that fall. The median increase in these programs was 13 per cent, significantly exceeding the overall 9 per cent growth in the city budget. Reflecting on this initiative's blend of the *Light's* editorial voice with news coverage, the editorial page editor commented on the synergy between these two aspects of newspaper journalism and what is happening in the local community:

If you have set the agenda well, have identified major needs in the community, then any conflict between the editorial and news roles of a newspaper will take care of itself.

Looking toward the future economic well-being of their state, the Huntington, W. V., *Herald-Dispatch* and West Virginia Public Broadcasting (WVPB) jointly explored "West Virginia After Coal." Coverage of the issue included a statewide public opinion poll, a six-day newspaper series, and creation of a comprehensive database that documented how little of the $ 18 million in coal severance taxes distributed to the state's 55 counties and 234 municipalities supported efforts at economic diversification and worker training.

Using new digital technology to create a three-hour, interactive "town meeting" from 10 different sites across West Virginia, "The Legacy Project" was broadcast on both the radio and television networks of WVPB during September 2000. These were the opening gambits of ongoing journalistic enterprise.

## THE ETHICS OF SETTING AN AGENDA

Daily and hourly decisions about the media agenda—what to include and how to play it, as well as what to omit—are among the most important ethical questions in journalism. Is the media agenda a valid effort to provide what the public really needs to know? One way of proving that the media agenda does provide what the public needs is to explicitly identify the civic utility of a news story.

An exercise that has proved useful in undergraduate journalism courses is one illustration of this idea of civic utility. For the first part of the exercise, the students cover three or four meetings of the city council and write their stories. Typically, these rather lengthy reports are a condensed "rearranged minutes" version in which the items on the agenda of the council meeting are reordered to reflect their news value rather than the chronological order in which they were taken up by the city council. For the second part of the exercise, the students select their best city council story—best in their own opinion, not necessarily the one that received the best grade. For each item covered in that story, written answers are required to each of these questions:

Who in particular among the general public is the primary audience for this item?

Why would they want to know / need to know about this?

On the basis of the answers to the first two questions, does the story contain sufficient relevant information? Too much marginal or irrelevant information?

Finally, the students rewrite their story on the basis of their answers to these questions. To put the matter in abstract terms, the students are asked to critique the civic utility of their reporting, and if they find it deficient, which they nearly always do, to produce an enhanced version. In some instances, the outcome of their critique is to shift substantially the prominence of an item on the media agenda. In other instances, the outcome is a change in the framing of the item or the addition of other aspects of the item to the news story. All these changes have important implications for what the public can do with information provided by the news media about their city council's actions.

This same kind of critique can be applied to other kinds of public affairs reporting and in an election year, particularly applied to how the interminable presidential campaign is covered. For decades, about one-third of the coverage has been devoted to the key issues of the campaign and the candidates' positions on these issues.

This leaves about two-thirds of the coverage devoted to spot news about the campaign and its hoopla, to speculations about who is leading the horserace at that moment and is likely to win, and to analyses of campaign strategy and similar information that Joan Didion described as "insider baseball."

During all these decades that issues have been relegated to a minority position in the news coverage, the issues also have been framed largely in negative terms as polarized and frozen opinions on which there is little common ground and little possibility of finding any.

Only rarely has this been a realistic account of the situation. In more recent decades, coverage of the candidates also has become increasingly negative. How much civic utility does all this information have? Vast amounts of money go into election-year coverage. What is the public dividend from that investment?

Of course, there are many other even more glaring examples in recent years of poor civic investments by the news media. A multitude of news organizations collectively spent tens of thousands of dollars camped out in front of Richard Jewell's apartment in Atlanta.

It is doubtful that the public gained an iota of information that it needed to know from this harassment of a man falsely implicated in the 1996 terrorist bombing at the Atlanta Olympic Park. Other names that are familiar from their appearance in the centre ring of a media circus are Elian Gonzalez, Monica Lewinsky, the Mendez brothers, O. J. Simpson, and U. S. Rep. Gary Condit. The list is long.

Journalism is a distinct form of mass communication precisely because it has a social responsibility for the nation's and the community's civic health. With the appearance of ever-larger media and communication companies, there has been considerable discussion about how the line between news and entertainment has become blurred and indistinct. Against this backdrop, Ed Fouhy warned one group of newspaper editors:

If we do not change, we stand a very good chance of becoming increasingly irrelevant, except as another form of entertainment where there are already many more attractive forms of entertainment.

The "change" that Fouhy had in mind was in enhancing the relevance of the news to the audience and public life. The declining audiences for news in all its forms—newspapers, national television and local television—underscores the need for change called for by Fouhy. But even among members of the news audience with considerable interest in the news, interest coupled with a strong belief in a civic duty to keep up with the news, there has been a dramatic decline in their attention to daily newspapers, network television news and local television news.

Access to the Internet and its myriad sources of news and information has stemmed, at best, a small proportion of this declining attention to news. Audience members complain that much of the news has little relevance for them as individual members of the public, and critics complain that much of the news does little to facilitate the process of democratic government at either the local or national level.

Public journalism with its call for journalism to make public life go well has proved highly controversial. Why the controversy? Isn't this call an explicit statement of journalism's longstanding implicit beliefs about its responsibility to serve the needs of the public?

# Bibliography

*Adhikarya Ronny*. Knowledge Transfer and Usage in Communication Studies: The U.S.-ASEAN Case. Singapore: Asian Mass Communication Research and Information Center, 2003.

*Becker Lee B., Jeffrey Fruit and Susan Caudill, with Sharon Dunwoody and Leonard Tipton*. The Training and Hiring of Journalists. Norwood, NJ: Ablex, 2001.

*Curry Richard O., ed.* 2000. Freedom at Risk: Secrecy, Censorship, and Repression in the 1980s. Philadelphia: Temple University Press.

*Cooper Dennis R.* "Basic Training for Third World Journalists." Ph.D. dissertation, University of Tennessee-Knoxville, 2001.

*Crook James A.* "Europeans Form Training Association with Help from European Community." Journalism Educator 45, no. 4 (Winter 2000).

*Davidson Terry*. "Ed Emery: Teaching Journalism in China." Community College Journalist 13, no. 4 (Fall 2002):

*Emery Edwin, and Michael Emery*. The Press and America: An Interpretive History of the Mass Media. 6th ed. Englewood Cliffs, NJ: Prentice-Hall, 2003.

*Failing Lynn*. "The Changing Scene in Communication Education." Media Asia 13, no. 4 ( 2000): 183-188.

*Hausman Carl*. 2001. Crisis of Conscience: Perspectives on Journalism Ethics. New York: Harper Collins.

*Jingming, Zhang, and Peng Jianan*. "Chinese Journalism Education: Slow Progress since 2000." Journalism Educator. 41, no. 4 (Spring 1986): 11-13.

*McManus John H.* 2004. Market-Driven Journalism: Let the Citizen Beware. Thousand Oaks, Calif.: SAGE Publications.

# Index